LOVE and MADNESS
My Private Years with George C. Scott

by

Karen Truesdell Riehl

gateway to **NetbookBiz**.com

The Green Room
Imprint of SANDS Publishing, LLC

LOVE AND MADNESS
My Private Years With GEORGE C. SCOTT

Copyright © 2003 by Karen Truesdell Riehl

ISBN: 1 59025 019 2

First Edition

Cover design: Cliff Vaughan

Inside Photos: Courtesy of Author

Author page photo: Jerry Bryan Photography

Published by SANDS Publishing, LLC
P.O. Box 92
Alpine, California 91903
Visit our Website: www.sandspublishing.com

Printed in the USA
0 9 8 7 6 5 4 3 2 1

Acknowledgments

Tammy Grimes, a great, true friend who taught me, "I ain't down yit."

Richard Riehl for hundreds of hours of editing and back rubs.

Lois Berning, Barbara Edlin, Peggy Hart, and Pat Sullivan for insisting, with loving encouragement, that I write this book.

Stephens College Alumnae office for their permission to use photos.

The Grimes and Glazier families for their lasting friendship.

Avenelle Kelsey for setting me on the road to writing.

Eric, for his wisdom.

Diana Saenger and Sandy Scoville for having faith in my story.

Dedication

To my daughter and to Dave.

For Richard, without whose support and understanding I could never have written this book.

And in Memory of Woolie and Nancy.

Prologue

≈

I was nineteen, and nothing mattered to me but loving George C. Scott.

For thirty years, while he became an international film and stage star, he remained an unmentionable part of my life. We never married. Some of my family members who know the story have been so ashamed, they remain to this day unwilling to acknowledge that George and I lived together and created a beautiful daughter.

I began making notes for this book as self-therapy twenty years ago. As my writing career developed, those notes haunted me.

I write now to rid myself of old ghosts. But I also have two added incentives: to give women in similar circumstances the courage to come out of hiding, and to let my daughter know that her mom and famous dad always loved her. She, too, has had to live in the shadows.

One

≈

On September 23, 1999, the phone rang. I heard my daughter's voice on the answering machine, "Pick up the phone, Mom. Pick up."

"Hi, Tracie. Is anything the matter?"

"It's Daddy. He died yesterday."

"Oh. What ... how?" For a moment I wasn't sure I understood what she was saying.

"I don't know. I'm calling my sister, and I'm going to ask Trish if I can come to the funeral."

"Let me know what you find out. How are you?"

"I'm okay."

The rest of that week every television anchor and radio news reporter told me again that George was dead. Each time I heard it I turned the volume up so I could be sure of what they said. It was true. He was dead.

The first time I saw George C. Scott was in 1952. He was twenty-six years old and about to strangle a defenseless old woman in a wheelchair. He was playing the part of Danny, the mad murderer, in *Night Must Fall* on the stage of the Stephens College Playhouse. His maniacal smile and fierce strength were frightening.

After the cast had taken their bows and the audience began to leave, I remained behind, staring at the closed curtain. My roommate watched me for a moment then nudged my shoulder. "What's the matter, Roomo, are you sick?"

"I keep seeing him and hearing his voice. He's incredible."

"If you're referring to George C. Scott, yes he is, in a scary kind of way." Sue moved toward the end of the row. "Now, come on."

"I think I'll sit here until tomorrow night's performance."

"Come on." She pulled at my arm. "We all get crushes on actors. It'll pass."

"It's not a crush. He fascinates me, that's all."

"Sure. Let's talk about it on the way back to the dorm. It's getting late. Classes begin tomorrow, remember?"

"Of course." I grabbed two discarded programs from under the seats in front of me. "Life begins tomorrow." I picked up another program on the way up the aisle.

"What are you doing, Trues, making a collection?"

"Yes, maybe."

We stepped out of the playhouse into the muggy Missouri evening and began our walk toward the dorms. Lampposts lit the path. I stopped under each of the first four of them to hold my program up to the light. I touched the letters of his name. *You are an amazing actor, George Scott. I have a feeling you are an amazing man.* I closed my eyes and saw his face. Sue finally took me by the arm and escorted me down the path to the dorm.

An hour later, while Sue slept, I sat on the alcove windowsill of our third floor room, studying the tree-lined path leading back to the playhouse and thinking about my life in the theater. We'd had a family joke about how mother had to pull me off the stage after I'd played a walk-on in Cinderella at the age of three. On the way home I said, "Mommy, I want to be an actress always." During my elementary and high school years I tried out for every show, volunteering for all the back stage work available. I spent Saturday afternoons watching double features at the movies. The stage and films were my life. I swore I'd never give them up for anybody or anything.

As I sat there on the windowsill, a feeling close to stage fright shook my body. In just a few hours I'd take the next step toward my professional acting career at the Stephens College Playhouse. George Scott could be one of my instructors. Or I might actually be in a show with him. Maybe playing opposite him. I wondered if he was as strong and fierce off the stage.

That night I dreamed I was with George rehearsing *Romeo and*

Juliet. We were so close together I could feel the warmth of his body. I wanted to touch him, to hold him. But when I looked at his face, his eyes were cold and vicious. He reached for me. Terrified, I ran away from him.

When I woke up the next morning soaked with perspiration, I had a vague feeling of uneasiness. For a moment I tried to recapture my dream. Then, remembering the exciting day that lay ahead, I let the dream go. The shower was on, and I heard Sue singing. After just four days of rooming together, we had become pals, already sharing clothes and secrets. I opened the bathroom door and yelled, "Good morn, Roomo. Don't stay in there all day." Sue answered by tossing out a handful of water. I pulled back the curtain, held up an imaginary camera, and clicked.

We skipped breakfast in favor of extra time for our hair and make up. But I couldn't keep my hands from trembling. When I tried to apply my lipstick, it smeared, and the tip broke off. Looking in the mirror, I saw a bright red streak beginning at my chin and running down the front of my new yellow blouse. "Oh, NO! Damn, damn, damn, damn, DAMN!"

Sue looked at me and began to laugh. "Good God, I thought something horrible had happened."

"It has, and it's not funny. Look at me."

"I am." She bit her lip in an effort to look serious.

"What'll I do?"

"Just wait a minute," Sue said soothingly. "I'll finish getting dressed, and we'll restore you. I don't know why you're so worried. All we'll see in this school are girls."

"But George Scott might be at the playhouse."

"I'm already getting tired of hearing about George Scott. I thought it was the theater you loved and that you didn't want any boys in your life."

"I do love the theater, and I don't want any boys in my life." I saw George's face in my mind. "But he isn't a boy. He's a man."

Changing clothes and repairing the damage took an extra twenty minutes. So I arrived late for my first class at the playhouse, my clothes wet from perspiration, and my hair limp from the steamy September morning. I wanted to hide so George wouldn't see me.

I needn't have worried. Another teacher stood at the front of the room. At the break I read the schedule and discovered George was a staff actor and didn't teach classes. The sharp stab of disappointment I felt surprised me. I had seen him only once on stage. I didn't know anything about him. But I did know I felt incredibly drawn to him.

The instructor advised the class to check the theater's callboard every day to find our assignments. Looking at the callboard the next morning, I had my answer. George was in the next show, and rehearsals were scheduled every afternoon from three to five o'clock. Dropping gym class would give me the free time I needed. I called my advisor, Miss Graham, and asked to see her.

Later that afternoon outside Miss Graham's office, I almost lost my nerve. I had never been a deceitful person, and I hated what I was about to do. But I had to. I might not find another way to be near George Scott.

Miss Graham was a woman of about thirty-five, with light brown tightly curled hair. She wore a navy blue cotton dress and sat behind an oak desk. "Hello, Karen. Sit down," she said as I entered the room. She smiled briefly and pointed to the straight back chair on the other side of her desk.

I'm glad to see you. What can I do for you?" she said in a crisp, no-time-to-waste voice.

I sat down and tried for a smile, but it probably looked more like a grimace. "I need to make a change in my schedule." The words were spilling out too fast, but I couldn't slow down. "I'd like to drop PE this semester. I need the time to watch the instructors and older students on stage at the playhouse. I can learn so much from watching rehearsals." That was the truth. I relaxed a little.

Miss Graham took off her reading glasses. She clasped her hands on her desk, her elbows resting on my file. "You know physical education is a graduation requirement, don't you? You'll have to take it sometime."

"Yes, I know, but my major is theater arts, and watching rehearsals can only help me."

"I'm not so sure you're doing the right thing, but we'll give it a try. However, you must keep your other grades up and take PE in the spring." She opened the file in front of her and made a note.

"Thank you, Miss Graham. You won't be sorry." This time I really smiled. "I promise."

The following day I controlled the urge to dance my way into the playhouse. At ten minutes to three I crept into the last row of the darkened theater and took a seat on the aisle. When George arrived, he walked so close to my seat I could feel the air move as he passed. It stunned me, being so close to him. The thought he might see me sitting there also embarrassed me. But the embarrassment changed to joy as I watched him onstage. I stayed through the rehearsal. After he left the stage I ached to see him again.

In my half-twilight sleep that night I imagined George caressed my face, neck, and arms. In the morning my body trembled with the need to be near him, to touch him, if only for a second. The revelation of these feelings shocked me. I had never felt that way before.

When I arrived at the theater that afternoon, I took an end seat again. I leaned toward the aisle letting my hand dangle casually over the side of the seat. As George passed me on his way to the stage, I pulled my hand up. My fingers lightly touched his pant leg. If anyone noticed, it would look like an accident. I knew it was a dumb thing to do. But I also knew I'd never forget the wonderful shock that passed through my body when I touched him.

When George wasn't on stage I used the time to work on my assignments. But when he appeared again, he had my full attention.

As Sue and I lay in our beds each night, I described his every move to her, telling her about his ability to create his stage character from the first time he picked up a new script. "Sue, he's a born actor. He's totally at home on stage. And his gravelly, sexy voice! He's amazing. He takes my breath away."

Sue reminded me she'd seen the show that first night and also studied at the playhouse.

"But did you notice his John Wayne swagger? Well, of course, you did. How could you not?" I didn't give her a chance to answer. "And did you see his gorgeous, thick, dark brown hair and his beautiful nose? And there's something more. A force about him. An intensity that's so strong. Sue, I've never felt so attracted to anyone. It's as if he has a strange power over me."

Sue sat up and turned toward me. "Trues, can't you talk about anything else but George Scott? I'm getting worried about you. You're letting your fascination control you."

"Don't be silly."

"You damned well know this can't go anywhere. He's a staff actor, he's married, and he has a baby." She emphasized *married* and *baby*.

"I know he's a teacher, and I'm only a student!" For the first time since we'd met, I yelled at Sue. "And I'm fully aware he's married and has a child. Anyway, he doesn't even know I exist. If he does, he thinks I'm pathetic. I never say anything to him. And when he speaks to me I just stand there gawking at him. I'm also aware that it's becoming obvious that I have a crush on him." I flopped back on the bed, rolled over on my stomach and jabbed at my pillow. "I can't help it!"

Sue tucked her red curly hair behind an ear and frowned. "Okay. Just, please, be careful."

By regularly skipping classes I created more free hours to spend at the playhouse. With the exception of theater class, my grades began to fall. At the playhouse they dubbed me "Sunshine" because I was so cheerful and worked so hard. I took any job that needed to be filled, sweeping, picking up trash, and scraping gum off the bottom of auditorium seats. I was completely happy working in the theater and being near George.

A month after the beginning of the semester I was cast as the other woman in *Death of a Salesman*. The walk-on part gave me a legitimate opportunity to watch George as he rehearsed the part of Biff. Now I had a legitimate reason to be backstage with him and to stand in the wings while he was on stage. I felt giddy most of the time and turned into a speechless empty head when he looked at me.

During productions when the actors were not on stage, they listened for their cues through the loudspeaker in the dressing room. A card table was set up in the center of the room where most of us played bridge. We handed our cards to another actor when we heard our cues over the speaker. Since I had such a small part, I spent most of my time at the table.

But while I tried to play cards, I watched George's every move. Each time he left the room for a stage entrance, I felt a deep loneliness, as if he'd be gone forever. When he returned, I wanted to run to him and welcome him back. At twenty-six years old, he was not only a talented actor, but also a fine bridge player. We were amazed at how he could stay at the card table until the last second, then dash on stage and instantly and totally be into his character.

Five-foot mirrors covered the walls on three sides of the room. So the other actors in the room could easily watch me watching George. It became the cast's backstage game. There were giggles, winks, and stage whispers announcing George's re-entry into the room. "Hey, Trues, guess who just came in?" someone would whisper in my ear. And just in case I hadn't heard, a finger would point in his direction. He didn't seem to notice, and though it became embarrassing to me, I couldn't stop watching his every move. On several occasions when he sat in front of his mirror, I looked at him and found him looking back. We both quickly turned way.

During costume changes, when his tall, muscular body disappeared behind a screen, I pictured him removing his clothes. I felt myself blush and hoped no one could read my thoughts. Several times the image of his nakedness drove me out the backstage door to breathe the cool air.

It was during this time that

I made friends during that time with Tammy Grimes, a petite blond from Back Bay Boston with a flair for comedy and a wonderful singing voice. She was a wise and honest friend, who warned me one day, "Trues, it's pretty obvious you have a crush on George Scott. I'd be careful if I were you. He's married."

"Am I making a fool of myself?"

"No, Trues. Not yet, but if you don't watch out you might."

In the late autumn I was cast in one of three one-act plays. At last I would be on stage exchanging dialogue with George! Life took on a new and merry glow.

Arriving at the theater early each day, I learned my lines by the second rehearsal. But the fear of forgetting my lines when I looked at him forced me to look down or away, instead of looking him in the eye, causing the strong character I played to appear weak.

One afternoon as I prepared to leave the theater after rehearsal, George was on the stage, waiting for me. "Karen, have you got a minute?"

My throat went dry. "Sure." I heard myself speaking an octave higher than my normal voice. I leaned my trembling body on the back of a prop chair. It began to sway and creak. I stepped away from it and tried for a smile, but I felt the corners of my mouth twitching.

He walked toward me. I leaned again on the chair in a vain attempt to keep my entire body from quivering. Terrified he might hear my heart's thunderous beat, I covered my chest with the script.

"Karen, I've noticed when you say your lines to the other actors, you look at them. But not when you speak to me. I know I have an ugly puss," he laughed, "but if you could bring yourself to look at me, it would help both of us, especially in scene two where we're arguing."

Oh, how I wanted to look into those beautiful eyes! But afraid I'd either go dumb or stammer something inane, I looked at the stage floor. "I'm sorry. I will." If he only knew how much I loved his face!

"You're doing it now. Karen, look at me. Are you afraid of me? Or do you just not like me?"

I did it. I looked right into his eyes. Dizzy and breathless, I backed away from him. Forgetting how close I was to the edge of the stage, I stepped into the air. George grabbed my arm before I fell and held me firmly in his arms to steady me. "You could have broken your neck! Are you all right?"

As he held me, I smelled the clean, sweet, aroma of his skin and white shirt. I felt his warm breath on my cheek and the strength of his arms. I wanted to stay there for the rest of my life, but I was sure he could feel my body shiver and hear my heart thumping. I pulled away from him. "Yes," I said in a breathy, squeaky, voice. "Thank you. I'll be more careful after this."

Somehow I maneuvered a jump off the stage. Head down, I walked as fast as I could up the aisle and out of the playhouse. I felt certain, if I looked back, he'd be standing there laughing at me.

I rushed back to the dorm and found Sue sitting at her desk studying. Throwing my books on the floor and my body on the bed, I recounted to Sue the events of the last half-hour.

"I can't stand myself! I threw away my chance to be near him. I could have talked to him, but instead I muttered and fell off the stage. When he touched me, I could barely stand it. I felt ecstatic and terrified, and hot and cold, and ..." I rolled over and hugged my pillow.

"My poor little Roomo. You've got it bad." Sue shook her head. Pursing her lips, she reached into her desk drawer and pulled out four chocolate éclairs. "I have four fattening pastries, a half pound of fudge, and two Cokes. Let's splurge on calories and talk about falling in love."

The next morning Sue stood by my bed holding a cup of coffee in one hand, nudging me with the other. "Wake up, lovely Trues. It's time for some serious talk."

I opened an eye and looked at the clock. "This must be serious. It's only 9:15. On Sundays that's still the middle of the night."

"We need to talk."

" I thought we talked last night."

"I know, but I didn't think I should tell you last night. This morning I think I should tell you. And yes, it's serious. So sit up and pay attention." Sue handed me the coffee cup and sat down on her bed facing me. "The news about George C. Scott is not good."

"Is he sick or something?" I sat up.

"No. I mean the talk on campus about him isn't good."

"I don't want to hear gossip about him. Besides, why are you telling me?"

"Because I'm the only one who will." Sue took two large gulps of coffee, looked me in the eye, and began to speak slowly. "He has a terrible temper. He drinks until he's drunk. I heard last summer he beat up a bartender. And he's loyal to his wife and baby, so you probably don't have a chance with him, anyway. But if it happens, it could be the worst thing you ever did."

"Who told you this?" Whoever it was, I wanted to hit him.

"Everybody at the playhouse knows everyone else's business. You know that. It doesn't matter if gossip is true or not, it gets passed around."

"He sounds unhappy. Besides, I've heard all those rumors, and I refuse to believe them. He's a great actor and a nice person. And I love him, and I do not want to discuss this anymore." I ran into the bathroom and turned on the shower.

I stood in the center of the bathroom for some minutes, filled with anger and hugging myself. Then I realized I'd said, "I love him." It surprised me, too. I did love him. The anger was gone, and I felt giddy again.

The last few days of rehearsals I found I could look into George's eyes and not forget my lines. In fact, it helped my performance. He held a Svengalian power over me that seemed to help my concentration. I did not know it then, but that power he held over me would continue for many years to come.

By the end of the show's run my grades had fallen into the danger zone. Miss Graham summoned me to her office. I arrived four minutes before the appointed time, standing outside her door until I had to knock. I knew being late would only add to my already bad image. I took three deep breaths and exhaled slowly, a trick that always calmed my nerves before going on stage. It didn't help at all this time.

When I entered her office, Miss Graham motioned to me to sit across the desk from her in the same straight back chair I had sat in first time. I straightened my shoulders and tried to swallow.

Hands clasped on top of a folder, she peered over her half glasses. "In the past few weeks your grades have dropped considerably, Karen. And I've been told you have been missing many of your classes." She raised her head and looked me in the eye. "You know grades will be out in three weeks."

Did I ever. "Yes, ma'am."

"Are you trying, Karen?"

I would now. "Yes, I am."

"Do you keep regular study hours?"

Of course, I didn't. "Well, yes, unless I'm in a play, or rehearsal, or something."

"Perhaps you are spending too much time at the playhouse?"

"Oh, NO ... I have to. I have to attend classes there, and if I'm in rehearsals ..."

"Is there anything else bothering you? Perhaps I could help."

Oh, if she only knew. "No, Miss Graham. I'm just working very hard at the playhouse. I can do better."

"I surely hope so. You know you must keep your grades up, or you won't be able to continue here. And we like having you, Karen. I enjoy seeing you on stage, but ..." She tapped her pencil lightly on the folder. "If performing in plays leaves you no time for other studies, it might be best not to take roles for awhile. Maybe wait until you have brought your grades up." She raised her eyebrows, smiled, and waited for an answer.

"But I'm majoring in theater, and I really need the stage experience."

She tapped again. "If, within two weeks, your teachers report an improvement in both your work and your attendance, I won't require any changes."

"Thank you. I will bring my grades up." I tried to wipe away the beads of perspiration on my upper lip without her noticing.

"I'm going to count on that." She leaned closer and spoke to me as if I were deaf. "And, Karen, NO ... MORE ... SKIPPING ... CLASSES."

I nodded.

"You may go now." Her unexpected smile was a relief. "Please study hard. We'd hate to lose you."

"Yes. Thank you, Miss Graham." Outside the door, I leaned against the wall to support my wobbling legs. Then I headed to the library to study.

For the next two weeks I devoted myself to classes and studying. Flunking out meant never seeing George again. I couldn't let that happen. I skipped meals to study, but I didn't skip classes. The minute I walked into the dorm room I sat down and opened a book.

Sue kidded me a lot about the new phase I was going through. "English lit, Hmmm? Does this mean you have a crush on your lit teacher?"

I gave her the meanest, narrow-eyed, tightlipped smile I could conjure up. "Very funny. The least you can do is encourage me on my new quest for knowledge."

The only treat I allowed myself was to stand outside the music rehearsal rooms and listen to Tammy sing. I was in total awe of her. She would sing as sweetly as a bird and then belt out a song with more energy than I'd ever heard. Several times I sat on the ground, leaned against the building, and worked on my assignments while I listened to her. Tammy actually made studying enjoyable.

When grades were posted three weeks later I found, I'd won the battle, with one D, two C s, and an A in theater history. Now I could return to my afternoon vigils watching George.

Two

≈

At Christmas break I traveled home to Seattle. My father greeted me at the train. His eyes twinkled as he trotted toward me. "Welcome home!"

I had a flash of guilt as he parked the 1946 Studebaker in our driveway. I knew my parents had given up many extras to afford my tuition. They never complained about it, which made me feel worse. But I also knew they didn't really mind the expense. They'd had me, their third daughter, late in life. Their hopes and dreams for me were huge.

My mother rushed out the front door. "Merry Christmas!" She embraced me, pulled back and looked at me. "You're thin. Don't they feed you? And you look tired. Have you been studying too hard?"

"Actually I'm not thin. I've gained nearly seven pounds." I slipped my arm around my mother's small waist, and we walked together into the house. "They feed me too well. But I'm looking forward to your good cooking."

When I entered the front hall and saw the flocked Christmas tree standing in the living room, I felt tears come to my eyes. I knew the blue lights had been turned on for my homecoming. My parents never wasted electricity. Turning on the tree lights before six-thirty topped their waste list. "Daddy, your tree is more beautiful than ever!"

"Well, thank you," he chuckled happily. He stepped to the tree and repositioned a bulb.

"You see, Walter? I told you it was your best yet." My mother repeated this every year, as though she'd never before spoken the words.

Putting up the tree had been a ritual in our family for as long as I could remember. My father took pride in buying the saddest looking tree on the lot, bringing it home to the basement, completely rebuilding it, and spraying it white. Then he'd bring it upstairs to surprise everyone.

A few minutes after I arrived my mother set out a platter of beef patties, a bowl of mashed potatoes, and a bowl of green peas on the dining room table. She sat down opposite me and smiled sweetly. "We're so proud of you." She reached across the table, patting my hand. "Aren't we, Walter?"

"I should say so!" He chuckled, buttered a piece of bread, and took a bite. "And happy you're in a nice girls' school, where you're safe and can concentrate on your studies."

We chatted through dinner. My parents asked about the train ride, my teachers, my favorite subjects, and my roommate. I answered each question in detail, carefully leaving out any reference to the male staff actors at the playhouse.

After dinner I stood beside my mother at the kitchen sink, watching Tippy, our twenty-five pound yellow cat, finish off the meat patties in her bowl. As my mother washed and I dried the dinner dishes, I studied her face and thought of the hundreds of times I'd stood working beside her. Sometimes I'd resented having to do it, but it had always produced our closest moments. I wished I could tell her about George.

Mother looked up and said, "I know you have a wonderful future. You're level headed and if you want it badly enough you won't let anything stand in the way. Someday we'll sit in the audience as you perform on Broadway."

Mother smiled sweetly at me and nodded her head toward the dining room door. "Your father has very high hopes for you. He thinks you and your sisters are close to perfect. Well, no one is perfect, but I hope you don't let him down. That would break his heart."

During my two weeks at home my parents showered me with love and gifts. Their pride in me showed when they met friends on the street. "Hilda, you remember our daughter Karen? She's home for the holidays from Stephens College. She's an actress! You'll see her name in lights one day." I wanted to run from these accolades, but mother kept a tight grip on my arm. I had to remind myself of how good they'd been to me. I owed them the privilege of letting them show me off. The abundance of their pride and affection should have made me feel warm and loved, but instead I felt a gnawing guilt as my longing for George increased each day. I only wanted to be near him. I didn't care about anything else.

In January, I was cast opposite George in *Petticoat Fever* in the role of the woman he left behind but who chased him all the way to Alaska. For several days I resented the actress who had been cast as George's fiancée. On the fifth rehearsal, Doug McCall, the director, re-blocked the scene where I arrived to surprise the hero.

"Karen, I want you to barge into the room, jump into George's arms, and try to kiss him. That will give him a chance to refuse your advances and make it obvious he isn't attracted to you."

During the next rehearsal I jumped into George's arms, but I didn't attempt a kiss. Doug stopped us. "The scene lacks reality without the kiss. I want to see you rehearsing it."

"Okay, you're the boss," George said.

The next rehearsal we gave each other an uncomfortable short peck and a quick hug.

During the rehearsal for the curtain call the cast stood in a row holding hands.

As George took my hand he looked at me. Our eyes locked for an instant. And my heart stopped. Then we both quickly turned away. The curtain closed, and we turned to the other cast members.

On opening night the first scenes went well. The audience loved George's comedic talent. They laughed at his every line and facial expression. When my scene began, I stood waiting for my cue to open the door and jump into George's arms. Did I really dare kiss him? If I did, I knew I'd forget my lines. Maybe he'd turn away. My body was freezing, and I felt faint. I heard my cue. I threw open the door. George opened his arms. I jumped into them, giving him a small peck. He quickly put me down, and continued the scene.

During his remarks after the curtain calls, Doug said, "That kiss was just right. Don't change a thing."

The second evening as I flung the door open, I saw George and nearly lost my courage. I hesitated before jumping, throwing the timing off. As I jumped I felt his strong arms surround me, holding me. I kissed him. His warm lips softened as he returned my kiss. It must have lasted longer than I thought because we began to hear catcalls, and he slowly released me.

During the director's notes after the show, Doug didn't seem angry, making only a brief comment. "Hey, you two, lighten up on that kiss. George, you're supposed to be in love with the other woman, remember?"

The third evening I felt in charge of myself and vowed there would be no more than a peck. But the second I saw him, I lost the battle. I jumped, he held me closer and more tightly than the night before, and we kissed. It was a long, grinding, passionate kiss. For a split second I forgot I was on stage.

After the show, Doug took us aside. "What in God's name do you think you two were doing out there? George, you know you're not supposed to enjoy that kiss. It threw everything off. It changed the whole story. I don't want to see anything like that again!"

Breaking a cardinal rule, I didn't stop to remove my stage make up. I raced back to the dorm feeling excited, happy, and humiliated. I had let my passion for George get out of hand. What must he think of me? I fell on the bed and hid my head under the pillow.

A few minutes later Sue burst into the room. "Trues, what were you doing? Trying to wreck the show? That kiss made George's character look like a fool!"

I raised my head and looked at my good friend. "I didn't mean to. Honestly. But when I kissed him, he kissed back, and I ... It won't happen again." I put my face in the pillow and sobbed.

Sue sat on the side of my bed, stroking my shoulder. "You poor kid. This is really turning into a mess. But you need to know that after the last two nights everyone on campus is talking about you two. They think you're having an affair. That's not good news for George. People are saying he may be fired."

"We're not having an affair. We've kissed on stage, and that's all."

"I know. Just control yourself. Go easy. Concentrate on your lines. If you want it to work out, it will."

For the rest of the show's run, George and I carefully avoided anything more than a quick peck on stage. We also avoided each other off stage. After applying my makeup I'd sit in the dressing room with my back to the mirror, reading my script, so I couldn't track him coming and going. He didn't look at me when we passed in the hallway. In the afternoons I stayed in the dorm while he rehearsed the next show. Except for classes, I kept my distance from the playhouse entirely. I thought I could put an end to the talk. I couldn't stand the idea that George might be harmed by rumors. It would be my fault. He didn't care about me. He was married. What if his wife heard the rumors? I'd really made a mess of things.

Two weeks went by. Then, one day after class George stopped me outside the theater. "Would you meet me off campus at the Town Coffee Shop in half an hour? There are a couple of things I'd like to discuss with you." I nodded. I couldn't find the breath or the words to speak.

As I walked the four blocks to the coffee shop, my emotions shot in several directions. Mostly fear. He'd never said anything to me that did not relate to a show. Now he'd tell me he knew about my stupid crush. He'd tell me to forget it, to stop making a fool of myself. He was a married man and loved his wife. Halfway to the café I stopped, turning back toward the dorm. I couldn't face him. No, I had to face him. I bravely turned forward again. I was on my way to have coffee with George. Oh, my God, I was really going to talk to George.

I arrived first, sliding into a rear booth. Then I slid out again and headed for the restroom. I stood in front of the mirror and mumbled to myself, "I knew it. I look horrible. My hair is frizzy as hell. Why did Sue and I give each other those home perms? I look like a freak with a huge mound of cotton balls on my head. And no lipstick." Then I saw the dark wet spots under my arms on a field of light blue. They were as obvious as a wart on my nose. Too late to worry. I'd just have to keep my arms tight to my sides. I flattened my hair with water and repaired my lipstick. I peeked out the door. He hadn't come in yet. I walked as casually as possible back to the booth.

By then fifteen minutes had elapsed. Maybe he had changed his mind. Maybe he was playing a joke on the stupid, lovesick coed. I sat still with my arms at my sides, feeling the wet spots grow. Another agonizing five minutes. I stood up to leave just as George walked through the café door. Sitting down quickly, I attempted to pick up the menu, but my hand trembled so badly I had to lay it down and put my hands in my lap under the table. George stopped a waitress, ordered coffee, walked to the booth and sat down, facing me. He looked at me for a long moment.

"Hello. I'm sorry I'm late."

"Hello." My throat was as tight as a canning jar lid, and my answer came out in a whisper.

George stared at his open palms. "Thanks ... for meeting me."

"Oh. You're welcome." I studied the sugar bowl and the salt and pepper shakers sandwiching the paper napkins.

"Karen, I, ah, think ... the show went very well."

The waitress put the coffee cups in front of us.

"Oh, I did ... do, too. Once we got the kiss ... organized." I tried for a laugh, but could only manage a nervous giggle.

He nodded, smiled, picked up the sugar cup and poured several spoonfuls into his coffee. His hands began to shake, and sugar spilled onto the table.

We both studied the spilled sugar, then looked away.

Keeping my hands under the table, I couldn't reach for my cup. I raised my eyes to look at George for a brief second and then focused back on the table. "How are rehearsals coming for *School For Scandal*?"

"Good. Good. It's a great show." He took a deep breath and cleared his throat. He began to reach for his cup, but stopped. "Karen, I, ah, have something I need ... I want to say ... to ask you."

"What?" I said, far too loud. This was it. He'd be kind, but tell me to get lost.

He swallowed hard and leaned toward me. "Karen ... I'm terribly attracted to you. And I need to know if you feel the same way."

My body was suddenly floating in space. I looked into his eyes, but I couldn't speak.

"Karen, did you hear what I said? Should I shut up, or ...?"

"Yes."

"Yes? Yes what?"

"Yes. I do. Yes, I ... feel the same. Yes."

George didn't respond. He smiled at me. We sat for a moment, staring at each other. Then we both smiled and leaned in closer. I felt so happy, I wanted to laugh or scream or kiss him.

My hand lay on the table now. He touched it gently with one finger. "I've fought my feelings. But it's driving me nuts. I don't know what to do about this."

"We see each other nearly every day." I looked into his eyes and saw the same yearning I felt. "I don't think there is anything we can do about it." Both my hands were on the table, only an inch apart. I wanted to touch him so badly my whole body hurt. "Or we can both try hard to ignore it, to forget it, or ..."

He squinted his eyes as if he were studying me. "Do you want to? To ignore it?"

"It would be the right thing to do." I pulled my hands away closer to my side of the table.

He stared closely at me. "Do you think you could ignore it?"

"I don't think it will go away." My breath was coming in little spurts.

He scrunch up his eyes, looked at me and leaned in closer. "Then let's not ... ignore it."

I nodded. "Okay." I had no idea what to say next. I guess he didn't either because we sat in silence with silly smiles on our faces.

He started to reach again for my hand, but pulled back. "We'll have to hide our feelings around other people. Gossip could get back to Carolyn, and I don't want to hurt her."

"Of course. You're right."

"We'll have to meet at night. Can you get out?" He asked.

"I'll get out." I was beginning to breathe normally again.

"I'll let you know when." He looked at his watch. "We'd better leave before someone sees us. I'll go first. You okay?"

"I'm fine."

He grinned at me. "Goodbye." He rose and went to the front counter. He paid the waitress, looked briefly at me, and left the café. I sat for a moment, then stood up, glad he had gone first so he wouldn't see my legs wobbling.

I walked slowly toward the campus. What had just happened? One of my fantasies? No! George just said he's attracted to me. "It's true. It's really true!" I said out loud. Suddenly feeling foolish, I stopped to see if anyone had heard. I carefully controlled myself the rest of the way.

I told Sue everything as soon as I walked in the door. "Roomo, don't tell me you've decided to have an affair. It's too dangerous. You could be kicked out of school."

I stood looking out our window at the path leading to the playhouse. "I refuse to think about that. I won't. If all I have is one hour with George, I'll be happy the rest of my life."

For the next few days George and I were almost too casual. Sue noticed and warned me. "Ignoring each other won't work either, Trues. Everybody is watching you. And, believe me, everybody is talking."

After Sue's warning I tried to look friendlier, sometimes greeting him with a "Hello." When I looked into his eyes, though, I saw the same desire I felt and quickly looked away. I wanted to be with him so terribly it frightened me. Now that I knew his feelings, it tortured me not to touch him, to hold him. If only we could meet somewhere, just be together for a while.

In the next show, Shakespeare's *The Tempest*, I had the role of the Spirit, Iris. During the read through, Doug explained, "You'll walk alone halfway into the auditorium on the ramp above the audience, stand there and deliver your soliloquy."

The thought terrified me. George overheard me telling Sue how vulnerable I felt, and he secretly memorized my lines together with his own. On opening night he stood in the wings, where he could listen to me. I walked gracefully to the end of the ramp, spread my arms to the heavens, and opened my mouth. Nothing came out. I had totally blanked. I couldn't remember one word of my speech. Standing with my mouth wide open and my arms stretched to the ceiling, I felt as if my body had turned to marble. After a very long moment George whispered my line from the wings. "Ceres, most bounteous lady ..." I heard something, but couldn't make it out, and stood mute.

"... thy rich leas of wheat, rye, barley ..."

Nothing from me.

Thinking he was too far away from me to hear him whisper, he spoke louder. "Ceres, most bounteous lady."

I heard him! So did most of the audience. I repeated the line but couldn't remember the next one.

He waited a moment and continued as loud as he dared. "... thy rich leas ..."

Again nothing from me. As the audience began to fidget, I prayed for a tornado.

He tried again, louder still. "... of wheat, rye, barley, vetches, oats, and peas." I repeated the line, continuing nearly to the end of the speech, and blanked again.

George shouted, "HER PEACOCKS FLY AMAIN." The audience looked from me to the wings and began snickering. I asked God to let me fall through the ramp.

"Approach, rich Ceres, her to entertain." I rapidly finished the speech, turned and walking regally back down the ramp, where I finished the scene. Wishing I could run straight out of the theater and continue running out of town, I walked backstage to the makeup room and sat, filled with humiliation and self-pity, waiting for curtain calls which I knew I didn't deserve.

After the curtain call George whispered, "Meet me at my car in half an hour."

I apologized to Doug, tried to look relaxed as I said my goodnights, left by the stage door, and headed for George's car. I knew where he parked, and I also knew the shortcut to get there. I forced myself to walk slowly down the path until I couldn't be seen from the theater. Then I ran.

I saw him grinning at me through the front window. He'd been waiting for me. The anticipation of the moment to come overwhelmed me, and I had to stop to breathe. Opening the car door I slid in beside him, not daring to look at him. When he touched my shoulder, I shivered. I lifted my hand to touch his, turned my head and looked into his eyes. Desire shot through me as his arms went around me. Our kiss was long and fierce. We held each other so tightly I thought my bones would break. Finally, I pulled slightly away. "I don't deserve you. I'm a disaster. I ruined the show. You must be ashamed of me. If you hadn't cued me, I'd probably still be there."

"Oh, my baby." He laughed and kissed my hand. "It happens to us all. Nobody in the audience knew the difference."

"Oh sure. Iris stands there like a wooden dummy, and the voice of Stephano speaks her lines. I can't face anyone. I ruined the show."

"You did not ruin the show. Now, be quiet, and let me show you what I think of the fair Iris." He pulled me close again and kissed me gently on my forehead. He kissed me on the neck, smoothed my hair back, and kissed my mouth. Then he pulled my hair back, squinted at me, and said in a harsh voice, "You belong to me now. You know that, don't you?"

"Yes."

After that evening we were together whenever possible. We met at George's car and drove to an isolated parking lot in back of a long vacated grocery market. "Not a very glamorous setting is it, Baby? I wish we could meet somewhere else, but I ..."

"It doesn't matter. As long as I see you. I don't care where we are. Just to look at your face and feel your arms around me is heaven. Let's not think of anything but each other. Now kiss me and tell me when you decided you wanted to be an actor. "

"I'll do just that, my lovely," he said in an Irish brogue. "But I'm not a-tall sure I want to waste time talkin'." He opened the glove compartment, removed a bottle of bourbon, took a drink, and offered it to me.

"No, I'd be expelled on the spot if I came in with liquor on my breath."

"I'll just take one for you, then." He held the bottle up in salute and took another drink.

Three

≈

When we were together, we controlled our passions. I was only nineteen and not ready to go any further. George knew how I felt and held back. But our need for each other made it nearly impossible for us to part. One night, when I finally looked at my watch and saw I'd missed curfew, panic hit me when I thought of the consequences.

"Don't worry, my baby, we'll get you over the back fence. No one will see you."

"George, the fence is six feet high with wrought iron spikes. I can't climb that."

As we neared the school, he turned off the car lights and drove to the rear of the campus. "Come on Baby, I'll help you."

I looked at the fence, wet from the evening rain. "George, it's slippery and dirty, and there might even be a moat on the other side. I can't."

He leered at me and gave my fanny a spank. "Yes, my sweet. It's designed to ward off wayward girls like yourself." He clasped his hands together. "Come on, be brave. Put your foot in my hands, and I'll boost you."

I took my shoes off and placed my foot in the center of his hands. He lifted me close to the fence, and I grabbed for a spike. Hugging it, I pulled myself up. My white blouse rubbed against the fence. I swung my left foot over and pulled my right foot up and over. As I did, a spike caught the hem of my skirt. "George, help! My foot is caught and I'm slipping."

"Drop, Baby, drop to the ground."

"It's too far. I can't." My body went rigid with panic.

"You have to. Just let go."

"I can't. I'd rather dangle here."

"Karen, on the count of three. Let go."

"NO!"

"Yes. One ... two ... three!"

I let go, my skirt ripped, and I landed in a sitting position. Relieved and dazed, I sat for a moment. When I looked up at George through the spokes, I saw him laughing.

"How can you laugh? I'm sitting here wet and dirty with a torn skirt and you're laughing!"

"You look as if you've been attacked by a mud monster. Are you all right?"

"Yes. I guess."

"Then, I'll keep on laughing."

"George, you're so mean. What am I going to do?"

"If I were you, I'd avoid your housemother." He laughed again and tossed my shoes over the fence. He grinned at me a moment. "I really love you a lot. Now get going." He walked toward his car, turned, and gave me a silly smile and a little wave.

I sat on the ground for a minute, watching him leave. I knew I should be mad as hell, but I could only smile at our antics and feel so lucky he loved me. I put my shoes on, pulled myself up, and walked toward the dorm.

Then I began to feel sorry for myself. This was wonderful. Just wonderful. Here I was, cold, wet, dirty, and miserable. I could be expelled tomorrow, but would anyone give a hoot? NO.

Luckily, nobody was at the reception desk. Removing my shoes, I ran for the backstairs, mindful not to leave wet footmarks. After tiptoeing up the stairs, I ran silently to my room.

Carefully opening the door, I stepped in and closed the door quietly behind me. I'd made it! I leaned against the wall.

"Hey Roomo, where have you been? As if I can't guess! I had to cover for you. It wasn't fun!" Her tone made it clear she was more worried than angry.

I began to remove my wet clothes. "I'm sorry. We just lost track of the time. It won't happen again. I picked up my clothes, stepped into the bathroom, and turned on the light. When I saw my reflection in the mirror I knew why George had laughed. My face and arms were streaked with black from the fence and mud from the ground. But when I saw my blouse and skirt, I didn't feel like laughing. Both were ruined. Black from the fence was on the white ripped blouse. My favorite dirndl skirt was no more. I looked again at myself in the mirror and smiled. It had been worth it. I'd been with George.

Now that I knew it was possible to return safely after curfew, I became bolder, paying little or no attention to the clock when we were together. Sue covered for me during the nightly bed check using every ruse she could dream up. She stuffed my bed. She turned out the lights, pretending to be asleep. At bed count she opened the door a crack and yawned, "Please be quiet, Trues is asleep, and we have a show tomorrow night." Night after night I missed the curfew.

After a month of telling lies on my behalf, Sue waited up for me. She sat studying a script in bed as I crept in. She put her script down and spoke slowly. "I have to talk to you."

"I know. I'm late again. I'm sorry. I hate that you have to lie for me, but ..."

"In the first place you look like hell." She got up, went to the bathroom and returned with a damp facecloth. "You're ruining your clothes climbing the fence. You're not getting any sleep, and you never study." She began to wipe the dirt from my face. "You may think this is none of my business. But I am involved. Trues, I lie for you two or three times a week. If I'm caught, we're both out of school. I think I've just about run out of excuses. Some night soon Miss Kelly is going to come into our room and check your bed."

"I really am sorry. I haven't been fair to you."

"You're damn right! And not fair to yourself. Look, if you get caught, you're kicked out of school. What happens to George? Nothing. He goes right back to his wife and on with his life. And from what you've told me about your parents, it would probably just about kill them."

"You're right. I've been selfish. Please don't give up on me."

"I'll never give up on you. But you've got to come out of the clouds and begin thinking straight."

"I'll try. I will. I'll get in by curfew from now on."

"I'll believe that when I see it. Now go to bed and take your biology book with you."

Though Sue was a wonderful friend to me, I knew she didn't like George. I didn't tell him I had confided in her, but in March I told him Tammy knew everything. He was relieved I had someone to talk to and glad it was Tammy. She became his confidante too, and the three of us became close.

Near the end of March George slipped me a note asking me to meet him behind the playhouse. He greeted me in high spirits. "My darling, I'm working on a way for us to be together. I hate this hiding as much as you do. There's an opening for an apprentice at the Mad Anthony Players at the Zoo Theater in Toledo."

"But what about you?"

"I've been offered a job as a staff actor. I'll take it if you're accepted as an apprentice. So listen, we have to work fast. The application will be posted on the callboard this evening before the show. Fill it out and submit it to Doug right away. You are one of the best actresses in the playhouse. I'm sure if you want the job, you've got it. Go back now, before we're discovered. I love you."

I kept watch and grabbed the application from the board as soon as the stage manager posted it that evening. I filled out the form, submitted it, and crossed my fingers.

Four

≈

Several weeks later in May I sat in bed one morning writing to my parents. I'd put it off long enough. They were the greatest parents in the world, and I was a selfish brat. I promised myself I'd make it up to them someday.

Dear Mother and Daddy,

I'm writing to warn you my grades are not quite what you had hoped for. I've been awfully busy at the playhouse, studying theater. SO, except for Theater History my subjects suffered from neglect. But I have a wonderful chance! I've been invited to work at the Mad Anthony Players in Toledo, Ohio, for the summer season. I'll only be an apprentice but the experience I'll gain will be priceless.

One other problem. I don't get paid. So I'll need a little money for transportation and room and board. Also, this means I won't be coming home. I'm disappointed I won't be seeing you. But this is a really big chance for me. And who knows, maybe I'll be discovered and go right on to Broadway!

Anyway, I hope this isn't too much of a letdown for you. I love you both very much and hope you'll agree to let me go.
Karen

Within a week, I found their reply in the mail.

Dear Karen,

Your father and I have talked it over, and though we have some reservations, we are going to let you go.

We will call you next Sunday afternoon to discuss the details.

We are disappointed we will not see you this summer and will miss you. But if this is what you want and you think it may lead to big things, we want it for you, too.

We look forward to talking to you on Sunday. About one, or so, our time. I think that's about three o'clock your time.
Love,
Mother
P. S. Daddy says to tell you hello.

Sunday morning I woke up early. For a moment I wondered why I had a feeling of dread. Then I remembered the phone call. I'd have to tell more lies to my parents. They'd always been so good to me. They trusted me. They loved me. And I loved them. I hated this. But if it meant I'd be with George, I'd keep on lying.

I was waiting in the dorm hallway when the phone rang at exactly three p.m. "Hello."

"This is Mrs. Truesdell. I'd like to speak ..."

"Mother, it's me."

"Oh. Karen. This is Mother."

"Yes, hi, Mother."

"How are you?"

"I'm fine. How are you and Daddy?"

"We're just fine. Daddy wants to talk to you."

"Okay."

"Here he is."

"Karen?"

"Yes."

"This is Dad."

"Hi, Daddy."

"I have a couple of questions about your summer plans." He sounded a little worried.

"Okay."

"Will there be older folks there to look after you?"

"Yes, Daddy, the producer, directors, and some of the cast will be older."

"Is anyone else going from Stephens?"

"One other girl in my theater department. We'll travel together so you don't have to worry about me."

"I don't feel real good about this. You say you'll be living in a boarding house?"

"Yes, Daddy, with all the other actresses."

"And the men will be living somewhere else?"

"Yes, Daddy."

"Well, you seem to want this an awful lot. I know you're level headed, and mother feels it'll be okay. I wish you were coming home instead. But ... well ... I guess it will be all right"

"Oh, thank you, Daddy. You won't be sorry, I promise."

"I'll say goodbye, then. Here's your mother."

"Karen?"

"Yes, Mother."

"I want you to promise you'll take good care of yourself, and if anything goes wrong, you'll come straight home." This was a familiar warning since sleepover days in junior high.

"Yes, Mother, I promise."

"Well, I guess we'd better hang up. Call us the minute you arrive. You can call collect. We love you. Goodbye. Daddy says goodbye."

"I love you, Mother. Goodbye."

I replaced the receiver and leaned against the hallway wall. How could two such great people have raised such a liar? I felt so guilty my body suddenly went limp. But I was also terribly relieved.

That evening, giddy with happiness, I sat with George in his car. "Darling, everything is working out! We'll be together all summer. I can't believe it. We can be together, really together. No more hiding."

"Yes, Baby, it'll be wonderful." He stopped and turned to face me. "But ... I'm afraid we'll still have to do some hiding. I haven't wanted to tell you, but Carolyn is coming, too. We'll be living with her brother and sister-in-law. It's the only ..."

I put my hands on his chest and pushed him away. "Your ... wife ... is ... going ... to Toledo?"

"It's the only way I can afford it."

"And she'll be there all summer?"

"Yes. There's no other way. Baby I'm so sor ..."

"You'll be living with your wife. We'll still be apart. Nothing will change."

Tears stung my eyes. I turned away.

"Baby, don't say that. We'll be together all the time."

"Oh, I'm sure we'll find some nice grocery parking lot to run to." My voice rose, and I laughed. "Or maybe there will be a dark cellar under the theater where we can hide."

"Darling, please don't ..."

"I don't even know now why I'm going."

"Baby, don't forget you'll be in summer theater. You may get to act professionally. This could be a great opportunity for you." He turned me to face him. He lifted my chin and wiped my tears. "Please don't worry, my baby. We will be together. I love you more than life. Nothing will stand in our way." He swept my hair back from my forehead, squinted at me, and kissed me almost savagely.

At the end of May the playhouse produced the last show of the year, *Ring Round The Moon*, a comedy by Jean Anouilh. George played the dual roles of the twins Hugo and Frederic. Cast as Isabelle, I was thrilled to have finally been promoted to a lead role opposite my love. And Tammy again showed her versatility playing the manipulating aristocrat Madame Desmermortes.

As always, the audience loved George's great sense of comedy. He could look outrageously silly one minute, exit, and come out immediately as the other serious twin. The reviews were excellent. We were all feeling pretty pleased with ourselves, but we were sad to be leaving Stephens and our family of actors.

George and Carolyn planned to travel together by car to Toledo. I would make the trip alone by bus. George, Tammy and I met for our last goodbyes on the porch of the playhouse. "Trues, don't forget to write me. You, too, George-o. And please, both of you, be careful. I love you, and I'm leaving before I cry." We both kissed her, and I clung for an extra minute. I felt lonesome for her already. What would I do without Tammy in my life?

After Tammy left, as the students and teachers said their farewells and took last minute photos, George and I sat together on the wooden railing, trying to appear casual. George whispered, "I'll see you in Ohio, my baby. I love you. I'll find a way for us to be together. I promise."

Wanting to throw myself into his arms and never let go, I leaned close to him and whispered, "I'll be there, no matter what! I love you." We stood up, gave each other one last brief smile, and walked in opposite directions.

When I returned to the dorm, Sue had just finished her packing. We sat on her bed, and she said to me, "Trues, do you remember the day you were in the shower, and I pulled back the curtain and took that picture of you?"

"Oh, yes. How could I ever forget? That was in retaliation for pretending to take one of you."

"Well, here it is. You can keep it or throw it away. But if I were you, I wouldn't show it to George.

I looked at it and slipped it into my pocket. "It's horrible. It makes me look like a hooker!"

We stood up and hugged again. "One last thing. Trues, please be careful about this thing with George."

"Thank you, Sue. You're a wonderful friend. But don't worry about me. I'll be fine. I love you, and I'll write you."

THE DEPARTMENT OF THEATER ARTS

presents

THE PLAYHOUSE COMPANY

in

RING ROUND THE MOON

By Jean Anouilh

Adapted by Christopher Fry

Directed by John Gunnell

Setting by Chandler A. Potter	Costumes Designed by Dorothy Groff	Properties by Jane Mehl

CAST

Joshua, a crumbling butler	William Cragen
Hugo, a young man about town	George C. Scott
Frederic, his brother	George C. Scott
Diana Messerschmann, engaged to Frederic	Joan White
Patricia Bombelles, Messerschmann's secretive secretary	Eugene Shewmaker
Madame Desmortes, aunt to Hugo, Frederic and Lady India	Tammy Grimes
Capulet, her faded companion	Marcea McCurley
Messerschmann, Diana's father, a melancholy millionaire	Sarge Bensick
Romainville, a patron of the arts	Robert Hurtgen
Isabelle, a ballet dancer	Karen Truesdell
Her mother, a teacher of the pianoforte	Ann Halloran
Lady India	Connie Brew

SCENE

The action of the play passes in a Winter Garden in Spring

ACT I

Scene 1. Morning

Scene 2. The same evening. Before the Ball

ACT II

The same evening. The Ball

ACT III

Scene 1. The same evening. After Supper

Scene 2. Dawn

Five

≈

I packed two suitcases, plus my theater trunk. I loved that antique, black-domed chest. It had been my father's special gift to me. He'd had it since he was a boy in Kansas. A week before I left for college he asked me into the basement room where he kept it. I expected him to relate more stories about his father's theater, but instead he said, "It seems you are the only one in the family interested in the theater, so I'm giving you this trunk."

His beloved trunk! I was stunned. I had no idea he even thought that much of my acting. I was thrilled, but what if I failed? What if something happened to the trunk? Daddy had had it for forty years. I couldn't gather any words to speak.

He smiled at me gently. "Maybe it will bring you good luck. Now let me show you some of my favorite mementos."

We knelt beside the trunk for most of that afternoon while Daddy reverently removed his memorabilia: a lock of hair from his first haircut at the age of four, his second and third grade report cards, a photo showing him at the age of twelve, playing the mandolin on the front steps of his grandfather's theater. "That was the first legitimate theater in Kansas," he boasted. He showed me a book of World War I poems and letters he had received from friends during the war. He touched each item tenderly as he emptied the trunk.

We sat together for three hours that afternoon. We had never been closer and sadly, would never be close again. Finally, with a large lump in my throat, I accepted the gift of his most prized possession and promised I'd take good care of it. That promise would later come back to haunt me.

When I arrived in Toledo, I took a cab to my final destination: a green and white wood frame, two-story boarding house on a street lined with oak and maple trees. I'd be staying there with the other actresses and apprentices. The driver carried my trunk and cases up the four stairs to the wide wooden front porch. I paid him and rang the bell.

A young female yelled, "It's open."

I pulled open the squeaky screen door and yelled down the hall. "Hello. I'm Karen, one of the apprentices. Is anyone here?"

Two young women stepped out from the end of the hall. "Hi. I'm Stacey, and this is Cricket." Stacey was tall and statuesque with thick, dark brown hair. When Cricket said hello, it was obvious how she had acquired her nickname. She clicked her tongue and giggled. Her entire face was a smile. A third voice yelled down from the second floor. "And I'm Amy Crawford. Bring your bags up, and I'll show you your room."

Amy was at the top of the stairs in her underwear. I guessed she weighed no more than eighty-five pounds and stood about five feet tall. She had short, tightly curled hair. Freckles covered most of her body. The way she flew down the stairs reminded me of Peter Pan.

Amy reached down to help pull my luggage up the last step. "Are you a full-fledged actress or a lowly apprentice?"

I slumped my shoulders as I put on a sad face. "I'm just a lowly apprentice."

Amy sat on her bed to put her shoes on. "Me, too. Yo-ho, heave ho." She pointed to the extra bed. "That's yours. Have you been to the theater yet?"

"No, I came here first. I'm going to change and go over."

"I'll go with you and show you around."

The amphitheater stood on the grounds of the Toledo Zoo. It looked huge by comparison to the 200-seat playhouse at Stephens. I was in awe, and I tried to keep my mouth from hanging open.

"This is so beautiful," I managed to say.

"Enjoy looking at it now," Amy warned me. "Because from the notices on the call board, we're going to spend every day and night working."

"That's okay with me. I'll be a slave to show business any day!" I did a deep bow toward the theater.

Amy opened the backstage door. "Enter, fellow thespian."

On the wall opposite the door was a poster board filled with pictures of past productions. While I studied the photos of *Othello, Angel Street, Winterset*, and *Harvey*, intimidation set in. "Amy, we're in real professional theater! I don't know if I'm that good."

Amy took my arm and giggled. "Too late for talent analysis now! Those are only photos anyway. It doesn't mean they were all great actors." She opened the door and cupped her ear dramatically. "I don't hear voices. Not even a ghost. Let's walk the stage and leave before Sir Scrooge arrives and sets us to work cleaning canvas."

Stepping onto the stage, I took a deep breath. "There's that special theater smell. I could stand here and breathe it in forever."

"Yeah ... great, huh?"

I stroked the front curtain, gazed up at the flies, ran my hands across some flats, and reverently touched the lighting board. Amy pointed out the graffiti on the backstage wall, where we would add our names before we left for the season. As we stood in the makeup room, my chest tightened, knowing George would soon be sitting in there. I wasn't sure I could wait.

On our way back to the boarding house we stopped at a food market. While I shopped for staples, Amy filled me in on the other apprentices and actors who had arrived. She told me Stacey had been hired to play leading lady parts. Jealousy hit me, knowing George would be playing opposite beautiful Stacey. But I couldn't let it show. No one could know about us. I had to keep my feelings hidden.

"The rest of us slaves will be cast when needed. Do you know anything about the male actors coming?"

"No, nothing," I lied, looking straight ahead, and adding quickly, "Let's go fix some dinner."

George and I had agreed it would be risky to contact each other. It was torture not to hear his voice. I couldn't concentrate on anything, but I went through the motions of settling into the boarding house. The first evening, after dinner, I met one of the boarders, who spoke for the landlord. Tall and willowy, Miss "Garbo" Clayson wore her white blonde hair swept up and fastened with a large, ornate comb. Her bright red and orange Chinese kimono touched the top of her 1940's-style brown and white spectator shoes.

"I know how it is with people of the theater," she told me as she snuffed out a half-smoked cigarette in the ceramic saucer she held. "I used to be one myself. I once acted in a show with Joel McCrea. Very nice guy."

She picked up a lighter from the kitchen table and lit another cigarette. "You've got free reign of the kitchen. Just clean up after yourself." As if demonstrating, she blew a small ash off the counter into the sink. "And please don't eat my food, which I keep in the lower left side of the refrigerator. I'd appreciate it if you could get in before three in the morning, pay your rent on Mondays, and get me free tickets to the shows." She winked, blew a stream of smoke at the ceiling, and left the room.

Monday morning Amy and I reported for work. If I couldn't be with George, at least I had the theater. I proudly swept, scrubbed, dusted, and scraped under the arms and seats of the hundred and fifty chairs that were assigned to me.

On my second day the actors began to arrive to rehearse for *Dark of the Moon*, the first production of the season. The leading role would be played by Jake Dengel. Jake and I became immediate comrades. He was a talented young man with a giant heart. He made me laugh.

At three fifteen on my third afternoon, the side theater door opened and George stepped inside. I stopped breathing. His eyes scanned the stage and rows of seats. Then he spotted me. We stared at each other, not moving. He turned away, jumped onto the stage, introduced himself to the crew, and asked directions to the dressing room. After a quick glance in my direction he left the stage. The crew went back to their tasks, so no one noticed my trembling body as I walked toward the stage door. I opened it quietly. Walked through. Closed it carefully. Then, nearly falling, I raced down the stairs to the dressing room.

George stood there waiting, his arms outstretched. I stopped a few feet from him. The anticipation of touching him was almost painful. "Hello," I said.

"Hello," he said with that big grin that I loved.

I jumped into his arms, my legs went around his waist, and the kisses were hard and passionate. "Baby, my baby, I'm so glad to see you," he murmured. "My baby ... my darling ... my baby." He put me down, stepped back, looked me up and down, and frowned. "Do you wear that red halter top often?"

"Yes, it's been so hot. This is the only really cool thing I have to wear. Why?"

"Don't wear it anymore. You look too sexy."

"Are you teasing?" I reached out to put my arms around him.

He held my arms to my sides. "No, Baby, I'm not."

"Well then, I'll wear it only for you."

"That would be fine." He raised his eyebrows and let my arms go free. He pulled the elastic, and the top snapped back. "I love you, Baby." He pulled me close. "I'm just so glad to see you. I've missed you. Sit down over here, Baby. We should talk about a few things."

We sat together on a prop bench. He gave me his address and telephone number, but I wasn't sure why, because he told me never to use it. I described the location of a city park I'd discovered, just a few blocks from the theater.

"We could meet there until we find a better place," I told him. "It's thickly wooded. I don't think we'll be seen."

"That's my baby!" He kissed me, barely touching my lips. "Carolyn seems happy to be with her family. For a while she won't be watching me too closely. She thinks we have a rehearsal tonight, so as soon as you're off work, we can meet at that park." He gave my halter another tug and let it snap again. "Then we'll find our special place in the woods." He held my face in his hands. "Oh, my God, it's good to see you. I've missed you more than you could ever know." He kissed my forehead. "We'd better get back upstairs, or we'll be missed. You go first."

That evening when Andy Fox, our stage manager, finally let the crew leave, I found George in the dressing room. He nodded and left by the side door. I followed a block behind him to the park. He walked into the thick woods, turned and held his arms open to me. My entire body filled with butterflies. I jumped into his arms with such abandon he nearly lost his balance when he caught me.

Sitting on the soft ground, he leaned against a huge oak tree, reached for my hand, and drew me down to sit on his lap. "Now, how is my baby?" His breath smelled of bourbon.

"Your Baby is so happy she can barely speak. Oh, how I love you. And this place is perfect! I think the woods are enchanted. Shall we live here forever?"

"Yes, my darling. Forever."

I returned to the quiet boarding house after midnight. I stopped in the kitchen to make a peanut butter sandwich before I crept up to the room I shared with Amy.

Amy opened one eye. "My gosh, Karen, where have you been?"

She startled me, and my response was slow. "I ... ah ... went to a movie. Probably the last one I'll see for a while. Go back to sleep, now. I'm sorry I woke you."

"That's okay. My alarm's set. We have to be at the theater by eight ... in ... the morning." Her voice trailed off as she fell asleep.

As I crawled into bed I told myself I'd better think up excuses for future late evenings. I lay awake thinking of all the wonderful evenings ahead with George in our special place. Thinking of him as I touched my body ignited such heat I could barely stand it. I wanted him desperately. But actually making love ... I remembered my mother's warning. "Stay a good girl until you're married. If you give it away to the first man who comes along, it can lead to a life of heartache." So far, George had been understanding and had not pressed me to go further than I wanted. But I knew he would soon.

During the next week I kept busy building the sets and rehearsing *Dark Of The Moon*. George and I met in the park the first five evenings. He waited for me under the same oak tree, and we sat holding each other on the soft leaf-strewn ground. Each time we met I felt sure it could never be that perfect again. But the next evening, feeling his strong arms and soft mouth and seeing the desire in his eyes reflecting my own, I knew our passion had grown even deeper.

"Tell me about you," George said one evening.

"What about me?"

"About your past."

"Wooo. My dark past." I poked him in the ribs.

"You know what I mean." He poked me back. "Your childhood. I only know that you grew up in Seattle, and you love your parents."

I told him about my first time on stage at the age of three, about school and the shows I'd been in. "Actually, my life has been pretty average."

He put his hands on either side of my face. "Baby, nothing about you is average!"

"So. It's your turn. Tell me all."

"There isn't a lot worth telling. My mother died when I was eight. I saw her leave with my father one evening. She wore a black raincoat and carried a black umbrella." George rubbed his temples and said, "I think she wore a black raincoat. That's how I remember her." He got up and began pacing. "My father said, 'Stay put. Your mom isn't well, and I'm taking her to the hospital.' I sat by my window all night watching for them. The next morning Dad came back alone. 'Your mother's not coming back.' That's all he said. He wouldn't tell me why."

George stared into the woods, as though he saw someone, and then shook his head hard back and forth. He walked a few feet away, rubbed his temples and turned toward me. "Of course she never came back. She was dead. But I couldn't believe it. I kept waiting. She hadn't said goodbye. For years I hated her for that."

"What happened then?"

"My older sister took care of me. She still does, in a way. I don't know what I'd do without her."

"What about your relationship with your dad?"

"I hated him. The older I got, the more I was convinced he'd killed her. Not really killed her, but with neglect. My aunt kept trying to tell me my mother loved me. That she never would have left me if she could help it. "

"Did you ask your father about it?"

"God, NO! The old broken-down drunk. We never talked. I

hate him. I left home and joined the Marines as soon as I graduated from high school."

"How did the Marines suit you?"

He laughed harshly. "Oh, it was perfect. They had me digging graves. It was so much fun I was tempted to jump in and cover myself up." He laughed again, then stopped abruptly to rub his temples. He looked so vulnerable standing there, his arms up by his head, smiling his sad, crooked smile. He walked to me and I held him.

After a few minutes we sat down again. I asked him if he had any further contact with his father.

"Nope. And I'm going to keep it that way." He reached into his pocket, pulled out a small flask and drank from it.

"I wish I'd known your mother. I'd like to tell her how grateful I am to her for giving birth to you."

"Well, my dear, I'm grateful for you." He kissed my neck. He kissed my mouth and neck again, and his hand moved to my breast. He stopped abruptly. "It's time to take you back to the boarding house, my love."

One very muggy evening in early July, a somber George stood waiting for me in the woods as always, his arms held out in greeting. We held each other for a long moment. Then he stepped back and took my hand. "My darling, Baby, I can't stay. Carolyn is beginning to suspect something. She said she'd wait up for me tonight. We'd better not meet for a day or so." He held my hand so tightly it hurt. "Believe me, I don't want it to be this way. But unless we want to be discovered, I've got to spend some time with her."

I wanted to ask, "Why? Why not tell her and get it over with?" But I made an effort to smile and said, "I understand. I'll miss you so much. But I agree, we need to be careful." He kissed me harshly, almost angrily, and held me so tight I couldn't take a breath.

"We'll be together very soon. I promise." He brushed my hair back from my face and looked at me closely. "You're mine! You always will be mine. Nothing else matters."

During the next few days my feelings of rejection and loneliness grew. I found myself picturing George and Carolyn making love. The vision continually forced its way into my thoughts. It became unbearable. I needed someone to confide in before I started screaming. I must have looked the way I felt because Jake stopped me in the makeup room after rehearsals one evening. Literally stopped me. He blocked the door so I couldn't escape.

"Karen, why don't you ever join us for dinner or party with us? Every time we ask, you're busy with something. Do you really want to be left alone?"

"I'm not really a loner. I've just had some problems."

Jake put his hands on my arms. "If you want to talk about anything, I'll listen. How about sitting on the back porch for awhile?"

"Yes. I'd like to do that."

We sat on a canvas porch swing, a prop for one of the coming plays. We sipped our Cokes and talked about everything but what was on my mind. Then, after a few moments of silence, Jake abruptly asked, "Do you have a crush on George?"

The question came so suddenly I felt panic. Oh, God, I thought. People know. I wasn't prepared for the question. I looked Jake in the eye, took a breath, and feigned surprise. "What makes you ask that? He's married."

"Well, just because one person is married doesn't stop another person from wanting him."

I stood up, walked a few steps, and turned to face him. "If I tell you something, will you promise not to say anything to anyone? I mean, promise!"

Jake nodded. "Yes. I promise."

I started talking slowly, and then much faster, as it all poured out. "George and I knew each other before we came here. We've been in love for months. We want to be together, but he has to wait for the right time to tell his wife. We love each other, we do, and we'll be together, we will. He's told me so often. He does love me. He ..." I stood in front of Jake and began to sob.

Jake offered a tissue from his pocket and guided me back to sit in the swing. After I stopped crying he said, "I knew you both came up from Missouri. That's no secret. And we know George is married. We saw his wife backstage on opening night. And most of us guessed the two of you were ... Well, you try so hard to keep your distance from each other, it's pretty obvious that something is going on."

"I didn't think anyone noticed. We've been so careful. At least I thought we were. Oh, God, I don't know what to do." I started to cry again. Jake dug into his pockets but couldn't find another tissue. He finally picked up a paint cloth from the swing and handed it to me.

Jake took both my hands in his. "Look. For a while, why not hang out with me? It'll confuse everyone. Maybe the gossip will die down, and it will give you and George time to think things out."

"Thank you. I've needed a friend."

Jake laughed. "Well, my friend, you now have paint all over your face."

Six

≈

I tried not to think about the lies George had to tell Carolyn. I knew he loved her and the baby. Many times I had fleeting thoughts of breaking it off. Very fleeting. I was so crazy in love that absolutely nothing mattered but being with George. I refused to think of anything else. I wouldn't let guilt take hold of me, and I pushed away all thoughts of consequences.

Our special place in the woods became our sanctuary. Near the middle of July we were enjoying one of our late night picnics. As I picked up the last bite of cheese, kissed it and placed it in George's mouth, I chattered on about our plans for the next Monday, the day of rest for actors and crew. "I can hardly wait for next Monday. It's going to be wonderful. A whole day alone together. Where shall we go? Can we go swimming? Or maybe rent a boat?" George held up his hand to stop me. "Oh, I know. I should shut up. But I'm so excited. I can't help it."

He put his finger gently to my mouth. "Baby, I have some bad news." He took my hand and looked into my eyes.

"What is it? You look so miserable. Is something wrong with Carolyn?"

"No. It's nothing like that. But I have to let you down about next Monday. I promised Carolyn we'd go to dinner with her brother."

I stood up and walked a few feet away. Of course, he'd have to be with his wife. She had to come first. I'd taken too much for granted. I didn't want to hear any more.

"She knows the theater's dark on Monday. She wants me home most of the day. Darling, if I'm not very careful, she'll begin to suspect something."

"LET HER! Maybe it's time!" My anger was so profound I felt ill. I turned toward him and spit the words at him. "Maybe it's time you decided who you want! I guess I should have expected this. After all, I am having a dirty affair with a married man who can't seem to make up his mind." I wanted to hurt him. I wanted to hit him. I wanted him to suffer.

"Darling, you don't mean that." He stood still, his arms at his sides. "Please. You don't mean that."

I began to say more when I saw defeat in his eyes. I had hurt him, and I realized then that we were both in pain. After a moment I went to him and took his face in my hands.

"Oh, my dearest, I'm so sorry. Please forgive me. I was hurt. I didn't mean it. I love you so. I love you. I can't bear to see you look so miserable. Please tell me you'll forgive me."

He held me. "Of course I forgive you. Will you forgive me? I love you, Baby. I'd die if I ever lost you."

"You never will. Never."

The next few days my duties included staying to clean the theater after the crew finished. George had two late night rehearsals. We met two or three times for a few minutes in the downstairs dressing room. It felt almost awkward. Neither of us said very much. We both felt cheated out of the approaching Monday.

I spent most of my free time with Jake. "Which do you want more," I asked him during lunch break as we shared a hamburger. "The theater or the movies?"

"Both, of course." He smiled, "I want it all. How about you?"

"Yes, me, too. I always have. Here, you eat the rest. I'm not hungry."

"You're not your cheerful self today. What's the matter?"

"George told me he couldn't be with me on Monday. Our first whole day off, and he has to be with his wife. He's having dinner with his in-laws." I reached for the hamburger. "I've changed my mind. Let me have another bite. I think I'll get big and fat."

He handed me the burger and said, "Well, he is living in their house. It would be pretty rude not to spend some time with them. And besides, the latest news is that all crews are on duty Monday to finish up the sets. You couldn't have been with George anyway."

"Oh, golly, why doesn't that news make me happy?" More than my words, I was sure my ironic smile said it all.

After we finished dressing the stage on Monday evening Jake and I sat on the stage door steps. "I'm sorry about the way things are going for you," Jake said. "But I'll tell you what. You look exhausted, and I'm hot and still hungry. Let me treat you to some ice cream. Maybe that will cool us off and help cheer you up."

I gave my friend a hug. "Let's do just that."

We had eaten halfway through our banana splits when George, Carolyn, her brother and his wife walked through the restaurant door. I crouched down in my chair, picked up the menu, and held it in front of my face.

Jake peered at me. "What are you doing? You look like you're hiding."

"I am. George just walked in."

"Why hide from him?"

"He's with his wife. I'm sure she doesn't know I'm in town. She saw me at the playhouse in Missouri. If she sees me now, she may begin to figure things out."

Jake covered his face with his menu. Then he pulled it down an inch to peek over the top. At the other table, they were all laughing. George sounded happy and relaxed. Jake covered his face again and whispered. "Well, we can't sit here hiding behind our menus all night. Let's leave money for the ice cream on the table, get up and go. Come on. I'll cover you."

Looking, I'm sure, as if we were trying to escape the bill, we kept our heads turned away from George's table as we walked a fast pace out the door. Outside, I continued the pace, walking ahead of Jake. "Now, what's the matter?" he asked, nearly running to keep up. "I don't think we were seen."

"*That* is the matter. Sneaking around. I feel like a thief. I never thought of myself as the 'other woman.' But I am. She can be seen in public with him. I have to hide behind a bowl of ice cream. I'm the dirty one, I'm ..."

Jake put his hands firmly on my arms. "Stop it! You're in a bad position. You have to hide now, but not forever. Didn't George promise things would change?"

"Yes. But I'm beginning to ..."

"You can't expect to have an affair with a married man and have everything be hunky dory. Come on." He took my hand. "Let's go listen to Cricket tell us again how she almost met Laurence Olivier."

The next day George told me he had spotted us the minute he'd stepped into the café. His first thought had been to suggest they go to another place. But he knew that wouldn't work. He'd been the one who'd suggested the restaurant. They'd wonder why he wanted to leave, since he'd have no good reason, and Carolyn would ask questions later.

He said it was hard not to laugh when he saw me hiding behind the menu. But then he realized I had been in a terrible position, and he felt guilty for having put me there. He had seen the escape and had wanted to run after me to tell me how sorry he was and how much he loved me. I was sure he meant his words. But they did not erase the sting of having to hide our love.

A week later Amy burst into our room and jumped on my bed. "Karen, did you see the callboard before you left the theater?"

"No, I left."

"You've got a part! You've got a part!" Amy jumped onto the floor and kept jumping.

"A walk on?"

"No. A real part! The slave girl in *Uncle Tom's Cabin!*"

"That's a walk on."

"I know. But Jeepers Crow, it's a start!"

Rehearsals gave George and me a reason to be together during the day. At breaks we met wherever we dared. When his arms went around me, I wanted to get closer, inside his skin, and stay there forever. "Being near you all the time is almost harder than not seeing you at all."

George would draw back and squint at me. "I know, my baby. I know."

"It's wonderful to be together on stage again," I told him one night. "But I'm worried about Carolyn recognizing my name in the program."

"Don't worry about Carolyn. She's probably forgotten the names and faces from the playhouse. Now come a little closer, so I can grab you and throw you to the floor just the way Simon Legree does to the slave girl."

The second Saturday evening in July George asked me to meet him in his car after the show. As always, as soon as I rounded the corner from the playhouse, I began to run. I ran all the way to his car and stopped a few feet away. With the glorious expectation of seeing him and touching him, my insides felt like a thousand bugs were jumping around in there.

I saw him grinning at me through the windshield. I walked slowly the last few feet, smiling back at his wonderful face. Opening the car door, I slid in beside him and closed the door. He grabbed me. He kissed me fiercely over and over again. He kissed my neck, my shoulder, and my lips again.

"Take a ride with me," he murmured in my ear. We drove on quietly for four or five minutes. I studied his profile and asked where we were going. He circled my shoulders with his arm and drew me close to him. "You'll see, my dearest." Taking the road through the center of the park, he continued driving on gravel that led to near wilderness.

He stopped the car and looked at me for a long moment. Then he pulled me to him more urgently than ever before. I shivered and murmured his name over and over until I was nearly screaming. He ran his hands over my body. He began to unbutton my blouse. Then he stopped.

"No. Not here," he whispered. He reached to the backseat for a blanket, opened his side door and got out. He came to my side, opened the door, and offered his hand. "My beautiful Karen." I took his hand and we walked to a huge pine tree. He spread the blanket on a bed of soft pine needles. He kissed my forehead lightly and looked into my eyes. Then he kissed me fiercely, holding me so tightly I could barely breathe.

He sat down on the blanket, and I sat beside him. He reached into his shirt pocket and brought out a scrolled, silver wedding ring. "My darling, this belonged to my mother. I want you to have it."

"George, it's beautiful. So simple and so beautiful."

"Let me put it on your finger." He took my left hand and placed it on my finger. "As you can see, my mother had large fingers. It's too big for you. We'll have it sized someday. But I wanted to give it to you tonight."

"Thank you. I love it. I love that you gave it to me. I love you."

We held each other, our kisses beginning sweetly and growing to such a fierceness I wanted to scream for wanting him. He put his hand inside my bra, caressing my breast. His other hand pulled my skirt up. He kissed my arms and hands and thighs. The passion was agony. He lifted me to meet him.

"Now, please," I pleaded." Now." I closed my eyes.

We were floating among the stars and moon, George saying my name over and over. I opened my eyes, and he was there. He whispered, " I love you, my darling Karen, I will love you forever."

We lay on the soft pine needle ground, our bodies entwined. I felt complete. And completely happy. We smiled at each other, giggled like children, and kissed sweetly. He kissed my shoulder. "You're crying, my darling." He gently wiped the tears from my face. "Did I hurt you?"

"I'm crying because I'm happy, and yes it hurt a little. But I didn't mind, knowing it was you."

He kissed my hand. "My brave Baby." He looked closely at my hand and kissed it again. "I love seeing that ring on your finger. It was meant for you. Stay here a minute, my sweet." He went to the car and brought back a bottle of wine.

We sat, resting our backs against the pine tree as he poured the wine into two glasses. He held his up. "A toast, my love. That we love each other as much in fifty years as we do this moment." We touched glasses.

"My dearest darling, there is no question about that. I will love you forever and beyond." I nestled my head on his shoulder, which felt so right. I was home, and I was sure we would love each other forever. "Tell me your dreams for the future," I said.

"Let's see." He squinted his eyes and looked down at me. "How about nine children?"

"Nine! How about two?"

He stroked my face. "And they'll both look like you."

"We'll live in an English Tudor style house. Of course, you'll be a very famous actor," I said with a British accent.

"As well as you, my deah."

"And we'll be frightfully wealthy."

"We'll have a ranch in Montana, and I'll teach you to ride, little lady." I laughed at his John Wayne imitation.

"And a beach house on Cape Cod, and a yacht for you, my lord."

"I should like that terribly, madam!"

"And I'd like to own an antique shop," I added. "Would you mind?"

"Not at all, if I may have five dogs."

He refilled our glasses and looked deeply into my eyes. "You are my only real wife. No matter what happens in the future." He spoke the words slowly as if I should memorize them. "Remember always. You are the only one I will ever truly love."

"I will remember always," I told him. It didn't occur to me not to believe him. If it had, I would have pushed the thought away.

About midnight we headed back to the car. I looked down to admire my ring. It was gone. "Oh, no. Your mother's wedding ring! George, it's gone! It must have fallen off when we were packing up to leave. It was on my finger when we were sitting with our wine." I ran back and knelt on the ground. George sat beside me as we sifted through the thick bed of pine needles and leaves. We pushed and piled the leaves, and repiled and sifted the pine needles again until it became obvious it was a futile search in the dark. Sobbing, I began to dig in the dirt with my nails.

He stood up. "We might as well give up, sweetheart. It's gone."

"No! I won't give up. I'll find it. I know I'll find it. Please help me." I clawed at the dirt and the piles of leaves. "I'll find it! I'll find it!"

He pulled me up and held me. "Baby, you're hysterical." He tightened his hold on me. "Stop! It's okay."

"No." I sobbed. "It will never be okay. I lost your mother's ring. How could I have done that when it meant so much?"

"Baby, Baby, stop." He started to walk me toward the car. "We'll come back and search in the daylight tomorrow. I'm sure we'll find it then."

"You can't be sure."

"No. I can't be sure. But we'll try. Now, come on, it's late, we have to get back."

A block before the rooming house George stopped the car. He kissed me lightly. "Darling, please don't let this ruin what we had this evening. It's only a ring, my love."

"It's not only a ring. You know that. We have to find it. I'll feel guilty all my life if we don't."

"We will. I'll meet you two blocks from the theater at noon. We'll drive out to the woods and look for it. We'll find it. I promise. I love you."

As I opened the car door to get out, he took my arm and pulled me back. "Do you know how to take care of yourself?"

"What do you mean?"

"You know, so you won't get pregnant."

"Well ..." I had just made love with this man and now I was embarrassed.

"Go in, take a hot bath, and wash yourself well. That ought to help."

My darling married man doesn't seem to know much more about sex than I do, I thought as I walked away.

After a thorough scrub, I crawled quietly into bed, my body shivering and aching. My tears wouldn't stop. For the remainder of the night, I lay reviewing the events of the evening. Making love with George was the most unbelievable and beautiful moment of my life. Then I lost the ring. That had been the worst moment of my life. It was too much to bear. Too much to think about. I fell asleep at five. Amy's alarm awakened me at six-fifteen.

We searched in the woods for two hours the next day, but we didn't find the ring. I felt ill, exhausted, and ashamed. I couldn't look at George, convinced he would never forgive me, and knowing I would never forgive myself.

That night after the show we were exhausted and went our

separate ways to sleep. I suffered horrible dreams all night. In the first one my mother and father were fighting over the silver ring. It fell to the floor, and Tippy the cat ate it. In the second dream George and I were digging again. Someone threw the dirt back in and tried to bury us. I woke up in the middle of the night, frightened and sobbing. Thank goodness Amy was a sound sleeper.

The next evening George had a pickup rehearsal after the show. "Darling," he said to me, "by the time I'm through here, it will be after midnight. Why don't you go on home? You look beat."

I found Jake in the makeup room and asked if I could buy him ice cream. After we'd settled ourselves at a table and ordered, Jake said, "You look awful. Did you have a fight with George?"

"No. It's worse than that. I lost his mother's wedding ring."

"How did you manage to do that?"

"He gave it to me the other night. It was too big for my finger, and it fell off."

"That's really awful." He touched my arm in sweet sympathy. "I gather you looked for it in the daylight."

"Yes. We both searched for hours. I feel sick about it. Having it on my finger was so wonderful. I loved it. And now it's gone."

"How was George about it?"

"Amazing. He said it didn't matter, but I know it does. My God, it was his mother's!"

"I don't know what to say. I wish I could help. Do you want me to go out and look for it?"

"Thanks, but I know it's gone. It's gone, Jake."

Then a terrible thought struck me. "You don't think it's an omen, do you?"

"Of course not. Don't think that way. Everything will work out for you and George. You know that."

"I hope you're right."

That night I slept, and in the morning I swore to myself I'd make up to George for the loss of the ring. Somehow.

Near the end of July I was cast in the show, *The Curious Savage*, a larger part than the slave girl, but not a lot of stage time with

George. He, however, had a lot of stage time with the luscious and sexy Stacey, and I hated it. I felt incredible jealousy. I wanted to yell, "Get away from him, you bitch, he's mine!" He belonged to me! Yet on stage he was with Stacey, and at home he shared a bed with Carolyn. I had to hide in the woods with him

The next production was a delightfully different story for me. I was given the part of Joanna Lyppiatt in *Present Laughter*. Now I could be luscious and sexy. George and I could flirt on stage. We could flirt backstage. We could make love after the show. I was in heaven. There was only one minor chord. George drank more heavily every night.

When I mentioned his drinking he said, "I have to. There's no way out of this mess we're in. I need to drink. And I'm not drinking that much. Leave it alone."

In my mind there *was* a logical way out. Tell Carolyn about us. But he was not in the mood to discuss it then so I let it go.

In August, halfway through rehearsals for the next show, *Brighten The Corner*, Stacey received a call from her father. Her mother was ill. They needed her at home. She left the next morning.

The playhouse director, Mark Tobin, caught me backstage that same afternoon. "Karen, I want you to take over the part of the wife. You haven't much time to prepare, but I know you can handle it. What do you think?"

That was the part of George's wife. Hallelujah! "What do I think? I think I'm very happy. I'd better get started."

"Well, good." Mark gave me the script Stacey had been using. The cues and blocking were marked. "I'll have George come in an hour early the next five days, and the two of us will work with you. I'm going to let you free of your apprentice duties this week. I think you'll be ready." Mark held out his hand. "I'm sure I've made the right decision. Check the call board for rehearsal times." I danced my way back to the scene shop thinking the career I'd worked for was finally beginning. Nothing could stop me now.

Seven

≈

That evening George was waiting in his car near the entrance to the woods. "George, do you believe it? I'm going to be the leading lady!"

Opening the glove compartment of his car, he said, "Just sit still a minute, Baby, I want to give you something." I thought he was reaching for his flask, but he pulled out a handmade paper star with my name across the front and pinned it on my blouse. "There, my baby, that makes it official. You're a leading lady." He kissed my hand. "You're going to be the best, most beautiful, most wonderful leading lady this town has ever seen. Let's drink to it." He pulled out his flask from under the front seat, took a drink, and offered it to me. "Here, Baby."

"I don't need a drink," I said, "I'm so happy I feel drunk."

He lit up a Lucky Strike and said, "Now, let's get to work on your lines."

We sat together in the car and worked for two hours, until we couldn't keep our minds on the script and drove to the woods, where we hurriedly undressed each other. Making love with George was always wonderful, but now that I was a leading lady I felt equal to him, and I allowed myself to become more aggressive. "You surprised me tonight," George grinned at me as we were dressing. "I loved it."

George worked with me on the script for several evenings. If it hadn't been for him, I'd have been too nervous to take on a large role on short notice. Since everyone was aware I'd been given the part, George and I could work publicly in the makeup room after the show. We worked on my lines, and he calmed my nerves.

"I'm not sure I can handle this," I said, more than once. "Maybe

I shouldn't have taken it on."

"Baby, all you need is confidence." Wearing that beautiful sideways grin of his, he knelt in front of me and took my hand. "Do not worry, my lady. Soon all the commoners'll love you. And, if you fall, I'll pick you up." He stood, picked me up and swung me around until I was dizzy.

In the next two weeks it became obvious George had been drinking before he arrived at the theater. I knew the rest of the cast and crew were aware of it, too. He came in later each evening, looking unkempt and slurring his words. I was embarrassed for him, but other than that it didn't bother me. I was convinced once he told Carolyn about us, the guilt would leave him, together with the need to drink.

Several times as I watched him stagger to the wings I wondered if he should go on. But the moment he made his stage entrance he seemed to sober up. Drinking didn't seem to hurt his performance at all. His timing didn't falter, his characterization didn't weaken, he never missed a cue, and he delivered his lines perfectly. He could memorize a script in three readings and never lose a word. It seemed to come so naturally to him. It was a wonder to me, since I always struggled to remember my lines.

"Can you believe that guy?" a crewmember whispered to another actor one evening before the show. "He comes in crocked and stammering, nearly tripping over his feet. He steps on stage and doesn't miss a word!"

His marvelous performances were also becoming well known. The theater sold out nearly every night. The local news people asked regularly for interviews, and his reviews were nearly all raves. Yet George never gave any indication that his career as an actor was becoming a reality.

And his heavy drinking continued. One evening it nearly took its toll on both of us. We met at his car after the show. I knew he'd been drinking heavily and was close to being totally drunk, so I urged him to sit and talk or take a walk. He insisted we take a drive instead, and started the car with one hand while he took a drink with the other.

It began to rain. When he pulled into traffic, the car skidded, nearly hitting a man crossing the street. I shrieked and asked him to stop. But he ignored me, sped up, and headed for the highway. He was breathing heavily and sweating. His driving became even more erratic as he passed between cars, narrowly missing both.

As I watched him, his face seemed to change. His skin tightened, and his eyes bulged. I felt as if I was witnessing Dr. Jekyll turn into Mr. Hyde.

I was terrified. "Please slow down, please."

"It's better this way!" he shouted back at me.

"I don't know what you mean. Please stop the car, and we'll talk." I reached out toward him, but he pushed me back.

"I don't want a future without you." He had one hand on the steering wheel. The other held a bourbon bottle.

"I won't leave you. Only, please, slow down. Please!" The wind and rain were heavy now, and a thin film of water covered the road.

"I'm tired of living this way. I don't want to hurt Carolyn. I don't want to live without you." He took another drink.

I tried to take the bottle from his hand, but he held it out of my reach. "Please, please slow down!" I tried to grab the wheel, but he gave me another hard push to the other side of the car.

"It doesn't matter any more."

The windshield began to steam up. When I tried to clear it with my hand, I only succeeded in smearing it. I opened the side window an inch.

"Nothing matters any more." His voice was a growl. He swerved the car to the left and headed for the oncoming traffic.

"No! George, stop! Please! Please!"

As we passed cars in the lane to our right, I saw a woman's face turn to us, her mouth opened in horror.

"This is the only way," he roared. "Nothing is any use."

"Please!" I screamed. "You're going to kill us. Stop the car!"

With the windshield foggy and streaked, the lights of the oncoming traffic blinded him. He suddenly swerved the car again, narrowly missing a truck. I was thrown against the dashboard and back to the side door. The car slid off the highway onto the left shoulder. An approaching car blared its horn and swung out of our way.

"Please," I screamed. "I'm begging you! Stop the car!"

He was quiet for a second. Then he slammed his foot on the brake. The car skidded in a half circle on the gravel. I fell hard against the side window. As he slowed the car to a stop, his face returned to normal.

George sat staring out the front window for several minutes. Then, he rubbed his temples and rested his head on the back of the seat. "I'm sorry. Oh God, I'm sorry, Baby. There's no way out of this. We're trapped." He looked at me, "Oh, Baby, you're hurt. Your head is bleeding. Oh, God." He pulled a handkerchief from his pocket and gently dabbed at my forehead.

"Don't worry," I said in a shaky voice. "It looks worse than it is. A cold cloth will take care of it."

"I might have killed you," he sobbed. Tears rolled down his face.

"Yes, you might have." I was too shaky and frightened to be angry. "George, that was awful ... terrible."

"I couldn't think of any way out of this mess."

"You think killing us is the answer?"

He pounded on the wheel. "That's just it. I don't have an answer!"

"I want you to turn the car around and drive me home." My fear had begun to turn to anger. I was about to tell him so, when I looked at him and saw the misery in his eyes.

"None of this is right. I hate lying to Carolyn. She's a good woman. But you're my life. If I lose you, I lose everything. Oh, God." He grabbed me, sobbing. "I love you. I love you. I've got to tell her. But I can't. I can't tell her."

"I know. I'm desperate, too. But killing ourselves is not the answer."

"I don't want to hurt you, Baby." He grabbed me as if my body was his lifeline and held me so tightly I couldn't take a breath.

"I know. But promise you won't try something like this again." My body shook, and I felt dizzy. "Please."

He drew back and looked at me as if he were searching my face for the answers. "I love you, Baby. I love you."

"And I love you. We'll find a way."

When Amy heard the door to our room open, she snapped on the bedside lamp. "What happened to you? You look awful. Were you in a wreck or something?"

"No. I ... we ... drove too fast and ..." The dizziness I had been fighting took over, and I nearly fell onto the bed.

Amy jumped out of bed. "Here, lie down and put your feet on this pillow. I'll get a wet cloth." She dashed down the hall to the bathroom, returned with a cold wet face cloth that she draped on my forehead. "You've got a huge bump. You may even have a black eye tomorrow. Guess we'd better get our stories straight. So, what happened?"

"Nothing, Amy. I fell off the backstairs, and I hit my head on the sidewalk. That's all."

She gave me a long unbelieving look. "Okay. I guess it's none of my business, so we'll just say I socked you when you tried to steal my autographed picture of Tyrone Power."

Close to hysteria, it took all my strength not to let go. "You're a good friend, Amy. Thank you for not asking any more questions."

After Amy turned off the light, I lay in the dark, trying not to review the evening. But I kept hearing horns and the screeching of brakes. Kept seeing nightmarish headlights coming toward me, and seeing George's face turn into a horrible mask.

I promised myself I'd find a time soon to try to reason with George when he was sober. I'd talk him into cutting down on his drinking. I'd convince him to tell Carolyn about us. But at the same moment I knew I wouldn't. I was in awe of George. I worshipped him. I'd stay with him under any circumstances.

George became increasingly more desperate. He held me more tightly and kissed me more fiercely every day. He repeated over and over, "It's not fair to either of you. I've got to do something very soon."

I couldn't seem to find the right moment to talk to him, so again I found solace in my friend Jake. Two days later on an ice cream walk, I reported the story of the near highway suicide. When I'd finished he said, "I wish you wouldn't go driving any more with George when he's been drinking. He might try it again."

"Jake, it isn't that he wants to hurt me."

"I know. But George in a car with a bottle and desperation don't mix. You've got to be more careful."

By the third week in August, George had formed a plan. He surprised me with it one muggy, late night in the woods. After we'd fed each other our picnic of crackers, cheese, and wine he said, "We're going to New York together, Baby. Carolyn can stay here with her brother. We'll both get acting jobs. No more hiding!" He held his bottle up high and then drank.

"You, my darling man, are crazy. Where do we get the money? We probably won't get cast in a show right away. What do we live on?"

"It'll work. It has to. We'll leave when the season is over." He swept my hair back and looked closely at me. "Please, Baby, say yes, please. It's the only way for us to be together."

I felt giddy to the point of bursting. "Did you just ask me to go to New York with you?"

"Yes, my dearest. Will you?"

"Please say it again."

"Will you join me for a short, or maybe a lifetime trip to New York?"

"Yes. Well, of course. Yes, YES!"

"Oh, my dear lady," he said in his best Irish accent. "You won't be sorry. I promise ye! Ye won't be sorry."

We gathered our things and headed for the car. I stood for a moment, memorizing the spot, feeling sad and regretful, as though I were leaving a dear confidant behind. This had been our hideaway. Our own quiet place where no one could touch us. Even with New York ahead, I knew I'd always miss this special place that had been ours alone.

The next day at lunch I shared a sandwich with Jake and told him my news. As I did, I realized what a good friend he'd been to us and how I'd miss him. "Jake, have you ever thought about trying New York?"

"Of course. Hasn't every actor? But I haven't the courage to go it alone. If I had someone to go with, I might."

I wanted to invite him to come with us, but I thought I'd better talk to George first.

I didn't ask George what he told Carolyn. It was enough to know she hadn't fallen apart and agreed to stay with her family while George got his start. I didn't expect or actually want him to tell her about us. I told myself it would be better for everyone. But in truth I was afraid she'd find out, and I didn't know how I'd handle that. If she had been aware of me, she surely would have said something by then. I had to stop thinking about Carolyn, or I might lose my courage and my chance to be with the man I loved.

Next on the agenda was the dreaded call to my parents.

"Hello, Mother?"

"Is that you, Karen? Why you sound as if you're right next door! Hold on, I want to get your father. She put the phone down. I could hear her yelling out the back door. "Walter, come in here quick. It's Karen long distance."

"Karen?"

"Yes, Mother. I'm calling from Toledo. I want to tell you my exciting plans. I'm ..."

"Wait a minute, honey. Your dad is sharing the receiver with me. Can you talk any louder?"

"Can you hear me now?" I heard my parents whispering about who should hold the phone.

Daddy yelled into the phone. "Yes. Fine. Go ahead."

"Mother and Daddy, I'm going to New York. Isn't that exciting?"

"Do you have a job there?" Mother shouted.

"No, not yet. But I'm going to live with Tammy, my friend from college. She's been there a while and knows the ropes. I'm going to look for acting work."

Daddy spoke now. "Well, I just don't know what to say. We'd sure like to have you come home for awhile. But if you're set on this, well, I guess it sounds okay."

It was Mother's turn. "Karen, are you all right? I mean, healthy and all?"

"Yes, Mother. I'm very healthy."

"Yes, well ..."

Daddy's voice. "So ... how are you on money?"

"I'm fine Daddy, I'm fine."

"Yes. Well I'll send you a little something to get you through."

"Thank you, Daddy. And please don't worry. I'll be fine. Just fine."

"Will you call us when you're settled?" Mother asked.

"Of course. Mother, be happy for me."

"Oh, I am, dear. I just ..."

"This is Dad. Your mother has a little cold, and she had to sneeze. So, we'll say goodbye now. You take care of yourself and let us know how things are going."

"I will, Daddy. I promise."

Mother came on again. "We love you, dear."

"I love you, too. Goodbye."

"Goodbye, honey. Goodbye, now. Goodbye."

When I replaced the receiver I was weak with relief and filled with guilt. They would have been devastated to know I'd been lying, that I was actually asking for money so I could go to New York with a married man. There was a second of questioning myself about what the hell I was doing. But only a brief second. Everything was going to be wonderful. It had to be.

The next day I received a letter from Tammy.

> *Dear Trues,*
>
> *I hope everything is going well for you. I'll be in New York starting in September. You can reach me through the Neighborhood Playhouse. If you ever get here, you can stay with me, and I'll show you around.*
>
> *I hope things are going well with George. Please be careful.*
>
> *I love you like a sister. Write to me.*
>
> *Tammy*

I happily put the letter in my pocket. I'd not only be with my love, but I'd be near my friend Tammy. "I'll see you sooner than you suspect," I said to myself.

A few days before the end of the season our director called me into his office. "Sit down, Karen. I've an interesting proposition for you." Mark leaned on the front of his desk facing me. "There's an opening for a leading lady in a winter stock company in Michigan. I've been hired as the staff director, so hiring the actors is up to me. I'd like to hire you for the season."

My pulse jumped. This is what I'd been working and hoping for all my life. It would be the beginning of my professional career. Oh, how I wanted to say yes. But accepting would mean I'd have to give up my plans with George. Unthinkable.

Mark went on talking. "It's an equity theater, so you'd soon get your equity card. It's a great opportunity. I hope you'll take it. It could very well be the beginning of a fine career."

"Mark, I'm stunned. It's a dream come true. And ... if things were different ... I mean ... I thank you more than I can say for offering it to me. But I have other plans for the fall and winter."

"I hope these other plans are important. Not many young actresses get an opportunity like this. And Karen, you have talent, beauty, everything it takes. I think you could go places. You may never have an opportunity like this again. Please take a day and think about it."

"Well, all right. Thank you. I will think about it. I'd better get going. You're a good friend, Mark. Thank you again."

"Karen, please, really think about this."

I did. I took a long walk by myself and thought about it all afternoon. I'd probably never get a chance like this again. But then, maybe I would in New York. Weren't all the great opportunities there? And wasn't George more important than acting? One minute I was ready to accept the offer, and the next minute I was filled with panic at the thought of losing George.

I told Jake about the offer before the show that evening. His advice was emphatic.

"Karen, don't be a fool. This is a once in a lifetime offer. Just think of the things it could lead to."

"But I can't take it. I'd lose George."

"You can't not take it. Don't you want a career in the theater?"

"Of course, I do. It's all I've ever wanted. But maybe I'll find it in New York. And in New York I'll be with George. And I can't let him down."

"He's a big boy. He can take care of himself. It could work out perfectly. He'll go to New York and get acting jobs and agents and things. You do a season in stock and then join him. You'll both have your own successes. AND that will give him time to get his divorce. "Come on, Karen, think straight."

"That's just it. I can't think straight. Everything has happened so fast. I have to talk to George."

As we sat in George's car that night, I told him about the offer and my talk with Jake. He reached for his bottle of bourbon and took a long drink. "Baby, that's wonderful. I'm so proud of you. Of course you're going to do it."

"But what about us?"

"Like Jake said, we'll both get some experience under our belts and get together later on." He took a pull on his bottle and stared out the side window.

"Is that honestly the way you really feel?"

"Yes."

"Look at me and tell me you want me to take the offer."

He turned toward me, but did not smile. "It would be great for you."

"Would it be great for you?"

"I'd miss you, but ..." His voice was so soft I could barely hear him.

"How much. How much would you miss me?"

He grabbed me roughly and held me to him. "Oh my love, don't leave me. I need you. If we're together, we can do anything. I love you. I love you."

"Of course I'll come with you. I only needed to hear you say it." We held each other in silence for a moment, and then I had a thought. "How about Jake coming with us? That way we could split things three ways. It would help all of us. And maybe we'd all find success. Wouldn't that be great?"

As he lit a cigarette, I studied his flat stomach, wide shoulders, long fingers, and heavily veined hands. His thin rugged features were compelling. There were moments when I didn't feel worthy of him and wondered why he loved me.

He took a deep drag on his cigarette and said, "If Jake can put up with us, I can surely put up with him. He's been a good friend to us, and we all get along. Sure, let's ask him to go."

The last two days all crewmembers were busy cleaning the theater, storing flats and props during the day, and packing their own things in the evening. So Amy and I had little time to talk privately. The final morning I sat on the porch waiting for George when Amy joined me.

"Well, I'll miss you and all the intrigue," Amy said. "Watching your love affair has brought unexpected excitement into this wannabe actress's life. While you're walking the streets of the big city, think of me struggling away at Smith."

"How long have you known?"

"Oh from about the second week, I guess. I knew for sure the night you came in with the big bump on your head."

"Did everyone know?"

"I think most suspected." Then, she looked at me seriously and squeezed my hand. "I really hope New York brings you happiness. Please be careful."

"And you promise to audition for *Peter Pan* someday."

"I promise." Amy's eyes filled with tears. "I'll really miss you. Please let's not lose touch. You're a terrific person. And you're so talented. I just have to say, I wish you hadn't turned down the stock job in Michigan."

"Amy, you know ..."

Amy held up her hand. "I know, I know. Love comes first. Well, give me a big hug." We held each other for a moment. Then Amy drew back and pointed down the street. "Look. Here comes your Sir Lancelot on his white charger. Only in this case it is a 1946 gray Chevy. I hope it makes it all the way to New York." I put my hand over Amy's mouth, kissed her on the cheek and ran down the porch steps to George.

We loaded my two cases on one side of the back seat and tied my trunk on the top of the car. "Goddamn, Karen, do you have to bring this trunk along?"

"Oh, yes. That's my good luck trunk. It's one of my prize possessions."

We slid into the front seat, and I shrank down out of sight. George reached over and pulled my head up. "We don't have to hide anymore. We can walk down the streets of New York, holding hands and smooching." He kissed me hard and started the car.

"Aren't we taking a chance? We're not out of town yet."

"I know. I couldn't wait."

Neither could I. I was free to love George without hiding. Everything to look forward to. I sat up straight, rolled the window to the bottom and took a deep breath of fresh air.

We drove to Jake's rooming house and found him waiting with a huge smile and one large suitcase. He loaded his things in the car trunk and jumped in the back seat.

The first few miles we were giddy, bidding farewell to our past, and looking forward to the future. A married man, a young wide-eyed actor, and me, a naïve, inexperienced woman in love.

Then George got serious and asked me how much money we had.

"Not a lot, I'm afraid."

"How much is not much?"

"Forty-five dollars. My father sent it to me. I told him I was going to New York to be with Tammy. I've done nothing but lie to them for months. I don't feel very good about it."

"When you're rich and famous you can pay them back. And, you're right, forty-five dollars isn't much. How about you, Jake?"

"I've got seventy-five dollars. I counted it before I left."

"I had to leave money with Carolyn, so together we have one hundred and ninety dollars. That's enough to get us there, rent a room and buy a few groceries."

"There's one thing we won't have to worry about." I straightened my shoulders and gave him an, I'm-so-proud-of-myself look. "That's sending your shirts to the cleaners. I bought an electric clothes iron yesterday! Now, I can ..."

"You did what?"

"Please keep your eyes on the road, George. I bought an iron to press your pants and iron your shirts so you can look tidy for all those auditions. I can do yours, too, Jake."

I was sure he'd pat my knee with pride. But instead he roared at me, "Didn't you hear me when I told you to save every cent?

What the hell did you think you were doing? Are you deaf and dumb? Damn it, don't you listen when I tell you something?" He raised his arm. For a second it looked like he might hit me, and I held my hand up for protection.

Jake sat forward in his seat. "Oh, come on, George ..."

"Stay out of this, Jake."

George turned back to me. "Say something."

"I hear very well," I said, biting my lip so I wouldn't cry. "And you don't have to swear at me." I was in shock. Had I heard right? He'd made it clear he was not proud of me and thought I was stupid. AND he yelled and swore at me. This was a new George, and I didn't like his attitude at all. I hoped he'd go back to being the other one.

Stopping the car by the side of the road, he took a deep breath. "Baby, I'm sorry. I wouldn't hurt you. You know we haven't got much money. And God knows when one of us will land a job." He looked at me, cowering by the passenger door. He drew me to him and cradled me. "I love you, Baby, but why in God's name did you buy an iron? You could have bought food. Why an iron?"

"We need an iron," I sniffled. "We can't afford to send your clothes to the cleaners, and I wanted something that would make us feel married."

"And an iron makes you feel married?" He shook his head, opened the glove compartment, pulled out a bourbon bottle, and took a drink.

"Yes. My mother taught me to be sure my husband looks clean and pressed before he leaves in the morning. Does that sound silly?"

"No, my darling. It doesn't sound silly. Just ask me before you spend any more money. Okay?"

"Okay." I had been strongly reprimanded. This had not been a great beginning to our trip.

He started to pull into traffic, slowed again, and stopped. "Your damn trunk is shifting around up there. Jake, get out and see if it's secure."

Jake tightened the ropes on the trunk and climbed back into the car.

"Is all well on top and in the backseat?"

"All's well, George."

Just outside Erie, Pennsylvania George said, "We're going to stop soon and buy you a wedding ring."

"Oh, I couldn't ... It was my fault your mother's ..."

He slowed the car and stopped. He took my chin in his hand. "I thought we'd gotten over that."

"No. I'll never get over it. I ruined the most wonderful moment of my life. I lost the most precious thing I've ever had. I ..."

"Ah gee, and I thought I was the most precious thing you'd ever had."

"Don't joke. I'll never get over it."

"Baby, nothing can ruin the memory of that wonderful moment."

"It doesn't. It's just that I really hate myself, and I think deep down you do, too."

"What? Hate myself?" he grinned.

"No. You know what I mean." I began to cry.

"Come over here." He pulled me to him and kissed the top of my head. "Yes, I'm sorry we lost it. But I think my mother would say something like, 'Wow, what a way for my ring to go.' Now, dry thy eyes, sit up, and look for a five and dime. You didn't think we were going to buy you anything that costs more than a dollar bill did you?"

From the backseat I heard, "I'm glad that's settled."

We stood holding hands at the jewelry counter in Woolworth's Five and Dime. "Pick out the ring you want, Baby."

"A wedding ring! I'll love it forever."

He grinned and did a deep bow. "Hurry, my lady. Choose from this dazzling display of treasure. Your carriage awaits without."

I studied each ring, trying several on, finally choosing a plain silver band. We paid the clerk and walked to the street. I began to open the door to the car. "Wait my lady! The curtain has not closed on this scene." He knelt on one knee and took both my hands in his. "My dearest, dearest lady, wilt thou consent to join me in a lifetime of love and happiness?"

"You're crazy, my sweet prince. You're a wonderful crazy man, and I'd be honored to become your lifetime beloved."

George stood up and placed the ring on my finger. He took my face in his hands and shook his head. "An iron! What am I going to do with you?"

"Love me?"

"That's right, love you." He kissed me sweetly and opened the front car door while Jake stood on the sidewalk applauding.

Pretending concern, I said, "I can't believe we didn't gather an audience. We gave a fine performance. Do you think we've lost our touch?"

"Nay, nay, madam. If we'd had the hat out, it would be full of gold coins."

I sat back, resting my head on the headrest. I'd never dreamed I could be so happy.

Ten miles later, the trunk began to slide again. Using some swear words I'd never heard before, George stopped, got out, and pulled the rope tighter. He stopped swearing, cheered up, turned the radio on, and we drove another ten or fifteen miles. Then he stopped the car again. "We're getting rid of the fuckin' trunk. Jake, help me get it down. Karen, remove whatever you want from the inside."

At first I thought he was joking. Then, I saw them remove it from the top. "Do you mean we just leave it here?"

"That's right Baby. Now get busy and empty it, or we'll leave it and everything in it."

"Oh, no. Please, George, I can't just leave it here."

"Yes, you can." He pushed me toward the trunk. "Hurry up!"

"Please don't make me leave it here. Please." I bit my lip and stood staring at him a moment.

"Do it!"

Realizing there was no way he'd change his mind, I opened my wonderful antique theater trunk and slowly removed my things. The winter clothes I'd worn at Stephens, my yearbook and photo album. I placed them in the back seat. My heart wept, and I felt terribly guilty. How could I do this? "Please, George, please," I sobbed, "let me keep it."

I thought if I pleaded with him long enough he'd change his

mind. It didn't seem like George to be so indifferent. He worried constantly about Carolyn, and his acting proved him to be sensitive to others' moods and needs. I thought I could make him see what it meant to me, but he said, "No, Baby, it just holds us back. Get in the car."

"You don't mean it."

"Yes, Baby. I'm sorry, but I do," he said more gently.

"But ..."

"Now."

I had no choice. He'd made his decision, and once George made up his mind, that was it. Defeated and hurting, I obeyed. George started the car. As we drove into traffic I prayed someone would quickly pick it up, would recognize its value as something to cherish, and give it a home. Watching through the rear window, as the trunk slowly disappeared from sight, I felt as if I were abandoning a child. I wept for the next hour.

Over the next few months I'd wake up many mornings with a feeling of heavy grief, realizing I'd been dreaming about Daddy's precious trunk.

Eight

≈

We drove straight through to New York taking turns at the wheel and keeping our windows open most of the time for some early September breezes. After twelve hours we were crossing the Manhattan Bridge. With our heads out the windows, we shouted to the city, "We're here, New York! Hi, New York! Is it really you, New York?" With George's one hand on the wheel and one eye on the road, we kissed, and sang, "New York, New York." And then shouted again, "Hello, New York. We're here!"

My practical side emerged immediately. "The first thing we ought to do, if, of course, it's okay with you, my lords, is to buy a *New York Times* and look for apartment ads."

George patted my knee. "Oh, my sensible Baby. You're going to make a wonderful little housewife."

My thoughts were so happy I could barely sit still. Was I dreaming or was this a dream come true? My one true love at my side, my best friend in the backseat, and soon to be a Broadway actress!

George was more animated than usual, yelling every word as if he were trying to get the attention of all the people on the streets. "I want to stand on 42nd street and walk down Broadway."

Jake rested his chin on the back of our seat and his arms on our shoulders. "I just want to walk up and down the theater district looking at the marquees."

I pointed to a drug store. "If you can maneuver the car to the curb in all this traffic, I'll go in and buy a paper and map of the city."

"Just don't buy any more electric clothes irons." George grinned at me.

I emerged from the drugstore happily waving the *New York Times* and a map. I jumped back into the car, opened the paper to apartment rentals, and handed a page to Jake. I read aloud from the third page, "Two rooms, furnished, with kitchen and bath. Ninety dollars per month, including all utilities."

We found it just north of the Hayden Planetarium. A brick apartment-hotel built in the 1920s and badly in need of paint, both inside and out. It had a desk clerk, an elevator, and halls filled with stale cooking smells.

I thought the manager was pretty trusting when he handed us the key to unlock the door to the apartment. But later, after my euphoria cooled, I realized there was nothing inside to steal. We opened the door to the tiny apartment, and I ran in. The kitchen took a fourth of one wall. I looked at the camp-size refrigerator, the small stained sink, the rusty cook top, and a twelve-inch workspace under four open shelves.

"Our first kitchen! Isn't it cute? And a table to eat on. A living room chair!" I didn't notice the rips in the fabric or the loose springs hanging from beneath the seat. Neither the water-stained, peeling wallpaper nor the holes in the rug caught my attention at the time.

George stood in the doorway, and Jake leaned against the kitchenette counter with his arms folded and an amused look, watching me dance through the apartment, touching everything with reverence. "Our first home. I love it. I love the table. I love the comfy chair." I danced my way into the bedroom. "I love the bed. I love the dresser. And you." I gave Jake a hug. "And YOU!" I jumped into George's arms, wrapped my legs around his waist, and we danced around the room and into the bedroom singing *Happy Days Are Here Again.*

George stopped abruptly, laid me down on the bed, and stood looking at me. "You belong to me. You won't forget will you? No matter what, you won't forget?"

"Of course I won't forget. Don't look so serious. This is too happy a moment to look so serious. Let's go down to the desk, right now, and pay our rent."

After paying the first month's rent we agreed on dividing up the space. George and I'd have the bedroom, and Jake would sleep on the pullout sofa, with dresser and closet privileges. The three of us then walked hand in hand to the corner grocery.

"George, when he asked you to register, what names did you sign."

"Why madam, dear madam, what could I sign but Mr. and Mrs. George C. Scott?"

My heart stopped. The words I'd waited to hear for so long! "Say it again."

"Mr. and Mrs. George C. Scott."

"Again."

"Mr. and Mrs. George C Scott."

"Just once more."

"Enough foolishness, my queen. Your king is a ravenous man. Come. It is time we stock the larder."

"Hey, aren't you interested that I signed Jake Dengel?" our roommate joked.

"Of course, I am." I kissed his cheek. He was becoming more like a brother to me by the minute.

After buying a few groceries and a bottle of wine, we sat down at the small wooden table to count our depleted funds. "It's not much," I said. "Maybe enough to get us through a week. We obviously need money soon." I stood up and tapped the table. "So, Sir. I've been thinking. You're the best actor in the group." I looked at Jake. "Not that you're not ..."

Jake held up his hand. "I agree."

I continued. "Thusly, you have the best chance to land a part. I'll be the breadwinner, while you pursue work in the theater. Once you're earning money, I'll begin to look for acting work."

"And that includes me. I'll help out while you look for work, George," Jake said.

George started up from his chair. "I can't let either one of you do that. You want a career in theater as much as I do."

I walked around the table, pushed him down into the chair and sat on his lap. "Of course you can. We need the money. And facts are facts. You are a better actor. You can pay us back when you're rich and famous. Right Jake?"

"Right."

I kissed George on his nose and handed him the paper. "Now, my love, while you're perusing the ads for dental assistants for me, I'll wash your clothes in the sink." I bit his ear lobe and batted my eyelashes. "My goodness, whoever was so smart as to bring an electric clothes iron?"

George grabbed my arm and smacked my rear. "I think my baby is gittin' a bit big for her britches. If she wants to tend to the wash, she will give her lord and master a proper kiss on his ugly mouth."

"I'm happy to obey my lord."

Jake, always our best audience, sat and laughed.

George's mood suddenly changed as he said, "Baby, before I check out the ads, I'll have to go downstairs and use the pay phone. I should call Carolyn and tell her I made it to New York."

I knew he'd have to call her, but at that moment, our perfect moment, his words hit me hard, and I resented Carolyn's existence. "I understand."

"You go ahead," Jake said. "I'll start looking for dental assistant jobs for our lady."

George didn't mention his telephone conversation with Carolyn upon his return to the apartment, and I didn't ask. But I knew he was having a hard time with his guilt because he pulled out his bourbon bottle and drank a third of it in four gulps. I knew if I remarked that bourbon cost more that an electric iron he wouldn't find it funny, so I kept quiet.

I awoke early the next morning. My back ached from the bumpy mattress. The room smelled of mildewed curtain fabric and bed linens. For a moment I couldn't remember where I was, until I turned and saw George lying beside me. "Please tell me this is not a dream," I whispered to myself. I closed my eyes tightly and snapped them open again. Nope. It wasn't a dream.

I slid quietly out of bed, put on George's shirt that lay on the end of the bed, brushed my hair, and carefully placed one drop of cologne on my neck. I hummed show tunes as I prepared a breakfast of toast, coffee and a bowl of canned pineapple. Jake woke up and hummed along with me. We were both in light, fun moods.

George woke up in a foul mood. "Karen, where the hell are you? I've had a lousy dream, and I need soothing."

"I'm right here, my love. I have your breakfast ready!"

"I suppose your mother dear taught you that, too."

"What?"

"That a good little wifey always has her hubby's meals waiting." He added in a stage whisper, "Whether he wants them or not."

"I heard that!"

"You were supposed to. Come in here. I hate talking to you through the wall."

I walked to the open door. "Hello."

His bad mood vanished. "Oh, hell, Baby, come over here, before I explode from wanting you!"

I closed the door and walked slowly to the bed, doing a bump and grind, one hand behind my head. He reached out, grabbed my waist, and pulled me onto the bed. He rolled on top of me, pinned my arms down, looked into my eyes, and said, "Repeat after me. George does not like breakfast."

I felt deflated, but echoed his words.

"But George does like Karen. Repeat."

"George does like Karen."

"George loves Karen. Repeat."

I repeated.

"George wants Karen."

"Karen wants George."

Later that morning we sat at the table, drank coffee, and read the newspaper we bought the day before. "I don't see any casting calls," George said. "I'm going to look up agents in the phone book. They probably won't let me through their front door. But it's worth a try. Do you see any dental assistant jobs listed?"

"In fact, I do! Not that I know how to get there. But if I do find it, I can use my last summer's job for a reference. I hope I don't get confused when to use my real name and when to use Scott."

"You're beautiful, but you're a klutz. Listen carefully, my baby." He pulled me onto his lap. "Do I have your attention?"

"You always have my attention." I kissed his mouth.

"You have to use your real last name on applications for Social Security and withholding. This is the only place where you have to use Scott. Don't forget we checked in as Mr. and Mrs. George C. Scott."

"How could I forget one of the most thrilling moments of my life?"

"And, my pretty, remember to remove your gorgeous wedding ring when you go for interviews. Are you sure you'll be okay alone on the streets of New York?" He waggled his finger at me. "You're not in Kansas anymore, Dorothy."

I stood in front of him. "Oh, thank you, Sir. Whatevah would I do without your guidance and protection? I'm hoping to find my way to town and back, but if I get lost, I'll take the yellow brick road." I curtsied. "Seriously. I'll be fine. Did you see anything, Jake?"

"There are a couple of clerking jobs and a movie theater usher/doorman. I'm going after that one first. At least I'll be inside a theater," he smiled.

We all wished each other luck, and I left quickly before I lost my nerve. I didn't feel as confident as I wanted them to believe. Descending the stairs to the lobby, I held my hand out to admire my wedding band. The dearest, most precious thing I'll ever own, I thought. I live in New York City with the man I love who will soon be on Broadway! We will always be together! I kissed my ring, skipped a stair and nearly fell into the lobby. I took a firm hold of the hand railing and walked sedately out the front door.

After walking three blocks, I found the entrance to the subway. I grabbed the banister and watched as the huge crowd rushed past me down the stairs. It looked as if everyone in New York had decided to take the subway at the same time. *I might get swept down there with them and trampled. No one would ever find me! I waited until the crowd thinned, then hurried across the sidewalk to the shelter of a building doorway.* I told myself walking would do me good. It couldn't be too far. And I could save a few pennies.

After I'd walked eight blocks I gave in. I found a coffee shop, sat on a stool, ordered tea, and asked the way to my destination. A very tired looking waitress about my age, said, "You've barely started, sweetie. You've got another fifteen blocks to go." I drank my tea and wrote the directions she dictated on a napkin. I wrapped my tea bag in a second napkin and began the next leg of my journey.

Another five blocks, and I began to get weary. I was grateful that the day was warm, and it wasn't raining. Without an umbrella I'd be a sorry sight. But I caught my reflection in a department store window and saw I was a sorry sight. The humidity had totally ruined any semblance of the hairstyle I had worked on so carefully that morning. My makeup had all but disappeared from wiping my dripping face.

While I stood peering at my disheveled self, I felt something being thrust into my hand. It was a small card. The handwritten words read: "If you need a job, we're here to help." An address and telephone number were on the back. Did I look that desperate? It gave me an eerie feeling to know someone was watching me. I shoved it into my pocket without looking around, squared my shoulders and kept walking.

An hour and a half later I sat in the office of Dr. Raymond Evans. "You walked into the office at just the right time, Karen. We need someone with your experience to begin right away. Rita will show you around. We can train you to be a chair-side assistant as we go along. I like your bright smile and eagerness. You'll make a fine addition to the office staff." Pudgy Dr. Evans sat behind an oak desk and spoke with a warm, soft voice. I liked him immediately, suddenly yearning to hear my father's voice and feeling a terrible pang of guilt about his beloved trunk.

"I'd like to see you here by eight o'clock tomorrow morning. Your hours will be eight to four-thirty, with a half-hour for lunch. We work half days every other Saturday. Your paycheck will be thirty-eight dollars a week until you're trained. Then, in six months, if all goes well, we'll boost it up four more dollars. How does that sound?"

How did it sound? Like Heaven! I thanked God for sending me to Dr. Raymond Evans. "That sounds fine," I said.

Nine

≈

Walking twenty blocks home from Dr. Evans's dental office didn't hold much appeal. I decided to use public transportation. But first I needed a lesson about how to board the train without being trampled. I stood a half block from the subway street entrance and watched as the masses rushed down the stairs. It seemed to be a matter of timing. If you joined the crowd and ran with them at exactly their speed, you'd be fine. You had to have firm footing and be sure you knew where you were going.

I gave it a try, talking myself through and trying to imitate the others as they purchased their tokens and elbowed into the front-of-the-line position. Finally, I stood squished shoulder to shoulder on the train, holding tightly to the hand bar. I found my way home with only one wrong stop, which was merely getting off, discovering my mistake, and boarding again.

Feeling like celebrating, I stopped at the neighborhood grocery and bought a bag of hamburger buns, a pound of hamburger, a tomato and three bottles of beer. When I walked into the hotel and past the three or four elderly people reading in the lobby, the room clerk greeted me. "Good evening, Mrs. Scott." I walked by him before I realized he was speaking to me. Startled, pleased, and embarrassed, I looked around at the readers, who were all staring at me. I looked back at the room clerk, smiled, and bumped into a lobby column. As I searched my handbag for my wedding ring, I said, "Excuse me," to the wood pillar and ran up the two flights of stairs, being careful not to trip on the worn carpet.

Entering the apartment, I put my packages on the table and went to the bedroom. George was lying on the bed asleep. I went to him, intending to kiss him awake, but when I leaned in to him and smelled his breath, I backed away. It wasn't just his breath. The smell of liquor emitted from every part of his body. I wondered how long he'd been drinking. We barely had enough money to buy groceries, much less liquor. But I rationalized, he'd probably walked all over New York looking for agents, was discouraged, tired and needed a drink to relax. I decided not to wake him.

When George woke up, he stepped to the open door and saw me at the stove wearing nothing but my panties and bra under an apron. "Don't wake me," he yawned. "I'm having the greatest dream of my life. This gorgeous woman is standing nearly naked in front of me with a spatula in her hand."

I went to him and pinched his bare behind. "You are a sexy good-for-nothing. Dinner is ready, and I have news."

"News and dinner can wait. But when I see my little wifey looking like that, I can't!" He grabbed me around the waist, slammed the bedroom door, and pulled me into bed. A healthy twenty-seven year old male is always ready for sex, and George was no exception.

Half an hour later he rolled onto his side and grinned at me. "Okay. Now."

"Now what?"

"Now, tell me the news."

"Oh, that." I pulled away and started to get up. "It can wait."

"Not for long." He tickled my ribs.

"No, I give up." I jumped off the bed, grabbed my robe, and ran into the other room and around the dinette table.

He ran the opposite way, caught and held me. He struck a dramatic pose. "Speak, madam, speak, before I expire from curiosity."

"Okay! It's not much. Just that I got a job!"

"Oh, my baby, I'm so proud of you." He grabbed me, and we danced around the room singing "We're In The Money," kissed, danced and kissed again when Jake opened the apartment door and stood watching us. "Does this mean good news?"

"Yes!"

We danced over to Jake, grabbed him, and the three of us danced. We danced to the table, where I had left the groceries and pulled out the beer. We danced to the drawer for the bottle opener and kept dancing as we drank our beers. Then, while I reported about my new job, we continued to celebrate with hamburgers and tomatoes.

When I finished my story, I turned to Jake. "You haven't reported on your day. Any success?"

"Gee I thought you'd never ask." He smiled. "Actually, yes, I am now an official member of the theater community."

"You're kidding!"

"Well, I'm not on stage, but I do get to take tickets and clean up after the audience."

"Congratulations!" I held up my water glass and gave him a huge smile, but my heart ached for him. Jake was a talented actor, and I hated to see him having to collect trash.

Then we made a few practical decisions. One: To ask Dr. Evans if I might have my mail sent to the dental office. That way I could give my parents an address. Two: Take turns cleaning the apartment and cleaning up the kitchen. Three: I'd keep the job of cook, since they both pleaded culinary ignorance.

There was a moment of quiet. George lit a cigarette and spoke softly. "The streets of New York did not treat me as kindly as they treated you two." He ran his fingers through his hair and gave us a cheerless smile. "No auditions are being held, this week at least. It's harder than hell to get inside a theater unless you know someone or have an agent. And the agents don't give you the time of day unless you're working."

Jake and I both offered encouraging words. "It's only a matter of time." "Sure, you're a great actor." "If we're not worried, you shouldn't be."

I forgot to tell them about the card I'd received on the street. Later, when I did think of it, I decided it wasn't important enough to mention, and I didn't want to dampen our happy mood telling about how inept I was on the streets of New York.

Jake left "to find some excitement," but I think he felt like a fifth wheel. Poor Jake. We both loved him, but our arrangement must have often felt awkward to him.

George and I sat on the couch listening to the radio. I rested my head on his shoulder. Elation hit again. I couldn't believe how happy I felt. We were sitting on our couch, in our own apartment. We'd just had dinner cooked on our own stove. Everything was perfect.

George took my hand and kissed it. "Now that you have a job and we're settled, I have to tell you something, Baby."

"My goodness, you look serious."

"This is serious. I didn't tell you before because I didn't want to ruin our first couple of days." He hesitated a moment.

"It can't be that bad."

"Well, it is, but ..."

"Come on, silly, spill it." I kissed his hand fighting the sinking feeling in the pit of my stomach.

"Baby, before I left, Carolyn told me she was pregnant."

The words didn't compute. "Say that again."

"Carolyn is pregnant."

Now the words were clear. My heart sank. I stood up and walked to the window, my back to George. "Please tell me this isn't true."

He came to me and circled me with his arms. "Baby, this doesn't change things."

I pushed him away. "Oh it changes things. It changes everything!" He'd betrayed me. I pushed him again and again, nearly to the other side of the room. "Why didn't you tell me before?"

He held my arms so I couldn't push him again. "Baby, calm down. Come sit down so we can talk."

"What good is talking going to do? Your wife is going to have another baby! When? Tell me when."

"In the spring, I guess"

"You guess?"

"I know."

"You will soon be a father for a second time. I'm in New York. I have a job I don't really want so I can support you." I was pacing the room. "And you're going to be a father again. What's the plan? Are we going to send Carolyn money from my paycheck? Gee, maybe I can be the godmother." I walked to the window. "I had planned to wash this window tonight. I thought it would be nice to see the view of the next building. But instead I'm told you're going to be a father again."

"I know it's ..."

Suddenly I was stung by the vision of him in bed making love to Carolyn, and I interrupted him. "Something just occurred to me, George."

"What?"

"To have a baby you had to have sex with your wife. And to have a baby in the spring, you had to be having sex with your wife this past summer while you were swearing your undying love for me. Is that not true?" It was all so obvious. He'd lied to me.

"Yes, but ..."

"Yes, but what?" I stopped myself before I asked if he'd enjoyed it. I shouted in his face. "Hey, I've got an idea. Why don't we all get into the sack together? Hell, we could invite some friends."

"Come on, Karen. That's beneath you."

"No, dear, it's not. Have you forgotten I'm your whore? I used to be your virgin whore. Now I'm just your whore." I felt like standing in the center of the room and screaming.

George reached out for me. "I couldn't just stop being her husband. Baby, you've got to understand."

"George, do me a favor." I backed away from him.

"Anything, Baby."

"Stop calling me Baby! You're going to have another one of your own, remember?" I ran into the bedroom and slammed the door. I sat on the side of the bed and hugged the pillow. Everything was wrong. Nothing would ever be right again. I was crazy in love with a married man whose family was growing larger by the day, and we were trapped in New York with no money. How did this happen? I suddenly felt very cold. I lay down, curled myself around the pillow and cried until I fell asleep. I dreamed all night about walking the streets of New York and seeing babies everywhere I looked.

At six-forty five I awoke feeling drained and tired. I lifted George's arm from my shoulders, slightly surprised because I hadn't heard him come to bed. I washed, dressed, and ran for the subway.

I tried to be the perfect dental trainee on my first day of work, but I failed. My state of mind and tired body made it difficult to grasp some of the office routines, and about once an hour I dropped a dental instrument.

At noon I knocked on my new boss's office door. He invited me in. I saw that I had interrupted his lunch, which made me feel worse, so I hurried to get the words out. "Dr. Evans, I want to apologize for being so slow and clumsy. I'll do better, I promise."

"No need for apologies, Karen. It's only your first day, and I think you'll be fine. Just have more confidence in yourself and read the pamphlets we gave you."

Having confidence in myself and reading had never been two of my strengths. The lack of these skills when I was a child had caused me to walk with my head and shoulders down. And the previous evening my love had told me his wife was pregnant, which left me wondering if he truly loved me.

No, confidence in myself was something I didn't have today. But I did need to ask a favor. "Dr. Evans, I wonder if it would be all right to have my mail sent to the office?"

"Is there a reason for that?"

"Well ... I ..."

He didn't pursue it. "How about we say, 'for now'?"

"Thank you so much. I won't bother you any longer, and I promise to do better this afternoon and tomorrow."

"I'm sure you will. You just keep that pretty smile. It's good for business. "

I didn't do much better during the afternoon, so I stayed until five-thirty reviewing what I had learned during the day, using up what remained of my energies. By the time I arrived home, I just wanted to sleep.

I opened the door to an empty, dark apartment. Perfect. I'd grab a shower and a nap before George and Jake got home. I took the shower, but my body wouldn't relax for the nap. I opened two cans of clam chowder and set them on the stove to warm later for dinner. I was sure Jake and George's tardiness boded good things. I filled a glass with tap water. Pretending it was wine, I sat down with the newspaper to await my family.

Jake arrived home at about seven o'clock with a large grin. "So, dear lady, would you like to hear my good news?"

"Indeed I do. Tell me."

"I'm now working the candy stand. At this rate I'll be head usher and candy stand manager in a week!"

I so wanted to celebrate with Jake. But my energy and enthusiasm had been sapped. And, looking at me, he could see it. Such a gentle soul, he warmed the chowder and served me a bowl and a slice of bread. At eleven o'clock he pulled his bed out and fell asleep almost immediately. I napped in the living room chair. At one-thirty in the morning a knock at the door awakened me. Expecting it to be George, I hurried to open it, but it was Fred, the night clerk. "You have a telephone call at the desk. It's Mr. Scott."

"Thank you. I'll be right down."

In my rush, the heel of my shoe caught in my robe, and I had to make a quick and awkward grab for the banister. I saw Fred watching, but he didn't laugh. Wonderful, I thought, now both the day and night clerks have witnessed my lack of grace.

"Hello?"

"Baby?"

"Yes."

"Baby, I've been inna fight. They rolled me. I haven' gotta dime. Come get me, Baby, please."

"Where are you?"

"I dunno."

"Look at the street signs."

Yeh, wayaminute ... Baby?

"Yes."

"Broadway an Thirty Fifth. Can ya ge' a cab?"

"Yes. Stay where you are. I'll be there soon."

"Good girl. I'll shtay here."

"Yes. Stay where you are. I'll be there as soon as I can."

I replaced the receiver and asked Fred to call me a cab, aware it would cost nearly every cent I had. I walked up the stairs and prayed to the gods to help me find my drunken lover and bring him home.

I found George sitting on the curb in the rain, his head in his hands. I told the cab driver to wait, and I crossed the street to my fallen lover. Blood dripped from his forehead. His clothes were wet and muddy. I touched his shoulder. "George, I'm here."

"I know. I'm ashame t' have you look at me."

I pulled his hands away from his bloody, swollen, face and sank down on the curb beside him. "Oh, my God. What happened?"

"I tole ja. They rolled me. And I think they bro' my nose while they were at it."

"I'll get you to a hospital emergency room."

"No. No hospital. Jes' let it be. We got aspirin at home?"

"Yes."

"Then Jes' help me up, and we'll go home."

When we arrived back at the apartment, it was nearly three o'clock. After cleaning George up, which included having to throw away his torn shirt and helping him into bed, I made coffee. I sat straight up on the couch so I wouldn't fall asleep and be late for work. At six a. m. I took another shower, dressed, ate the rest of the clam chowder, and left for work.

A week or so later, George told me what happened to him that day. He had awakened that morning as I dressed. But after our words the night before, he thought it best to pretend to be sleeping. He watched me leave to earn money to support us. He dressed and had coffee with Jake. An hour later he left the apartment and headed for a newsstand. He bought a newspaper and carried it into a coffee shop. After ordering a coffee he took out his pencil. There had to be something. He'd happily audition for radio commercials. Anything. Just one audition so he could tell me about it. Then he read an ad for auditions at the Round And About for male actors age 18 to 30. That address was probably off-off-off-Broadway, but who cared? He circled the address and started walking south.

Twelve long blocks later he decided he'd better take the subway if he wanted to get there at a reasonably decent time. The train carried him within two blocks of the address. He stood on the sidewalk and stared at the Round And About. It was a restaurant. Maybe they did dinner theater. He pushed open the door and stepped into a fog of stale cooking smells. He followed the sound of voices and soft music to a room so dimly lit at first he didn't see the couples on the dance floor. Small tables circled the floor. Women sat at the tables. The men dancing were dressed in swimming trunks. When the music stopped the couples either disappeared through a door marked "Private," or separated, and the woman sat down at a table. He observed for a while then decided there must be some other way to earn a living.

He stopped outside and searched the paper again for possible auditions. He spotted a cattle call for extras. It read, Males and females of all ages. Report to lobby of the Henderson Hotel by 7 a.m., Wednesday, September 12. He'd missed it, but maybe they'd need people for tomorrow.

When he finally found the hotel, it was jammed with people. A rope, with guards on the other side, held a crowd of curious fans away from the lobby. He fought his way to the rope and asked a guard. "Where should I report if I want to be an extra?"

"You're a little late buddy. They signed up all the extras they needed by eight a.m."

The guard hushed the crowd and turned away from him.

He watched them film a robbery for the rest of the afternoon. At least he could tell Jake and me he'd seen a filming, even if he hadn't been in one. After three shots of bourbon, he felt better and decided to walk the theater district. Seeing the marquees only reminded him how badly we needed money and how few acting jobs were available. At ten o'clock he stopped in a bar and ordered a boilermaker. After finishing the bowl of nuts, he ordered another boilermaker. He thought about me at the apartment, waiting for him. And of Carolyn and his daughter, still living with Carolyn's brother. He paid for his drinks and left. He crossed a street, tripped on the curb, and fell to his knees.

He decided to stop at another bar and have another belt for the road. He drank a shot. In the back of the room three men were throwing darts. He'd always been good at darts. Suddenly he realized how badly he needed to take a piss. He rushed to the bathroom, but there was no urinal. He used the washbasin. A woman walked out of a stall. She gasped and dashed out the door. Two men ran in and grabbed him. They dragged him out of the bar and threw him on the sidewalk, where he had passed out.

Ten

≈

Is this Tammy Grimes?"

"Yes."

"From Brookline, Massachusetts?"

"Yes. Who's this?

"If you're sure you're Tammy Grimes from Brookline, Massachusetts, I'm Karen Truesdell from Seattle, Washington."

"Trues? TRUES?"

"That's me." I was so glad to hear her voice I nearly wept.

"How are you? Where are you? You're not in New York, are you?"

"Yes, I am. In fact, I'm in a pay phone about five blocks from your apartment at this very moment."

"Can you come down here? That is, are you free to ...?"

"Yes, he's in New York with me. But I'm alone this evening. I'd love to see you."

Tammy opened her apartment door, and we wrapped ourselves in a warm hug that lasted a long moment. Then we stepped back and looked at each other. We laughed and hugged again. Tammy took my arm and led me into her tiny apartment. Theater posters and black and white photos of famous people filled the walls. A small, mended oriental rug lay in the center of the wood floor. Along one wall there were two mattresses and several pillows covered with assorted fabrics. A steam radiator stood under the one window.

"Gee, Trues, you look thin. And what's with the nurse's uniform?"

"I'm a dental assistant, ma'am," I saluted. "I earn all of forty dollars a week."

"Well, my friend, that's more than I make. I barter for nearly everything. We all do down here."

We walked the few steps across the room. Tammy bowed. "You are now entering my kitchen. It's set up only for gourmet cooking, as you can see." She opened the cabinet over the sink and proudly lifted out two saucepans. Opening the small refrigerator, she retrieved a small bottle of white wine. "I even bartered for this bottle of wine that I'm about to open in your honor. She stepped back into her sitting room. "Here, sit on my one chair."

I started to cry.

"Oh, God, Trues, did I say something? Leave it to me. I'm always saying the wrong thi ..."

"No, it's nothing you said," I sobbed. "Tammy, it's awful. I don't know what to do."

Tammy walked to her bed, returned with a tissue box, and handed it to me. "Now, tell me."

"I really don't know what to say."

"Okay, I'll ask questions."

I nodded.

"I gather this has something to do with George."

I nodded.

"Okay. You're living together. His wife found out, and ..."

"No, she didn't find out. She's PREGNANT." My sobs were fading into sniffles. "George told me a couple of nights ago. He's known since before we left Toledo." I began to mindlessly tear the tissues into small bits and throw them on the floor. "He says nothing has changed. But it has changed. My God, he's going to be a father again. Maybe they'll have twins and he'll be a triple father. I mean ..." I began to sob again. "Oh, you know what I mean."

Tammy sucked in her bottom lip to keep from smiling. "Yes, dear Trues, I know what you mean." She waited for me to stop sobbing. "How was it before? With you and George I mean, before he told you?"

"Heavenly." I blew my nose. "We found a darling little apartment. And we're so in love. And I got this job. Everything was perfect. Except it wasn't really, because George knew Carolyn was pregnant. And ..." I began to sob again.

"Look, Trues, I think we have a lot of talking to do. Why not stay the night and go to work tomorrow from here. You can call George. Maybe he needs a night alone to think, too." Tammy poured two glasses of wine and handed me one.

"I want to, but I'm afraid George would just go on a drinking binge." I took a sip of wine. "He drinks an awful lot. Last night he stayed out all night, and I had to go get him."

"You what?"

"He called me from a phone booth in the middle of the night. He'd been in a fight, and they took all his money. At least he said they took his money. But I think he may have spent it all at a bar. After he told me about Carolyn being pregnant, I don't know what to believe. Anyway, I called a cab and went to pick him up. The cab driver was a nasty crank. He asked me what my husband did for a living. I said he was an actor. He said, 'It figures. I get a lot of late night calls from so-called actors. They're all a bunch of bums, if you ask me.'

"I wanted to say he's not a bum and I love him, and I didn't ask your opinion, but I was afraid if I insulted him he'd make me walk." My sobs returned, and Tammy brought another box of tissues from the counter.

"I found George, dirty and bloody, and so forlorn looking. I just held him and got him into the car. Then the cab driver said, 'Hey, don't let that dirt and blood get on my seat. It stains bad.' I could have belted him. When we got to the apartment, the cab fee was so high it took nearly every cent I had, except for subway fare today and the dime to call you. Now, aren't cha glad you asked?"

"That's quite a story."

"That's not all. I think George's beautiful nose is broken. He refused to go to emergency." Big sobs again. "We couldn't have paid for it anyway."

"Is George good to you? I mean is he gentle and kind?"

"Oh, yes." I took a deep breath. "Well, sometimes he gets mad. He has a temper. But he'd never hurt me. I'm sure of that. And I'm sure he loves me. But he loves Carolyn, too, and he feels so guilty and ..." I took a gulp of wine.

"I'm going to start dinner. I'll bet you haven't eaten in a while. I have a can of delicious meat stew and half a loaf of fresh bread that my neighbor gave me. We shall feast, my dear. But before we eat, you'd better call George. Yes. I have a real telephone! There are times I wish I didn't. Everyone uses it. But they always leave a dime, and that helps me pay the monthly. And it certainly makes me popular. I'll just step into my bathroom and give you some privacy."

I hated asking the desk clerk to call George to the phone. I promised myself we'd get a phone installed as soon as I had the money.

George growled into the phone so loud I had to hold it from my ear. "I don't understand why you're not coming home. Are you trying to punish me?"

"No, of course not. I just want to spend some time with Tammy. I'll be home tomorrow after work. Isn't Jake there to keep you company? You'll eat, won't you? Not just drink. But eat?"

"Jake is working nights now, or have you forgotten? And if you're not coming home, what I do is my business." He hung up just as Tammy came out of the bathroom.

"Oh, God, I feel so guilty. He needs me. I know he won't eat anything. In fact there isn't anything to eat except some crackers."

She gave me a wry look, "He'll probably drink his dinner anyway."

"Tammy." I gave her a warning look.

"Sorry, sorry."

Silence for a minute.

"I really ought to go home."

"That's a great idea. What are you going to do, walk the thirty blocks? Besides, George is a grown man. He can take care of himself for one night. And I think you'd be a lot better off if you stayed here. We could have dinner, a long talk, and a good night's sleep. Tomorrow you can ask your boss for an advance. Come on, Trues, you know I always know best."

"Well, maybe."

The longer I stayed with Tammy that evening the guiltier I felt. George was home alone and needed me. About ten o'clock I suddenly made up my mind. "Tammy, I love you for this evening and the comforting words, but I just have to get back to George."

Tammy laughed, "I figured you'd leave." She picked up my coat and wrapped it around me and placed fifty cents in my hand. I started to refuse the coins when she said, "You can pay me back. I can't have my friend walk the streets of New York without emergency money. Take care of yourself, Trues, and stay in touch."

The apartment was dark when I walked in. Thinking George was asleep I tiptoed to the floor lamp and turned it on. He was sitting at the table staring at his wrist where he was pointing the tip of his switchblade.

The scene frightened me, and for a moment all I could do was stand there.

He seemed startled by the light being turned on and rose suddenly, dropping the knife. "What the hell?" he growled.

I took a step toward him. "I'm sorry, honey, I'm sorry. I thought you were asleep."

"Well, I'm not!" He picked up the knife and tapped it on the table. "I thought you were going to stay at Tammy's."

"I was but I missed you. I wanted to come home and take care of you."

"No one has to take care of me. Jesus, do you think I'm helpless?"

"Of course not." I walked to him and put my arms around him. "I just wanted to be home with you. Are you mad at me?"

"He swept my hair back off my forehead and squinted at me. "Shit, Baby, I love you so."

Our kiss was hard and fierce.

"By mid October, the three of us had settled into a routine. Jake worked from seven to midnight, I worked from eight to five, and George walked the streets chasing acting opportunities, becoming more discouraged every day.

At night we played the radio. Our one source of entertainment, it was also a comfort, a constant in our strange existence. We kept it playing all night. The hottest record that autumn was Tony Bennett's "Strangers In Paradise." We liked to think he sang it just for us and adopted it as our song.

George often waited for me in the evening at my subway stop.

He'd stand on a landing halfway down the stairs, grinning, arms outstretched. I was sure there must have been a hundred women who would gladly have jumped into them. Then we'd walk the New York streets holding hands and dream of the day we'd see our names in lights and have enough money to move out of our tiny rented apartment.

One or two days a week, when I left the dental office at five, Jake would be standing outside to greet me. I loved being with Jake. We seemed to bring out the child in each other. "Let's take a city bus," he'd say. "We can watch the people for future acting reference."

"Okay, but only if you behave yourself and don't clown around."

"Why, of course. I'm always quiet and gentlemanly," he said, ever so meekly.

"Sure you are. Are we going to speak Baltic or Asian?"

"I feel in a Baltic mood."

"Here's our bus."

At rush hour the buses were always jammed. We stood in the center of the crowd and talked to each other in Russian-sounding gibberish, just loud enough to gather an audience. We were quite good at it, and even tried to engage our eavesdroppers in conversation. They shook their heads and tried to make us understand they didn't speak our language. We pointed to different spots in Manhattan and looked quizzically at them. Our fellow passengers mumbled, "Sorry." We shrugged, smiled, did a little bow and left the bus.

We laughed and sang the rest of the way home, thinking of how we had really put one over on those poor, unsuspecting people, and of how surprised they would be when they saw us in a show on Broadway. Sometimes I felt that Jake and I had hatched from the same egg.

Once, on a weekend morning, Jake opened our bedroom door to speak to us, walking nearly to the bed before discovering he'd interrupted our lovemaking. George waved him off, Jake retreated rapidly to the other room, and I felt as if I'd been caught doing something cheap and disgusting.

The three of us treated ourselves to a shared pound of hamburger once a week. We had soup and bread the rest of the time, unless Tammy dropped by, as she often did, carrying a basket of food to share with us. There'd be a knock at the door, and we'd be greeted with, "George-O, Trues! Mum sent me more cans of food, and I've come to share." Like a weekly Santa's helper, she'd unload cans of stew, beans, brown bread, biscuits and honey.

On most Sundays, George, Jake and I relaxed, read the New York Times, ate pancakes, took long walks, and picnicked in Central Park. The crisp, October air and colorful leaves were medicine for our woes. I was in paradise most of the time, proudly walking hand in hand with George, laughing, and wishing time would stand still.

When Jake had matinee duty on a Sunday, George and I had our picnic alone. We'd spread our blanket on the ground, stand back and admire our perfect spot. I'd often ask him to impersonate the people we watched go by. George could catch the essence of people immediately. I'd sit on the blanket, watching him walk behind someone, mimicking them. It was better than going to the movies.

One Sunday afternoon in the park he declined his usual miming performance. "Later, my love. Right now I'd like one of those perfect sandwiches you slaved over."

"Perfect. That seems to be my favorite word lately. Perfect. New York's perfect, you're perfect. I even like my job." I took out my camera. "So, stay where you are, my perfect hero, and let me take a picture of this perfect moment."

George struck a dramatic pose. "So you're going to photograph my Barrymore schnoz, eh? Commence, my love! Let the rabble agonize in their jealousy when they gaze upon this incredible proboscis!"

We sat on the blanket, and I opened the sandwich bag. "Here, my lord. One perfectly shaped bottle of ice cold, perfect Coke. One perfectly square peanut butter sandwich and two perfectly round Oreo cookies."

George caught my hand and kissed the palm. "My dearest, you are perfect. I love you more than life. You know that, don't you?"

"Yes. I do. And I keep thinking what might have happened if I hadn't come home from Tammy's that night. When I walked in and saw you with your switchblade open, I ..."

"Sshh. Don't ever think about it again. I wouldn't have done anything to myself. I was just feeling blue and guilty. Besides, you carry it with you now."

"It feels strange, though. Little innocent me with a switchblade knife in my pocket."

"It may save your life some day, Baby. If anything happened to you ..."

"Well, it's not going to. And I have faith we'll be together for good very soon. After the baby's born and Carolyn gets on her feet, you'll ask her for a divorce, just as you've promised. I can wait a few months for the love of my life." I reached for his hand. His watch was gone. "Did you forget to put your watch on this morning?"

"No, Baby, I pawned it yesterday."

"George, you loved that watch."

"Do not trouble yourself about it, my lady. 'Twas only a trinket. Someday we'll replace it with one festooned with diamonds and rubies. Now, come close to me. We'll cuddle and watch mundane people walk by."

We sat for a few minutes in silence. Then he said, "I honestly don't know when I'll be able to bring in some money. When I go to a casting call, the line stretches around the block. By the time I get inside they've ended for the day. This acting business is a very hard nut to crack."

"But you will crack it. I've got total faith in you. And you must have faith in yourself, too. Say it. I will crack it. I will crack it."

He displayed his Barrymore profile again, put his hand to his forehead, and said in exaggerated cadences, "I will crack!"

"You're a fool."

"I know, but you love this fool, right?

"Right."

Eleven

≈

November was not a good month. The loan company repossessed George's car, which actually was a relief since we constantly had to find new parking places for it and really never used it. And Jake moved out. Which was not a relief.

For several days I'd had a feeling that he wanted to tell us something. He seemed worried and distant. He'd start a sentence and then say, "Nothing important." He finally made the announcement on a Sunday morning, when we were lounging after our pancake breakfast. He put his section of the New York Times down and said, "I love you both, you know."

George looked up. "How come the sudden burst of affection, Jake?"

"Well, I've been thinking. It's time I moved out and gave you two some privacy."

"No, Jake. It's wonderful with you. You're family." I loved him like a brother. The thought of his leaving panicked me. Who would I confide in? "You're my best friend."

George walked to the stove, poured another cup of coffee, and leaned against the drain board. "Listen, I can understand wanting your own life. If that's what it is. But you know we love you. It won't be the same without you."

"Well, thanks, I'll miss you, too, but I need to do this."

Then, my practical side emerged. "Where are you going to live? Do you have enough money?"

"I found a place to stay, and yes," he gave me a sweet smile, "I've got enough money."

He was really doing it. He was moving out. I felt as if someone had died. "When are you moving?"

"Tomorrow, if that's okay with you. It's my day off this week, and I'll have time to move."

I tried to keep my voice from shaking. "So soon?"

"I know this is sudden, and I don't want to leave you two with no money."

We both spoke. "Don't you worry about us, we'll be fine."

"We have plenty."

"Well, I guess it's settled then. I'll move out tomorrow."

I bit my lip and began to clear the breakfast plates from the table.

The next morning I woke up with a sinking feeling. Jake was leaving today. My heart hurt at the thought, but I told myself to keep a brave face for his sake. And no matter what he said about "dropping by often," I knew it never would be the same. We'd drift apart.

I went to work late that morning. I wished I hadn't. I watched Jake pack his things. No one could think of anything to say at breakfast. Or maybe Jake and George couldn't talk because they had big lumps in their throats like I did. There were kisses and hugs, and he left.

A few days later George and I moved to a one-room unit, sharing a bathroom down the hall with another family. I hated sharing a bathroom with strangers. I hated having to wait, hated the mess people left, and I hated the lack of privacy.

We still had a kitchenette, two chairs, a table, a bed, a dresser and each other.

When I returned home from work one evening in late November, I opened the door to our room and felt a chill. It wasn't the cold air. I had a terrible foreboding.

"Hello, my love!" I called out. "Are you in here? Hey, my darling. Turn on a light. I've brought wonderful gifts called food and drink." That was odd. George had always greeted me on payday. "Hello," I tried again. "Honey? George?" Silence.

I set the groceries on the table, removed my coat, then put it back on. The apartment was freezing. As I began to put the food away, I saw an envelope addressed to me in George's handwriting in the center of the table. My heart pounded, and my hands trembled as I removed the note.

My Dearest,

I have gone to Toledo for a few days. When I called to wish Carolyn a happy Thanksgiving she begged me to come for the holiday. I knew the day meant nothing to you, and it seems to mean so much to Carolyn. I'm thumbing, so it may take a while. Think of me.

I love you always.

Yours,

George

Relieved of my initial fear, I half fell into a chair. At least he wasn't leaving me for good. Then it sank in. He would be gone during Thanksgiving. He'd be with her. I felt anger, rejection, and disbelief. What did he mean by "the day meant nothing" to me? For weeks we'd talked about sharing our first holiday together. Or maybe I had talked about it, and he hadn't heard. Could he really think I didn't care?

I looked at the turkey breast slices, the rolls, potatoes and canned peas I'd spent too much money on. Picking up the yellow chrysanthemum I'd planned for a centerpiece, I ripped off the petals. I was still standing by the table an hour later, the flower petals spread on top, spelling George.

The knock at the door was a welcome interruption. "Mrs. Scott. This is Larry, the day clerk. There's a long distance phone call for you at the desk."

"Thanks, Larry. I'm coming."

This had to be George. He was coming back. He'd changed his mind and was coming back. I ran down the stairs, sprinted across the lobby to the desk, and picked up the receiver.

"Karen?"

"Oh, hi, Daddy." I recognized my father's voice.

"My goodness, you sound almost disappointed to hear from me. You must have been waiting for an important call."

"Daddy, there is no one I'd rather talk to than you and Mother,"

I lied. "How are you?"

"Well, we're fine. We haven't heard from you in quite awhile, and you know your mother and me. We begin to worry. We also want to wish you a happy Thanksgiving. I imagine you're going to your roommate's sister's house to celebrate?"

"Yes, Daddy, that's right. What are you and Mother going to do?"

"Your sisters and their families are coming here. Aunt Ella and Aunt Florence will be here, too. We'll surely miss you. I'm going to hand the phone to your mother now. Happy Thanksgiving. Here's your mother."

"Karen?"

I held the receiver away from my ear. Mother yelled into the phone, as if the phone lines needed some help to carry her voice all the way from Seattle to New York City.

"Yes, Mother."

"Well, we sure had a hard time getting through to you. I guess everyone and their cousin is calling relatives to wish them happy Thanksgiving tomorrow. Karen, are you all right?"

"Yes, Mother, I'm fine."

"You sound funny."

"Everyone sounds funny to you on long distance."

"Well, what are you doing? I mean, besides working in that dental office. Have you seen the Rockettes?"

"Not yet."

"You know when Daddy and I visited New York we saw the Rockettes. They were wonderful. Are you warm enough? Is the flu going around there? It is here. I hope you don't catch it. I hope you're drinking lots of water with lemon, and ... ohh!"

"Mother?"

"Karen, this is Daddy. Your mother wants me to wish you a happy Thanksgiving for her. She says she's going to send you some lemons. Well, that's it from here then. So, happy Thanksgiving. We both send our love."

"Bye, Daddy. Happy Thanksgiving. I love you both. Goodbye." After I hung up, I realized I'd been yelling, too. I looked at the desk clerk. "Thank you for the call, and happy Thanksgiving. And thank you for putting the calls for Karen Truesdell through to me. My parents don't know I'm married."

"Oh, sure," he winked.

I wasn't sure if he winked because he suspected I really wasn't married, or he understood about not telling my parents. Either way, I really didn't care.

Thanksgiving morning I used the lobby pay phone to call Tammy. She didn't answer. I bought a newspaper and returned to the room. I thought it was quite a coincidence that my mother had asked about the flu. I felt like I might have it. It was probably for the best that Tammy wasn't home. I might have given it to her. I put on my warm pajamas, made tea, and went back to bed. I felt terribly nauseous, and realized I'd felt sick for days. As far as I knew, the flu hadn't been going around. I napped until afternoon and felt better. I dressed and decided to take a walk before twilight.

As I returned through the lobby, the desk clerk told me I had another long distance call. "Thank you so much!" This had to be George.

I dialed the operator and was connected to Jake. "Karen! How great to hear your voice!"

"You, too. How are you?"

"I'm fine. I'm in Wisconsin. How are you? I miss you."

"I miss you, too. Why are you in Wisconsin?"

"Just home for a few days to rest and think about my future. How's George?"

"He's in Toledo with Carolyn for a few days."

"Oh. Is that okay with you?"

"It doesn't seem to matter if it's okay with me or not," I growled. "I'm sorry. I'm just feeling sorry for myself."

"I don't blame you. Has he found any work in the theater yet?"

"No, and he gets more discouraged every day."

"I'm sorry. Well, tell him hello for me and good luck."

"Thanks for calling, Jakey."

"Happy Thanksgiving."

"Yes. Happy Thanksgiving."

After I hung up, I felt sorrier for myself than before the call. If only Jake were there to hug and talk to, I knew I'd feel better. I went up to the room, got my coat, and headed outdoors in hopes another walk would help me feel better. It didn't. Everyone seemed to be walking with someone. Laughing. Or at least smiling. A light shower began, soon turned to freezing rain, and then to sleet. It was a truly miserable day!

When I returned, I sat on the couch with more tea, and tried to read a library book. I fell asleep and woke up at twelve-thirty a.m. When I looked at the time, I felt a bit better. At least Thanksgiving was officially over.

When I awoke the next morning I felt as nauseous as the day before. I dressed and went to the local market, where I bought two lemons and a coke. On the return trip I used the elevator, something I never did. I couldn't face climbing the stairs feeling so miserable. I squeezed a lemon into water and lay on the couch. I not only felt awful, but totally alone. If I could just get my period, I thought, I'd feel better. It was just bloat. Just ... Oh, NO!"

I got up and walked around the room hitting at my stomach. George would kill me! Oh, that's great. I might be pregnant, and my first thought is that George would be angry. So much for his instructions to "take a bath every time we have sex. It will wash out all the sperm." It was probably a false alarm anyway. I'd feel better tomorrow. Maybe George would be back tomorrow, and we'd walk in Central Park. Maybe Monday I'd go to work and everything will be fine. Maybe, maybe, maybe we'd all become millionaires. If I would just get my period!

Dear Mother and Daddy,

Thank you so much for the Thanksgiving call. I loved hearing your voices. I had a great day at Tammy's sister's house. She has two adorable children. I played with them all afternoon and dreamed of having several myself someday.

I am having a wonderful time. And yes, I plan to see the Rockettes soon. In the meantime, I am meeting all kinds of great people and going to parties nearly every weekend night. Don't worry about me staying warm. Our apartment is cozy, and I wear the flannel pajamas you sent.

You'll be happy to know New York is flu free, and I feel very healthy. In fact, I seem to have a huge appetite and have even gained a few pounds.

I will write again soon. Don't worry about me. Tammy and I take good care of each other, and a doctor lives down the hall.

I love you both,
Karen

On Monday morning, Laurie, the dental receptionist, couldn't help commenting on my physical appearance. "Karen, you look a bit rocky this morning. Too much turkey?" Laurie always looked bandbox perfect, and I suspected it pleased her to find someone looking unkempt.

"Yes, that's it. I ate too much, drank too much, and overdid it in every way. I'm just having too much fun." I went into the bathroom, put my head down by the toilet seat, sucked a slice of lemon, and gave myself a pep talk. "You're fine. You're fine. Just keep sucking lemons all day, and you'll be fine."

When I stood up I nearly fell back again, weak from lack of food and nausea. I dampened a paper towel with cold water and put it on my neck to jump-start my body. My ashen face looked back at me in the bathroom mirror. It was no wonder Laurie had made the remark. I looked as if I'd been pulled from a grave. I combed my hair, put a bit of lipstick on my cheeks, and practiced a happy greeting for our next patient.

"Good morning, Mrs. Hanson. How are you today? I'm fine. I'm just a bit pregnant. No, I'm not married. No, I haven't told the father. Oh, he'll be just tickled."

That afternoon I called Tammy and asked her to meet me at a coffee shop near the dental office. Two hours later we sat in a booth facing each other. She took a long look at me. "Trues, you look awful. Are you sick?" She took two spoons of sugar and stirred them into her coffee.

I felt nauseous again, watching the spoon go around and around in the cup. "No, I don't think I'm sick."

"Then ... Oh God, don't tell me. How long?"

"I should have had my period ten days ago. I kept thinking I was tired because I've been working so hard. But now I'm sick every morning."

"Does George know?"

"No. He's been in Toledo with Carolyn over Thanksgiving."

"Okay, let me get this straight." She studied me with one eye closed. "George has been whooping it up over the turkey table with Carolyn, while you've been throwing up alone in New York." She smiled ironically and stirred another spoonful of sugar into her cup.

"It's not like that. Carolyn needed him, and ..."

"And you don't? When is he coming home? Actually, where does he call home, your place or Carolyn's?

"Please don't put George down. I thought you were his friend, too. I love him, and he loves me. I'm sorry ..." I stood to leave. "I'm not feeling well. I have to go. I'll call you." I ran out of the café.

On my way home I thought about Tammy. She was a good person, she wanted the best for me, and I knew she was fond of George. I also knew it must be hard to understand why I stayed with a married man when it didn't look hopeful. My only answer was that I loved him and I couldn't, wouldn't, consider life without him.

Forty minutes later I opened the door to our room and found the lights on, the table set, and George standing in the center of the room, his arms open for me. "Oh, my darling, I've missed you so," he said. "I worried you might be lonely or afraid."

I dropped my coat on the floor and flung myself into his arms. "You're home!" We kissed and held each other for several minutes. Then, abruptly, George stopped, swept my hair back from my forehead, squinted his eyes, and looked fiercely at me. "You're mine. Still mine."

"Yes, of course."

After removing each other's clothing as fast as we could and making love, we ate a dinner of crackers, cheese, wine and Hershey bars. It was the first food I'd gotten down in days. Then we sat in bed reviewing the past week.

"I'm sorry I left so suddenly. Carolyn sounded miserable. She misses me and isn't feeling well. She had terrible nausea, which she seems to be over, but she's lonely and worried. I just thought it was a good idea to keep her happy over the holiday. I knew you wouldn't mind. And I was able to borrow some money. We now have enough to have some fun."

Whatever I'd said in response to that would have sounded snide and selfish, so I just nodded and asked, "Who loaned you the money?"

"It doesn't matter. Now, tell me about your Thanksgiving. Did you see Tammy?"

"Well, I did, but ..."

"Wait." He jumped out of bed and ran to the closet. "Before we go any further, I almost forgot. I brought you a present, my love." He returned to the bed, carrying a small flat object, wrapped in a napkin. "Here, my dearest, open it." He slid back into bed next to me.

Aside from my wedding ring, it was the first gift George had ever given me. "I'm so nervous, my hands are trembling. I can't imagine what it is. Oh ... it's a ... chicken bone?"

"No, my darling. It's a turkey bone. The wishbone. It's for us to make a wish. Our wish for our future."

"Is this from Carolyn's turkey?"

"It doesn't matter where I got it. I got it for you. I thought you'd appreciate my thinking of you."

"I do. It's just that ..."

"I even thought you'd get a kick out of my swiping Carolyn's wishbone. God, I nearly froze to death getting home to you. You're all I thought about the whole time I was gone. But you only care where I got the fucking turkey bone."

He rolled over toward the wall. "This is some homecoming."

"I'm sorry."

"And I'm sorry I tried to please you." He turned off the light.

I really couldn't think of anything to say that would make a difference. After my last four days of hell, he'd handed me Carolyn's turkey bone. I laughed until I cried, partially because I felt so sorry for myself, and partially to let George know how awful I felt. He either didn't care or slept through my hysterics. I finally fell into a twilight sleep. I woke again at five.

Hours later that day, I pulled myself wearily up the subway stairs on my way back to the apartment. My feet hurt, I was nauseous, and my head ached. I'd feel better when I got to the apartment and saw George. I wouldn't tell him yet about being pregnant. We needed a problem-free evening together.

I stopped at the corner market and splurged on a steak. I'd prepare it just the way he liked it. I opened the apartment door. George sat at the dinette with a full ashtray and an empty bottle of bourbon.

I left the groceries in the kitchenette and started toward him. "Hi, sweetheart."

He stared at me for a moment and held out a small card and a photo. "What the hell is this?"

I took another step and began to reach for the note. He got up, lurched toward me, and shoved the card in my face. "It looks like my little Baby didn't waste any time bein' lonely when her daddy was away."

In a horrible moment I realized what he held. It was the card that had been shoved into my hand on the street the day I was looking for Dr. Evan's office. "If you really need a job –" The other item was the photo of me in the shower Sue had taken at school. "Where did you find these?"

"I needed a little cash and was looking in pockets. It was worth the look."

"Those are nothing," I began. "That photo is of me in –"

"I know it's of you, Baby. I've seen you naked, remember?" He took a step closer to me. "What I want t'know is, how many other guys have seen you naked? An' how much money did ja get for your services? Maybe you don't work for pudgy Evans at all. Maybe you jes' whore all day."

"George, please. You don't know what you're saying. Let me explain."

"That's right, Baby, you explain to daddy." He stepped closer and raised his hand to hit me.

I ran behind the chair. He grabbed for me and stumbled. The skin on his face was ashen and taut, and his eyes began to bulge. I hadn't seen his face that way since Ohio, when he had nearly killed us on the highway. He stumbled again and muttered. He started to take another step, but a knock on the door and Tammy's voice stopped him.

"Trues, you in there?"

I ran to the door, opened it, and Tammy stepped inside. She looked at George holding a dumbbell in the air and dropped her basket of food. "George, what are you doing?"

"Jes get out of the way. This is between her majesty and me." He took another step toward me.

Tammy tried to step between us. "George, for God's sake, don't hit her."

He gave Tammy a push. "Get out of the way." He raised his arm.

I grabbed the iron skillet off the stove and jumped on the bed. Tammy jumped on the bed after me. Still holding his barbell, George made a lunge toward us.

Tammy screamed. "Don't hit her, she's pregnant!"

Her words obviously didn't register with him, or they surely would have sobered him up. I raised the skillet and gave him a light tap on the top of his head. He looked dazed for a second and then lunged for us again. "Hit him again, Trues, hit him again."

My heart was pumping so hard it rocked my body. I raised the pan high and hit him again as hard as I could. He slumped to the floor. We stood on the bed looking down at him. "Trues, his head is bleeding."

We climbed off the bed and knelt on either side of him.

The horror of it hit me. I had actually knocked George unconscious. "My God, my God, Tammy, what have I done?"

She leaned closer to him. "He's breathing. He's okay. We'd better get out of here for a while. He's going to be mad as hell when he wakes up."

"Should we just leave him like this?"

"Yes. He'll be all right. Come on."

Tammy and I sat in the neighborhood cafe for an hour before we ventured back to the apartment. When we opened the door, we found George lying on the bed with a towel on his head. We crept in and over to the bed. George opened one eye.

I leaned close to him. "Are you all right?"

"No, my head hurts. Hi, Tammy. Baby, what the hell did you hit me with?"

"The frying pan."

"You sure it wasn't the whole stove?"

Tammy put her arm around my shoulders and guided me toward the door. "I'd better get going. You going to be okay, Trues?"

"Yes, I'll be fine. He's probably forgotten why he was so mad at me."

"Okay. Good luck. Call me tomorrow. I love you."

"You, too. Thanks for saving my life."

"Sure, anytime."

I closed the door behind Tammy and went to George. "Can you sit up?"

"Help me, Baby."

He sat up. I sat beside him on the bed.

"Baby, why did you do that?"

"I thought you were going to hurt me."

"Oh, my baby, I'd never hurt you. You know that." He looked vulnerable and sad. "Don't you?"

I nodded, but I wasn't sure.

"I'm glad you're not any stronger." He gave me a forced grin. "You might have knocked my head off."

"I'm sorry. When I saw you lying there ..."

"It's all over now, Baby. I'll tell you one thing." He rubbed the top of his head. "It definitely sobered me up."

I wet the towel again and sat down next to him on the floor. Gently holding the towel to his forehead, I said, "George, I have to tell you something. This might not be the time, but I've a feeling the right time will never come."

"Okay. Things probably can't get any worse. What is it?"

"I'm pregnant."

He sat silent, staring straight ahead. He got up, walked to the sink, poured a glass of water, and swallowed four aspirins. "You know, Baby," he laughed. "Jokes like that could shock me into sobriety for the rest of my life." He walked to the couch and patted it for me to sit beside him. "Now, tell me what you were going to say before the jokes."

"George, it's not a joke. I'm pregnant. And, believe me, I know it's a horrible mess."

"Jesus! You have some timing! First you hit me on the head with a frying pan and now you tell me you're pregnant."

"Yes."

"You are telling me this is no joke?" He massaged his temples. "You're pregnant?"

"Yes."

"As in, having a baby." He shook his head as if to clear it. Then he laughed, got up and slapped his hands together hard. "Well, hell, let's celebrate. Let's think about our bright future. I'll have three kids and no money! How does that hit you? Maybe you and Carolyn could start a nursery school. We'll call it Carolyn and Karen's school for unwanted infants." He laughed and danced around the table.

"George. STOP IT! We need to talk. We have to figure out what we're going to do."

He stopped suddenly, sat down on the bedside, rubbed his temples and looked at me grimly. "There's only one thing to do. We get rid of it."

"Get RID of it?"

"Of course, as soon as possible. How far along are you?"

"About a month, I think."

"There ought to be a doctor somewhere in this city that will do it for us." He stood up abruptly. "Jesus! How could this happen?"

"Well ..."

"Oh shit, I don't mean that. I mean now. It couldn't happen at a worse time." He turned around in a circle. "Ah, shit." He squinted at me. "Ah, SHIT!"

"I didn't get pregnant on purpose, George." Now I was getting angry.

"I know." He combed his fingers through his hair. "I know. We'll get rid of it. I'll find someone."

"I knew you'd be upset." I stood up. "But are you saying Carolyn gets to keep her baby, but I have to get rid of mine?"

He turned to look at me. "Well, of course. Yours isn't ... well ..."

"Important?" I took a step toward him. "Supposed to be? Legal? What?"

"I didn't mean it that way." He reached for me, his arms outstretched.

I pushed his arms away. "I did. And I might remind you, George. It's your baby, too." I walked to the stove and turned it on. I picked the frying pan up from the floor, put the steak into the pan and began to fry it.

"What the hell are you doing?"

"I'm cooking dinner. When things get this bad, there is only one thing to do. Cook a good steak and eat it."

"I suppose that is a direct quote from your dear mama."

We looked at each other across the room. George, bleary-eyed, with a large bump on his head, and me, still in my uniform and torn stockings. "We're both a mess you know," I said.

"Yeah, two messes in a mess. Hey, that's a good title for a show!" George laughed sardonically. We stood looking at each other. "I know one thing. This mess is madly and forever in love with the mess standing over there." He walked to me and opened his arms.

I walked into his arms. "I love you so, and I'm so sorry I hurt you."

"I deserved it." He stroked my hair. "You're my love forever. We'll work things out."

Tammy Grimes and Karen Truesdell sunbathing at Stephen's College 1952-53

Tammy Grimes and Karen Truesdell signing yearbooks at Stephen's College 1952-53

The sweater Karen knitted for George

Above and below: George C. Scott and Karen
Truesdell at Stephen's Playhouse (1953) in *Petticoat*

George at Karen's home
in Washington 1983.

George clowning
around with his
famous
"Barrymore" pose.

Jack and Felicia Lemmon in
California with
George and Karen (1983).

Twelve

≈

During the next week I was too tired and nauseous to argue about the baby, especially about "getting rid of it." If there were ever a test of our love, that was it. Only once again did we discuss it briefly. George said, "Please, let's try for an abortion. There are lots of doctors who do it. You just have to find one. It would be expensive, but I'd find the money."

"NO!"

George spent long hours walking the streets, looking for acting jobs. He'd sit at the dinner table tired and discouraged. He woke up often after having nightmares and would walk the room or dress and leave for a while.

Midweek Tammy called me at work. She asked me to join her for lunch, and I happily agreed. I had missed her and badly needed her emotional support. We met at an inexpensive cafeteria and fell into each other's arms. "Trues, I've been worried about you. How are you?"

We picked up our trays and found a corner table. Tammy leaned toward me. "How are you feeling?"

"Fair to crummy. I guess I'm supposed to feel this way. I mean the nausea. I read an article that said a lot of nausea early in the pregnancy means the baby has a good chance of going full term."

"How do they know those things?"

"I don't think they do, but it makes me feel better to think I'm suffering for a good reason." It was good talking to Tammy about my problems. I took several large bites of my sandwich and thought about dessert.

Tammy seemed hesitant to ask the next question. "Do you have any plans? I mean for the next few months?"

"Not a one. I don't know where to go or what I'll do. I just know I'm having this baby." It felt good to say that out loud.

"Okay." She sipped her coke and spoke slowly. "I have an idea. If you don't like it, you can tell me to stop talking."

"Go ahead."

"Well, first a question. Have you thought about getting into a home for unwed mothers?"

"Unwed mother. Well, if the title fits."

"Maybe I shouldn't ..."

"No, go on. It's just that for a second ... You know. Anyway, tell me. I don't know anything about them."

"Okay. I didn't either, until I was talking to my mom."

"Oh, Tammy, you didn't tell your mom!"

"No. I didn't. I just said I had a friend who needed somewhere to go. Anyway, there is a home for unwed mothers in Newton, Massachusetts, not far from where my folks live. They take care of you for free, if you have no means of support, until your baby is born."

"I wonder what it's like." I suddenly had a very lonely feeling. "But since I'm a beggar I can't be a chooser, right?"

"I don't think they can force you to stay if you want to leave. Why don't you think about it?"

"That would mean leaving George. I don't know."

"Do you want your baby, or do you want George?"

"Both."

"I'm still hungry. Let's get some ice cream."

"Your best idea yet."

That evening I didn't tell George about Tammy's idea. I thought I'd write and get the particulars first, since he seemed especially edgy and depressed. Not a good time to broach a subject like leaving him to save the baby.

We were both tired and in bed by ten thirty that evening. I fell asleep soon after we turned off the light. I slept soundly until my dreams turned vivid and ugly. Someone had buried me under a pile of sand. I needed to take a breath. I wanted to yell for my mother, but I couldn't open my mouth. Something held my head down when I tried to raise it. I had to get some air or my lungs would burst. I pushed hard to sit up. Something pushed back. I began to panic. This was not a dream! Something pushed against my face. Something held my arms and legs down. I had to breathe. I kicked as hard as I could. I couldn't move. I couldn't open my eyes. I had to take a breath, or I'd pass out. No. I'd die. I pushed hard, freed my knee, and jabbed straight up.

I heard George cry out. He released one arm. I clawed at his arm and neck and kicked again. He freed my leg. I still couldn't breathe. I had to get the thing off my face. I kicked again. My other arm was freed. I pushed at the thing. A pillow. I gave one huge kick with both legs and pushed against the pillow. It came off.

I took in several deep breaths and choked. Gas! I smelled gas! I opened my eyes and saw George. He tried to grab me, but I rolled out of his reach and jumped off the bed. I ran to the window, pushed it open, and took several deep breaths. Coughing and gagging, I inhaled again and again. I knelt on the floor with my head out the window. I heard him turn off the gas and felt him kneeling beside me, gasping the fresh air.

It wasn't a dream. My wonderful dearest had tried to KILL me! We sat at the window breathing heavily, both staring straight ahead out the window. My body shook as I sobbed. Then came the terrible nausea. I took several more deep breaths. After a long while, my body stopped shaking, and my mind cleared. I pulled myself up and looked down at him. "You tried to kill me, George. Goddammit! You just tried to kill me!!"

"There's no other way," he said. "We'd be better off dead."

If I had been confused, afraid and angry before, that comment really did it! Strength returned. "I don't want to die, GEORGE! I want to live. Pregnant or not. If you want to die, you'll have to die alone."

"GOD, THAT WAS A STUPID AND TERRIBLE THING TO DO!" I had never felt such anger. I punched his shoulder. "Stupid and arrogant." I punched him again. "You could have been polite enough too ask me if I wanted to die or not." I realized that was a silly thing to say, but I was so distraught and worried that maybe he was a little crazy. I hit him hard. "You're always saying how you wouldn't hurt me. No, you wouldn't hurt me, you'd just KILL me!" I was crying and punching. George did not move. He didn't even put his hands up to protect himself. He just sat there, while I gave him several more punches.

"I hate you for doing that. Now I'm afraid of you. Do you want me to be afraid of you?" I hit him twice. "Do you want me to hate you?"

"No. I don't want that." He spoke quietly, almost inaudibly. "I never wanted that."

"You just wanted me dead."

"It's the only way out."

"Not for me, it isn't." I suddenly had a feeling I should be somewhere else at that moment. "What day is it?"

"Don't worry. It's Saturday. Old Pudgy won't need your services today."

I kicked his back with my bare foot. "Don't you dare call him Old Pudgy. If it weren't for him we'd be dead from hunger. But then you'd have your wish, wouldn't you?" I walked unsteadily to the closet and took out a skirt and sweater.

"What are you doing?"

"What does it look like, George? I'm dressing. I'm going out. I've got to walk and clear my head."

"I'll come with you."

"Over my dead body! And that wasn't meant to be funny!"

"But Baby ..."

"NO! I want to be alone and think. Try not to jump out the window while I'm gone." I slammed the door.

As I walked down the front steps I thought, "It's a damn good thing I'm going for a walk and not to work today. What a hideous joke, slaving to support a man who tried to kill me."

Mid-morning I opened the apartment door and found George sitting at the table. "You were gone a long time. I was worried."

"About what? That I wouldn't fall under a moving truck?"

"Oh, shit!" He put his head in his hands.

I removed my coat, hung it in the closet, and walked to the refrigerator. I removed two Cokes, set one on the table, and leaned against the sink facing the room.

"George, we're going to talk. Sober."

He stood up and started toward me. "Oh, Baby, you know I'm sorry."

Billing Address:
SYLVIE M OBRIEN
6338 Kabletown Road
CHARLES TOWN WV 25414-4675

SYLVIE M OBRIEN
6338 Kabletown Road
CHARLES TOWN W

Shipping Address:
SYLVIE M OBRIEN
6338 Kabletown Road
CHARLES TOWN WV 25414-4675

Your order of September 21, 2005 (Order ID 002-1123889-5603212)

Qty	Item
	IN THIS SHIPMENT
1	Love and Madness: My Private Years With George C. Scott Riehl, Karen Truesdell Paperback *20 -* 1590250192

This shipment completes your order.

"No, I don't. And do not come near me. Sit down. Over there."
I pointed to a straight chair by the table." He obeyed.

"I have decided to take charge of my life. To make my own
decisions. And the first decision I have made is to keep my baby."

"But we have no choice."

"Yes, we have. More to the point, I have."

"What do you plan to do?"

"There are homes for girls in trouble."

"Oh, Baby, no. That would make me feel like ..." He started to
rise.

"Sit down and be quiet. This has nothing to do with how YOU
feel." I took a sip of soda and a deep breath. Putting the bottle
down, I folded my arms and spoke as if I was speaking to a 6-year-
old child.

"There's a home in Newton, Massachusetts for unmarried,
pregnant girls. Tammy told me about it. She grew up near there. I
intend to go there, if they'll have me. I'll quit work as soon as I can
make the arrangements. I'll take my paycheck for train fare and
spending money."

George stood up and took a step toward me. "You sound like
you've made up your mind. You had it all planned out. You weren't
planning on consulting me at all."

"Yes, I was. But after this morning you've lost your rights
where my baby and I are concerned."

"Baby, I don't know what to say." He studied his hands as if he
were counting his fingers and shook his head. When he looked at
me there was pain and disbelief in his eyes, and if I hadn't been so
angry I might have caved in.

"There is nothing to say. And, George, please do not call me
Baby! You'll soon have two babies. Three children. That ought to
be plenty. Now, I am going to eat a good breakfast and go to
Central Park. If you want to join me, and promise not to kill me,
I'd like the company. If you don't, that's okay, too."

I turned my back on him. My hands shook as I reached for a
bowl and the box of cereal. My head ached, and I felt ill, but I
stiffened my shoulders and my resolve. I couldn't show any
weakening. George had to see that my decision was final. I poured
milk on my cereal, closed the refrigerator, carried my bowl to the

table and began to eat without a word or a look in his direction.

He decided to join me for my walk. I remained quiet throughout our time in the park, afraid of wavering if he said anything kind and loving. I was determined to go through with my plan.

Before we went to bed that night we talked about our close call with death. He was shocked he'd done it. When he promised there'd be no more episodes like that again, I tried hard to believe him. But I knew I'd be wary, even afraid of him, for a while. As was his habit, he laid his arm heavily over my shoulders and pulled me close. I wondered if this symbolized an act of protection or his need to be protected.

I turned on the radio. The station was playing "Strangers in Paradise."

In the next four weeks he tried only three times to change my mind, twice begging me to stay with him. "We'll work it out. I promise we'll work it out." The third time he said, "When we're married and have money, we'll have other children. Just not this time."

"Yes, this time," I said.

In early December, knowing we wouldn't be together much longer, we decided to have some New York fun. We used some of his mysterious loan money and bought tickets to see our first Broadway show, *Arms and the Man*. George had been drinking heavily during the day and had to leave twice to be sick. He enjoyed himself, but I'm not so sure the people seated around him enjoyed themselves. We saw the movie *Annie Oakley*, and when Doris Day sang "Once I had a Secret Love," we kissed.

One morning George thumbed to Hoboken, New Jersey to watch the filming of *On The Waterfront*, starring Marlon Brando. He was completely enamored with Brando's talent.

December was cold, and I was glad I'd packed my warm winter fur coat. With the collar up, I snuggled down and took long walks alone to do some clear thinking. As much as I wanted to be with

George those last weeks, my mind churned when I was near him. Several times I almost lost my resolve. I felt lonely for him when we weren't together and muddled when we were. But I knew, both for the safety of the baby and my health, I had to leave him until our child was born.

Mother and Daddy had called a few days earlier to wish me Merry Christmas and ask if I'd received my gifts in the mail.

"We sent the box early, to be sure you'd get it in time," Mother yelled.

"Did you find the one for your roommate?" Daddy asked. "It's just a little something for her. But it's a surprise, so we won't tell you what it is."

"Yes, I got the box. Thank you."

"Karen, did you get to see the Rockettes?" Mother asked for the fifth time, including the three times in her letters.

I decided to lie. "Yes, and they were wonderful!"

"I'm so glad. Now tell me." Her voice softened. "How are you feeling?"

For a second I thought Mother was psychic, then I remembered that she always asked about my health in that voice. I was tempted to tell her, but a change of subject would be better. "Oh just fine. And New York is so beautiful during the holiday season. May I open your gifts early?"

"Can't wait, huh?" daddy chuckled. "You never could."

"Well, Merry Christmas, dear. We'll miss you."

"I'll miss you, too. Merry Christmas." I wanted badly to add, "I want to come home."

"Merry Christmas." They yelled into the phone together.

Our first Christmas, which turned out to be our last one for twenty-five years, was a disaster. I threw up most of Christmas Eve and the next day. We decorated the standing lamp with tinsel and two glass balls we'd stolen off the tree at Macy's. It looked pathetic.

We promised not to buy each other a gift. I cheated and bought George a pair of slippers. I was hoping he'd cheat, too. He didn't. Instead, he yelled at me for spending money on "slippers, of all things!" I cried. He apologized.

We celebrated Christmas dinner with two cans of turkey soup and my famous peanut butter sandwiches. We had saved an ice cream bar for desert. I knew George hadn't had enough to eat, and since I was nauseous anyway, I put it in front of him. He insisted I eat it. I shoved it back, and he returned the favor. By the time we stopped arguing the ice cream had melted away.

Nothing was at all like the Christmases I had known growing up. At home the house would be bright with decorations and warm with good feelings and turkey and pie baking in the oven. My married sisters and their families would be there, happy, laughing together. There'd be no secrets. I felt homesick, pregnant, sick, and very sorry for myself.

New Year's Eve was worse than Christmas. We took the subway to Broadway to watch the people. I felt faint when I stood in the overcrowded subway, so we got off two stops early. In an effort to feel festive, I had worn my best dress shoes from college. By the time we'd walked three blocks, blisters formed. I tried to ignore the pain, but I finally sat down on the curb, removed my shoes, and began to walk barefoot. This infuriated George.

"Can you tell me one good reason why you wore tight shoes for a long walk?"

"I didn't expect it to be a long walk. And I didn't know my feet had swollen. It's our first New Year's Eve together, and I wanted to look pretty for you."

"Well, for whatever stupid reasons, you have succeeded in ruining New Year's Eve. We're going home." Quickening his pace, he walked toward the subway station.

I limped behind him crying, and angry that he blamed me. What he needed was another good bop on the head with a frying pan, I thought.

By the time we got back to the apartment, he had cooled off. We toasted each other at midnight with the last Coke and beer in the refrigerator and went to bed.

The end of January, I gave Dr. Evans two-weeks' notice. My uniform was beginning to feel tight, and I knew it wouldn't be long before I'd be an embarrassment to the office.

The time for leaving George was marching on me, and I became increasingly depressed. But a lovely surprise! Unbeknownst to me, Tammy had called her mother in Brookline, Massachusetts, to ask her if I could come there for a while. So on a day when I especially needed a miracle, one arrived at our apartment door.

Tammy's mother could have been Little Red Riding Hood, standing at my door, wearing a red wool cape over a full dirndl skirt, and holding a basket of food. She wore her hair in a Dutch Boy cut and her voice was lyrical. "Hello, deah. I'm Woolie, Tammy's mother," she said in her cultured Boston accent. She appeared to be my fairy godmother. She had the dearest face and the sweetest smile I'd ever seen. She stood about five feet, two inches tall in her ballerina slipper shoes and said, "How do you feel? Oh, don't answer that. I know you must feel awful. I've come to help you. May I come in?"

"Of course." I stepped back. Removing her cape, she brought out a canister of tea, a tin of Scottish cakes, and a jar of honey from her basket. We made tea together and sat down at the table.

We talked about Tammy. She told me about their home in Brookline, about her family, and about New England. Had I ever been there? No, I hadn't. Would I like to go? It was then I knew she was my guardian angel. She had come to save my life. She took my breath away with her kindness and held my shaking shoulders as I wept. Someone cared! This dear, dear person cared. And she continued to care and remain my close friend until she died.

The last weekend before I left, I took one of my solitary walks. I watched the Christmas lights reflected on the icy streets, while I rehearsed what I'd write in the long overdue letter to my parents. "Dear Mother and Daddy. I am entering a home for bad girls, because I am." Better not be too flippant. It might give Daddy a heart attack. "Dear Mother and Daddy. I have been invited to visit Newton, Massachusetts, for the holidays. You can reach me at the Florence Crittenden home for unwed mothers." That would give Mother a heart attack. "Dear Mother and Daddy. Don't worry about me. I am going to Massachusetts for a few months with Sue. We are tired of New York and plan to be successful brain surgeons." I started to laugh out loud, nearly tripping on some black ice. That would be fitting, I thought. "Pregnant woman found dead from fall on ice. No real reason for death except depression."

Poor Mother and Daddy. They'd always been good to me. And I'd done nothing but lie to them for over a year. How would they feel if they knew the truth? They'd probably blame themselves. "Where did we go wrong? Did we give her too much? Too little?" It was better they didn't know. I could take care of myself. I didn't deserve more. I was scared, and God knows I needed them, but I didn't deserve them. That evening I wrote a letter to my parents and told them more lies.

The day before I left New York, Tammy paid us a last visit. She handed me a red basket and spoke, lovingly, as a mother would to her child. "Here are sandwiches and fruit. You eat! You're eating for two now."

"Tammy, thank you for so many things. I miss you already."

"Dear Trues, just give me a great big hug and say you'll write to me. I'll be in touch with Mum to check on you. Maybe I can be there when the baby arrives. I love you." We hugged hard and long before she turned and left.

George and I hired a cab for the ride to the train station. We sat in the back seat, holding each other in silent desperation. How could I do this? How could I leave my love? I couldn't! Yes, I could. For the life of my baby. It surprised me to realize I had finally grown up enough to care about someone other than George and myself.

We both wept. We kissed while we were weeping. The kisses were wet and salty. We dried our eyes and kissed again.

Crying again, I said, "I have to do this."

He half closed his eyes and studied me closely as he so often did. But this time his eyes were filled with anguish. "I know," he said quietly. "How can I live without you? My whole body aches for love of you."

"I know. I know my love. I can barely stand this. But we will see each other soon. I promise. We'll be together."

He kissed me long and hard. Then he held me at arm's length and said, "I promise, my dearest. We'll be together. I promise."

"George?

"Yes, my darling."

"It's all right if you call me Baby."

One side of his mouth went up in a half smile, but the look of sadness remained in his eyes. "I'll see you soon, my baby."

"ALL ABOARD!"

"I have to go."

"I know."

I pulled away and walked toward the train. I stopped, looked back, pointed to my dime store wedding ring and mouthed, "I love you!"

George stood motionless as his eyes filled with tears.

I ached to yell to him, "Stop me! Please don't let me go. I can't stand this." But I knew I'd still go.

'Death of a Salesman' Is Moving Production; Tragic Willie Loman Comes To Life

Arthur Miller's play, "Death of a Salesman" opened last week at the Playhouse. It is an ambitious production for any theatre group to present, for a great deal of sensitivity and understanding, as well as talent, is necessary to make seeing it a memorable experience.

However, director John Gunnell has succeeded in translating the script into a vivid and moving production. Willie Loman's tragic story comes to life and seems to reach over the footlights and pull the onlooker into it.

By the third act the observer feels as if he knows Willie and his family very well, and wants to do everything possible to prevent the inevitable ending.

But, of course, nothing can be done, and when the lights go up the audience is quiet, thinking, beginning to see life in a new perspective. The spell is so strong that it's a full minute before one's mind returns to the theatre, and applause begins one of the finest tributes an audience can pay a production—the moment's silent appreciation before applauding. William Cragen is magnificent as

Willie Loman, a salesman who "rode on a smile" all his life, dreaming of wealth and success, and never obtaining either.

His devoted wife, Linda, is portrayed by Frances McCrory, a fine actress who gives the role the warmth and understanding it needs. Their sons are played by Richard Shepard and George C. Scott, who are both excellent in their parts. The fine supporting cast includes William West, M. G. Mehl, Eugene Shewmaker, Karen Truesdell and Don Smith.

Special credit should be given to Chandler A. Potter's settings and to the special lighting effects, both of which add to the production. Alberta McCreery is in charge of costumes and properties are by Jane Mehl. "Death of a Salesman" runs through October 25.

1952 newspaper review of *Death of a Salesman* with George and Karen in roles

1952 newspaper photo of George and Karen in *Present Laughter*

Have Leads In Coward Play

KAREN TRUESDELL, VELLA DAVENPORT AND GEORGE C. SCOTT

The Misses Truesdell and Davenport and Mr. Scott will have the leads in "Present Laughter," the Noel Coward comedy which the Mad Anthony Players will present in the Indoor Theater of the Zoo, starting tomorrow evening for a week with matinees on Saturday and Sunday.

Thirteen

≈

"TICKETS!"

I raised my hand above my coat just high enough for the conductor to take my ticket. He punched it, put it back into my hand, and I lowered it into my coat sleeve. He must have been used to that by then. I hadn't looked at him since I'd sat down eight hours before. He probably thought I was either hiding from the police or a marathon weeper. I was sure I'd have scared him if I had looked at him, with my puffy face and uncombed hair. I probably smelled bad, too. My head ached, and I wondered if I'd ever be able to straighten up again.

During the trip my thinking was not constructive. My thoughts were only about Poor Me. I was a wreck, filled with self-pity, guilt, fear, remorse, and though I was learning fast, ignorance of how the real world works. As the train slowed, I had a giant panic attack. I barely knew Tammy's family. What if they didn't like me? What if I didn't like them? What if they're not here to meet me? What if, after all this, I lost my baby?

The train came to a jerky stop. I'd get some answers soon.

Three sweet faces welcomed me at the Back Bay Station. Woolie, her sister VeeVee, and Tammy's 9-year-old nephew, Scott. The name jolted me. At first I thought they were playing some sort of horrible joke, but his name truly was Scott. He proudly helped me carry my bags.

We drove to Woolie's big brown shake New England home. It had a homey look on the outside and a comfy feel on the inside, with overstuffed furniture and natural woods. Luther, Tammy's father, and her sister and brother were equally warm in their greetings, but I couldn't help wondering what they really thought of this girl who had lived with a married man and wound up pregnant. The first evening went swiftly. When I finally closed the bedroom door and lay between the fresh sweet-smelling sheets, I allowed myself to cry once again. I only wanted to go home to George.

The next morning I wrote to George, telling him about the wonderful family that had taken me in, and about Woolie, who danced and sang her way through preparing dinner. A modern dance student, she wore a leotard, skirt and dancing shoes. I told him about Luther, a soft-spoken lover of gardening, and about Tammy's tall, Boston-classy sister, Nancy and her gentle fun-loving brother, Nick.

During the next few days I tried to make myself useful doing household chores, but I felt uncomfortable forging ahead without asking how they wanted things organized. I felt like a nuisance, having to ask how the washer worked, or if she'd like to have her floors vacuumed.

George called a week after I arrived. How was I? What were my plans? He'd moved to a cheaper room. He missed me. He loved me. He'd call again when he could. I felt so lonely and empty after I hung up, I almost wished he hadn't called.

One evening we had a dinner guest named Phillip. A family friend, he was a thin, dark-haired, Harvard graduate. He was congenial, even charming. But sitting across from this carefree young man, I missed George all the more.

A few days after he came to dinner, Phillip called to ask if I'd like to take a ride with him in the country. Woolie urged me to go. "It would be good for you to get out of the house." So I went with him and wasn't as bored as I thought I'd be. The end of that week he came by again. He returned again a few days later.

And then one evening I heard Woolie whispering with Luther in the next room. Whispering always made me curious, so I listened from the hallway. He was asking her how long I intended to stay, and she was defending me in my plight. I couldn't blame him. He had to share his home and board with a pregnant waif he barely knew.

The next morning I told Woolie I felt I should leave, that I was in the way.

"You're not in the way, deah." She placed a cup of her favorite chicory coffee on the table in front of me and said, "But maybe there's another way you can have some freedom." She made several calls and found me a job in the city, selling gloves and handbags at Filenes department store.

Nancy worked in Boston, so most mornings I joined her on the subway. During the day, I stood behind the glove and handbag counter wearing a forced smile. But my guilt made me vulnerable to paranoia. Each time I saw the other employees talking, I was convinced they were talking about me.

Tammy came home for a weekend in March. I cried with joy when she arrived. She made me laugh and she sang to me. As I sat on her bed, she stood belting out the song, "Johnny Jones." "... and then he'd kiss her once again and row, row, row, right up the river, he would row, row, row ..." I asked her to sing it over and over again.

She didn't have news of George, but she entertained me with stories about her theater friends. She was my golden person, and I wept when she left.

Even though I worked during the day, I knew I was still underfoot. And, of course, my stomach continued to grow. So when this pitiful parasite could no longer handle the guilt of sponging off Woolie and Luther, I decided it was time to enter the home for unwed mothers.

I also realized I was taking advantage of Phillip. I should never have gone driving with him. I should have discouraged him the first evening. But he was such a dependable person, with a strong shoulder to lean on, that I let it continue.

I wrote to George nearly every day for several weeks. It was sometime during those weeks that I received one short letter from him saying Carolyn had lost the baby. My first reaction was guilt. Had she found out about George and me, and had that led to her miscarriage? Then anger. Had George given in to his weakness and guilt and told her? Why? To get back at me somehow? I wondered if she hated me. I'm sure she hated me. I had ruined her life. I had caused her to lose her child, while mine was still alive.

After I read the letter, I told Woolie about it. After listening to my every word, she told me, "Don't blame yourself. God works in many ways. It's for Him to punish."

I appreciated her kindness and understanding, but that didn't really make me feel much better. God had punished Carolyn for my mistakes.

The first week in April, I entered the Florence Crittenden Home. Woolie had made the appointment for a Thursday afternoon. I packed my things Wednesday evening, then sat on the bed and looked at the lovely, yellow room. Woolie gently tapped on the door and asked if she could come in. We sat together on the side of the bed. "Don't worry." She patted my hand. "It will be all right."

"Woolie, I owe you so much. You and all the family. I'll never forget what you've done for me. How can I ever repay you?"

"You pass it on someday. That will be our thanks."

"I love you, Woolie."

"And I love you, too, deah."

"May I ask you something?"

"Of course."

"Where did you get the name Woolie?"

She laughed in her quiet gentle way. "My father gave me the nickname. He thought I was woolly minded." She patted my hand and gazed at me so intently I felt she could see my soul. At that moment I felt closer to her and trusted her more than anyone I'd ever known. She was the least woolly minded person in the world. She saw everything clearly. She made me feel almost okay.

At one in the afternoon Woolie rang the bell on the heavy wood front door of the Florence Crittenden Home. The door was opened almost immediately by a small woman who appeared to be about sixty years old. She was wearing a flowered dress that hung nearly to her ankles. "We've been expecting you," she said. She exchanged greetings with Woolie, smiled, took my hand, and guided me into the hallway. "I'm Mrs. Stanley. Now, if you'll both come with me into the office, we'll do some paper work and get acquainted." As the front door clanged shut behind me, I thought at least her name isn't Igor, and there don't seem to be any bats flying around.

The house's interior reminded me of a 1940s prison movie set. The walls were gray and empty. The floors were a shiny, slate gray. Every click of a heel or whispered word echoed through the halls. The smell of institutional food filled the place. I hated that smell from the time I was in grade school, and I was afraid my gag reflex would start. I swallowed hard. I'd have to get used to it.

We sat across from Mrs. Stanley while she opened a new folder. She jotted down a few words and then handed me a sheet of paper and a pen. "Please fill out this form and sign at the bottom."

I signed the form swearing I was pregnant with no means of support.

Then she read me the list of house rules:

1. No smoking anywhere, except in the smoke room on the first floor. The smoke room is closed at nine p.m. and opens after breakfast daily.
2. Meals are served in the dining room. Breakfast six-thirty a.m., Lunch eleven-thirty a.m., Dinner, five-thirty p.m.
3. The weekly task sheet is posted outside the dining room. Please take note.
4. You will be held responsible for keeping your bunk area neat and clean. Clean sheets are dispersed weekly.
5. Please shower daily.
6. Lights out at nine-thirty each evening, unless there is entertainment in the main hall.

After she finished reading the list, she said, "We strongly recommend that you don't tell anyone your last name or your hometown address and telephone number. After you leave here, you will want to start a new life. Believe me, you won't want your experience to follow you. If, of course, you choose to tell, that is your own concern. You may have visitors any day between 1 p.m. and four p.m. On Sundays you may leave with your visitor between one and five." Her eyes twinkled. "And we advise you to go easy on the sweets. They're not good for you or your baby. But I'm sure the girls upstairs will tell you more about that. They'll fill you in on any questions you might have." She smiled and stood up. "Now it's time I take you up to the dorm room."

Fear struck hard. "Oh," was all I could manage.

Woolie and I walked to the front door. She hugged me and said, "You call me if you need anything."

I wanted to say, "I need you to take me with you now." But I only replied, "I will." I bit my lip hard as I could. This was no time to show what a big baby I could be.

"I'll be by to visit you on Sunday." She hugged me again, patted my cheek, and left.

I stood looking at the closed front door. This was the most alone I'd ever felt in my life.

Then Mrs. Stanley took my arm. "Come, dear. I'll show you the way to the dorm. I'm sure you're anxious to meet the other girls."

That was the last thing I wanted to do. "Thank you," I said, and followed her up the twenty-five stairs and down the hall to the dorm room, where she left me standing at the door, while she announced the arrival of the new girl. She patted my arm and told me cheerfully, "You go right in. They're waiting for you."

Peeking around the corner, I saw a room with tan walls and cracked linoleum, filled with pregnant women lounging on cots. I was alone no more. I stood awkwardly in the doorway for a moment.

This had to be a nightmare. I'd wake up soon and be back at Woolie's house or maybe in George's arms, or even home in Seattle, sitting on my mother's lap. I did not belong here. I peered at the inmates, waiting for something. I had no idea what.

Finally a fleshy, dark-haired girl looked up and broke the silence. "Hi. Come on in. Make yourself at home. I'm Sophia. There are two empty cots. Take your pick. There's an orange crate beside the cot for your stuff. Your locker's over there. This is rest hour. At two o'clock we have recreation hour. That means we walk downtown." She went back to reading her magazine and chewing her candy.

A redheaded girl who looked no older than thirteen, sat up, and in a singsong voice filled with sarcasm added, "Yeah, walking a mile every day makes a healthy mama in every way."

Without looking up from their reading everyone joined in. "A healthy mama means a healthy baby."

"HA! All they want is a healthy baby to give to someone else," one girl said.

"Let us carry the load, and they give it away," another added.

It seemed rehearsed, as if they had chorused these words many times before. I wasn't sure if they meant it or thought they were just being funny. But after that greeting, I wanted to crawl into my locker and not come out until the baby was born.

I chose a cot in a corner, thinking I'd have some solitude there. I unpacked my things, lay down on my cot, and closed my eyes, trying to erase the feeling of being trapped in hell.

In the afternoon, and every afternoon thereafter, we walked to the drugstore by twos, in a line like second graders. It's a wonder they didn't suggest we hold hands and skip. Twenty pregnant girls, skipping down the street holding hands. That would have frightened the neighbors. I soon discovered we disgusted them enough as it was. The city council had tried to rezone so that Ms. Crittenden would have to move her pregnant girls out of the neighborhood. As we walked down one side of the street to town, we watched our neighbors cross to the other side to avoid us. We figured they thought illegitimacy was contagious.

One day before our walk, when Sophia and I were standing outside the home waiting for the others to join us, a young mother with two small boys crossed to our side of the street, heading straight for us. She looked as if she'd just emerged from church, wearing her proper light blue wool suit and clean white gloves with white hat to match. When she was near enough for us to hear, without raising her voice, she carefully enunciated, "Sluts." She nodded to the two little boys, who ran up to us and took turns spitting on our shoes. Then she took their hands, and without looking back, recrossed the street. I stood there, stunned, staring at the saliva slowly sliding down the side of my brown loafers. Now we knew why we had been advised not to stand outside the home unless we were all together.

But being together in the home did not necessarily mean we were "together." There was a social system, and the pecking order had nothing to do with who you were, or how you lived on the outside. It had everything to do with whom you went around with on the inside. If you were fortunate enough to be accepted by the leaders, which I was, no one dared laugh or torment you, and you'd probably be the lucky receiver of bags of confiscated cookies and candy.

After a week, the girls accepted me into the inner circle, and we began sharing stories. We'd gather together in the dorm room after the lights were out, gorge on forbidden goodies, and tell our tales. We were careful not to disclose our last names or hometowns. It was awful to hear how many of the girls had had unhappy love affairs and been thrown out by their families.

"My father whipped me," Gina told us, "Look, I'll show you the scars." She removed her blouse to prove it. It seemed the people closest to all of us had been the cruelest.

Roselyn denied being a "bad girl" like the rest of us. "I was raped," she claimed. The rest of us felt sorry for her, whether or not she had truly been raped or if she just couldn't face the reality of her situation. But we still joked about her behind her back.

Judy, a large square-jawed girl of about twenty-five, said she'd always yearned to be more feminine. "I proved I'm a female," she laughed. "Now I just can't show my face around my own home town anymore."

Mollie wanted us to know that all her maternity smocks came from Bergdoff's, and Susan seemed more concerned about her zits than being unmarried and pregnant.

Marci carried her Bible in front of her like a shield, announcing at least every other day, "You're all going straight to Hell." We wondered where she thought she would be going.

Hearing about others in the same boat was therapy, but we were still in that boat. It was a select club, and like any special group of people who've shared hard times, we understood each other as no one else ever could.

I missed George so terribly I could barely think his name without crying. It had been weeks since the letter about Carolyn. I hoped that meant he was busier auditioning than drinking. But I knew better.

Mail time was bleak. Few of the girls expected letters, some of the families didn't know where they were, and other families didn't care. Everyday I rushed downstairs to the letter cubbies in high hopes, only to climb back up the stairs depressed.

Supportive, understanding people surrounded me. But I only wanted George's arms to surround me. I was desperate for just one letter or phone call to reassure me of his love. I wouldn't allow myself to think I'd never see him again.

Mother and Daddy were faithful writers. I had written to them, telling them how happy I was in a cute little apartment outside of Boston. I gave them the post office box that Mrs. Stanley had supplied. Their letters were full of love, good cheer, and hope they would see me soon. I felt so guilty reading them I could only read half a page at a time.

My favorite time of day was in the evening after dinner. The six of us on cleanup duty would squeeze our bulging bodies into a tiny area where the sink and cupboards were, turn up the radio, and sing along with the latest hits, substituting our own raunchy words:

"Hello, young ladies, wherever you are;
Being faithful will not get you far;
There's only one thing a boy wants to do:
To screw, zip back up, and leave you."

We felt terribly clever, and laughed ourselves into coughing fits.

Once a week we had hot dogs for dinner. We'd save a weenie, give it a male name, and take turns slicing it ceremoniously with a serrated knife. It was a lot more fun tormenting Jerry or Frank, than snipping away at a hot dog. The girl closest to her due date had the privilege of making several extra stabs. Our ceremony would end as we'd hum the funeral dirge, carry the cutting board to the garbage can and toss in the pieces.

Phillip came to see me nearly every Sunday. He'd arrive at two o'clock on the dot, drive me as far as the four hours allowed, and return me five minutes before curfew. We had fun together. No heaviness, no trouble. He was my friend. I had the awful feeling he wanted to be more than that, so I talked about George constantly. I felt no attraction to Phillip, and tried, without being rude, to let him know it.

The turnover at the Florence Crittenden Home was constant. About every week one of the girls would go into labor. They'd help speed things up by taking large doses of laxatives a night or two before they were due.

On our afternoon fresh air walks we would head straight to the drugstore for candy, magazines, cigarettes and castor oil. The drugstore was small, with one clerk. If he had been observant at all, he would have noticed that Florence's fat girls bought castor oil every seven or eight days. We guessed he thought pregnant women were always constipated.

The procedure was the same for all of us, although we didn't force anyone to take part. The girl who was a day or two away from delivery would drink half the bottle of castor oil with an orange juice chaser. We'd keep her walking until she went into labor. It was a painful and risky thing to do. But after months of waiting to get out of our pregnant prison, we tended to do painful and risky things.

The morning after a girl had given birth, there'd be a note pinned to the announcement board outside the dining room: "Girl. 5 lbs. Mother and child doing fine." We'd stand with our arms around each other and give a cheer. A sad silence would follow, knowing we'd never see our sister again. Our ensuing conversation was always the same.

"I wonder how she feels."

"I hope she's not scared."

"I wonder if she has someplace to go."

"I hope she finds a good guy this time."

"Yeah."

Then we'd rush upstairs to divide up her old maternity smocks. That afternoon another girl in trouble would join us.

Only years later did I admit to myself the fine care we had at the home. Physical exams and deliveries by one of the best OBs from the Boston General Hospital who volunteered his time. Psychologists and counselors held group and individual weekly therapy sessions. We were not grateful at the time, convinced the therapists were there for the sole reason of pressuring us to sign our children away for adoption.

The staff took the extra effort to prepare a diet table. We hated it, reasoning that fattening food was our only solace. After hours we'd gorge on the contraband we hid beneath our cots. The staff members were wise and compassionate enough to let us think we were getting away with it.

And Mrs. Stanley was the best of them all. She was the first to greet us when we checked in, our constant protector while we were there, and the one who rubbed our backs as she rode with us to the hospital.

Fourteen

≈

Florence Crittenden had been my home for nearly four months when one Sunday in July I woke up with a feeling of dread. Today was the day I had planned to tell my parents of my pregnancy. Make a clean breast of it and clear my conscience. It turned out to be another cowardly mistake. I should have wrestled with my conscience some other way than laying it on them.

I had written to my married sister, telling her everything. I included in the envelope a letter for Mother and Daddy, telling them about New York and George, but not about my pregnancy. I asked my sister to read it to them. I knew it was one nasty task to put on a sister's shoulders, but I had to prepare them for my call. My sister reported to me later that she had read them the letter, and it had, indeed, come as a terrible shock for them.

So, on that day in late July, with Phillip and Woolie on either side of me, I called Seattle and told my parents I was eight months pregnant. I cannot remember the exact words we exchanged, but I do remember it as an emotionally wrenching conversation.

I cried my way through the next few days, as I'm sure my mother did. The letter she wrote me was devastating.

> *"You have broken our hearts. We gave you everything, and you treat us this way. After all the hopes and dreams we had for you, you lied to us. You're a bad, deceitful girl. No decent man will ever look at you now. You've ruined the family name. You're no better than a guttersnipe. You must give the baby up for adoption and never speak of it again."*

That was that. I felt as if I deserved every word.

On an afternoon in late August I proudly purchased my bottle of castor oil. That evening after dinner, and as my friends circled around me, I held the bottle high, toasted them and chug-a-lugged it. Instantly, I wished I hadn't as it wasn't at all what I had expected. Drinking it was horrific, and trying to keep it down, even worse. I wanted to lie down, but my conspirators reminded me I had to keep walking. They practically dragged me around the room. If I had had the strength or the time between trips to the bathroom, I'd have slugged them all with the castor oil bottle.

After all my insides had drained out, and only the baby was left, the labor pains began. I begged the girls for mercy.

But they reminded me of the rules. "No hospital until it really hurts."

"This HURTS!" I shrieked at them.

When the pains became frequent and hard, I heard myself cry for my mother, until I remembered her letter and knew that she hated me.

My baby girl was born in the charity ward of Boston General Hospital. I opened my eyes and wanted more than anything on earth to see George's face. Instead I saw Phillip's. He stood beside my bed, smiling at me. He looked almost comic, holding a bouquet of wilted summer flowers. His eyes were bloodshot, and he looked exhausted. "Well, good morning," he said. "How do you feel?"

"Fine, I guess. How long have you been here?"

"Since about five this morning."

"How did you know I was here?"

"Woolie called."

"You didn't have to come."

"I wanted to. Here, these are for you." He handed me the wilted flowers. "Well, I guess I'd better go and let you rest." He kissed my cheek. "I'll come back this evening, if that's okay."

"Yes. That'll be fine."

After Phillip left, I looked around. Ten white iron beds with white covers, white walls and white linoleum floors. The room resembled a huge barn. There were no pictures on the walls, no flowers in vases. The room smelled as if it had been recently scrubbed.

Two other women occupied beds. We took care not to look at one another openly. Having a charity ward baby meant you were poor and unwanted.

Woolie was my next visitor. She brought me a thin, red leather belt. "To show you what a nice little waist you have now, dear. When you're released, I want you to come up to the farm for a few days. We'll talk about what you should do next."

In the middle of my morning nap I heard a singsong voice. "I have a lovely baby girl here. I have a lovely baby girl here." The nurse stood at the open door, rocking a small bundle in her arms. "Don't you want to hold her? She's very pretty."

I had promised myself I'd wait a few days before I looked at my daughter, to think things out. "Don't look, or you'll be hooked," my friends at the home had warned me. But as the nurse came to the side of my bed and leaned so close, I could smell the sweet baby scent, I lost my resolve. "Yes. I do want to hold her."

The nurse put her in my arms. Our baby. George's and mine. Our daughter.

"Oh, sweet baby. I hope you'll be glad you were born." I whispered to her.

I had no idea about a name. None of us ever talked about naming our babies. A name made the child a reality. We knew if we thought about it as a living being, it would be hard to let it go. And we were urged constantly to think of that alternative. So, for most of us, our thinking didn't go past giving birth. After that it was like looking at a blank wall.

I didn't want my baby to go another minute without a name. As I looked at her, I remembered my sister's favorite name. "Hi, baby girl. Hi, Tracie," I said as I kissed her tiny fingers.

That afternoon I wrote George a short note. Our daughter had arrived, and her name was Tracie. I'd be staying with Tammy's family for a few days.

A week after I was released from the hospital, Phillip arrived at Woolie's farm in New Hampshire and asked me to marry him. It was far too soon to make a decision like that, and I wished he hadn't asked me. I didn't love him. But I owed him. He had been a wonderful friend to me when I desperately needed a good friend. I owed him my life. I owed him my loyalty. I owed him everything. He'd been there when George had forsaken me.

Phillip must have known I didn't love him. I had talked constantly for months about how much I loved George. But I began to think maybe kindness would prevail, and that I could grow to love him. Maybe he'd be a good father to my child. Maybe I'd stop loving George. Maybe I would die soon.

So, just ten days after I'd given birth to George's baby, I agreed to marry Phillip. He slipped an engagement ring on my finger, and all seemed well with the world. Except my heart still ached to be with George.

After Phillip left the farm that evening, I knocked on Woolie's bedroom door.

"Come in."

I sat on the side of her quilt-covered bed. "Woolie, I have something to show you." I held out my left hand. "Phillip asked me to marry him."

She took my hand, glanced at the ring, then looked at me intently. "Oh, my deah, it's so soon. Too soon to make such a decision."

She was giving me a way out. She was saying what I wanted her to say, but I didn't dare listen. If I stayed too long in her room, I'd lose my resolve. I had given him my word. It wouldn't be right to turn my back on him. I had to marry him. If I didn't, I'd hurt him and my family again. "I told him I would."

"But you're not happy, dear. I can see that."

"Phillip is a nice man. And besides, I owe him so much."

"Oh, my dear, that is no reason to marry him."

But, I thought, it is the reason. I have to begin to repay my debts. "Well, I am. I'm going to marry him." I kissed her cheek and hurried out of the room.

The next day, George called Woolie from New York. He told her he was coming up to see me and the baby. He had some good news. I should have been ecstatic at the thought of seeing my love after being so long apart. I wasn't. I was miserable. I was engaged to another man.

Seeing him step from the train the next morning filled me with such pain I couldn't move. He was there in front of me, my passion, my love, my life. I had dreamed of this moment for months. He held out his arms. I felt if I touched him, I'd explode. He walked to me, enveloped me in his arms, and I was home. Then he stepped back and grinned. "Baby, it's so good to see you." He kissed me lightly and turned toward Woolie.

She held out her hand. "And I'm Woolie, deah. It's good to meet you at last."

He hugged her and said, "We owe you so much."

After we returned to the house, Woolie left us alone in the front room.

"Baby, I've got some news. Carolyn is divorcing me. She found out about us several months ago."

"Was that what caused her to lose the baby?"

"I don't know. Probably, in part."

"She must hate me."

"She doesn't blame you. She blames me. She hates me."

As I sat with him, I knew I was being disloyal, both to him and to Phillip. Everything was upside down. It wasn't supposed to be this way. He told me he was getting a divorce. He would be free. We could be together. And I loved him so.

Then he reached for my hand and saw the ring on my finger I'd so carefully hidden.

"Son of a bitch! Is that an engagement ring?"

"Yes. But ..."

"Yes, but what?"

"I love you."

"You've got a great way of showing it. Goddamn, you work fast." He stood up, walked across the room, turned toward me, and began laughing. "Well, well, it looks like you've got a good thing going." He ran his fingers through his hair. "That was fast. I have to hand it to you. That was fast." He laughed again. "Maybe you never loved me in the first place. I guess we were just a joke."

I wanted to rip the ring off and run to him. My body wouldn't move. I had hurt us both by believing I should be loyal to Phillip. I loved George. I owed it to him to explain, to say something. But I just sat there.

Why hadn't I removed the ring before I saw him? Did I want to repay him for the pain I'd felt for the last few months? No. I loved him. I wanted to throw the ring away. But I couldn't move.

Woolie came into the room, carrying a tray with a teapot, cups and cookies. "Let's have some tea before we go out to see Tracie. I'll bet you're hungry, George."

"Yes, I am, thank you kindly. Here, let me help you."

We drove out to Tracie's foster home, where she would stay until I could provide a home for her. Mrs. Merrick greeted us at the door of her small white, wood house. A robust woman in her fifties, she wore a full-length apron, with two pockets stuffed with baby toys. Woolie sat on the porch while George and I followed Mrs. Merrick through the tiny, scrubbed kitchen, past a little boy, about three years old, in a high chair, who she described as her "special un-adoptable child." I took a second look and saw he had Downs' Syndrome. She led us to her front room, excusing herself. "I'll get your daughter for you."

Our daughter. The most incredible words. We sat on the couch and waited.

Mrs. Merrick brought us our baby, dressed in a pink jumper, wrapped in a pink blanket. "Here's your sweet girl," she said. We both held up our hands to receive her. Mrs. Merrick walked out of the room. Then I guided Tracie to her father's lap. George and I sat close together, our bodies touching, while we both kept our hands on our child. We looked at each other with tears in our eyes. The three of us were together for the first and the last time for many years.

George was silent while he studied her. Then he turned to me. "She's beautiful. She looks like you ... beautiful." We laughed and talked to her for nearly an hour, until George said it was time for him to catch the train back to New York.

Mrs. Merrick stood on her front porch, holding Tracie as we drove away. I waved to her, and then turned to look at George. His jaw was set, and he stared straight ahead out the front window.

Woolie tried to make small talk as she drove us to the station. But George and I both just sat there silently. George got out of the car and walked to Woolie's open window. "Thank you for everything," he said. "When I get back to the city, I'll call your daughter and remind her of what a terrific mom she has."

"Give her my love. And you take care of yourself."

"I will. Thanks again."

He kissed her cheek, and without looking in my direction, walked in long fast strides toward the train. He was close to the platform when I realized he was truly leaving. I nearly fell out of the car in my rush to catch up to him. "George, please! I ..."

In his eyes I saw the same pain I felt. I wanted to scream, "I love you. I'll always love you. Take me with you."

But I was engaged to Phillip, so I said nothing.

"Have a good life, Baby." He turned and climbed onto the train.

Fifteen

≈

The next day Phillip and I called my parents to tell them we were engaged. They were elated, and, I'm sure, astounded that their worthless gutter girl had snagged a man. And not just a man. A Boston socialite. One of the most sought after, eligible bachelors on Boston's North Shore. Happy days had returned to the Truesdell household.

Mother sent me money to buy proper clothes for the many parties and introductions. Woolie and I made the rounds of elite dress shops. The essentials were easy to find, but we had to search for the perfect formal gown. When I tried on the red taffeta, off the shoulder, ankle length, totally top-of-fashion gown, I felt uncomfortable. But Woolie told me, "You're tall and regal. The dress is regal. It's perfect."

Phillip had a lovely, warm family. Very social, very classy and very, very "nice." I didn't know it then, but Phillip had told his parents my sordid story long before I met them. They were not happy with his choice of brides, especially since he had his pick of nearly every debutante on the North Shore. I was damaged goods. But they made the best of it. They were good people.

There was one gala and several introductory get-togethers. During the round of parties I learned how handy the plastic smile could be. I'd dress, do my hair and makeup, and, just before leaving the guest room at Phillip's, I'd stand in front of a mirror, put my fingers in the corners of my mouth, and pull up. As an actress I could force a happy expression into my eyes. I'd keep that look on my face all evening, letting it go only after I returned to my room. I don't think anyone ever guessed I wasn't thrilled speechless to be marrying the catch of the decade.

After the round of parties and introductions in New England, I left Tracie with Mrs. Merrick and flew to Seattle to prepare for the wedding. The flight was similar to the train ride to Boston. I cried for six hours. The plane was taking me closer to a marriage I didn't want, and further away from the man I loved.

Mother had been happily busy. Everything was organized. "You don't have to do a thing but think about beginning your life with Phillip," she told me.

That was fine with me, since my heart wasn't into planning that wedding. But neither did I want to think about beginning a life with Phillip.

One day in early October, the phone rang at the Truesdell house. My father answered it, then immediately began yelling into the phone, "NO, you won't talk to her. You're nothing but a dirty, rotten snake-in-the-grass."

It was George! I ran down the stairs.

Daddy bellowed on. "Leave my daughter alone. She's going to be married to a fine man. NO! Never! Not as long as I'm alive!"

Just as I tried to grab the phone, he slammed the receiver down.

Mother came running from the kitchen. She saw me in the hallway. "Go to your room! We'll deal with this."

"Please, Mother! I ..."

"GO!"

I climbed the steps to my room, closed the door, and stood at the end of my bed. I turned around several times, trying to think, but couldn't get a thought into my head. Empty of any thoughts at all, I pulled my overnight case from the closet and packed some underwear, George's switchblade, and a book. As I was about to leave the room, I stopped, took the red gown from the closet, stuffed it into my overnight bag, and closed it. I picked up my jacket and purse and started down the stairs.

Mother and Daddy were sitting in the living room on the sofa. I didn't say a word or look at them. My hand was on the front door knob when Mother yelled, "Where do you think you're going?"

"Away. I'm just going away." I stood still, looking at the closed door, my hand on the knob.

Mother stood up. "Where ... away?"

"I don't know," I heard my voice say in a controlled monotone. Maybe I'll go to California. I've always wanted to see California."

I waited for someone to say, "You may open the door now."

"You're going to George. You're going to that terrible man."

I replied honestly. "No. I'm just going."

"NO you are not!" She took several steps toward me.

Daddy still sat on the sofa, looking at the floor, saying nothing.

Mother took another step in my direction. "You've already brought disgrace to this family. You will marry Phillip as planned."

"It wouldn't be fair to him. I don't love him."

"You don't love him! Bunk! You should kiss his feet for looking at you!"

I knew she meant I was a slut. A dirty girl. Not good enough for any decent man.

The words didn't hurt anymore. But not being with George did. I had to leave. "I can't stay here," I said quietly. My hand was still holding the doorknob.

"You open that door, and you'll kill your father. Look at him. Look at him. You're killing him."

I looked. His face was ashen, and his body was shaking. It frightened me. I didn't want to hurt anyone any more than I already had. I surely did not want to kill my father. He looked at me and said, "You are a disgrace to this family."

"All right. I'll marry Phillip." I turned and climbed the stairs to my room.

For most of the ten days before Phillip and his parents arrived, I stayed in my room, ate little, and felt nothing. But I pulled myself together to greet and escort them around Seattle for the four days before the wedding. On the day of the ceremony my sisters dressed me. There was no giggling, no toasts, and no silliness.

On my wedding day, I adjusted my face to a smile, walked down the aisle on my father's arm, and recited vows as instructed. When I told myself to smile, I did. I was an actress, pulling off the part of a lifetime. I was charming. To some, I'm sure, I looked like a very happy bride.

After the wedding we drove to a cabin in the Cascade

Mountains. The crisp weather was perfect for long walks and talks about our future.

The second day after we returned to Boston, I called Jake. I wanted to explain my situation to him, but I couldn't do it in front of my new husband. Phillip was a kind man, but he was also a controlling one. He followed me wherever I went. Knowing I was calling the man who'd lived with George and me, he wouldn't leave my side. So if I wanted to talk to Jake, I had to do it with Phillip listening. It might have been for the best. I probably would have broken into tears. The conversation was stilted and brief.

"Hi, Jake. This is me. Karen. I have something to tell you."

"I'll bet I know what it is! You and George got married."

"No. I married someone else."

"Oh. God. That's hard to believe."

"Well, it's true. I just wanted you to know."

"I hope you'll be happy."

"Thank you." Oh, how I wanted to tell him everything! If I could only sit with my dear Jakey over a bowl of ice cream, he could have set things right. But I knew things would never be right again.

For the first four months Phillip and I lived in a posh Boston apartment that he had shared with a roommate. The four rooms were in a new high-rise, had a romantic view of Boston, black and white angular furniture, and a kitchen equipped with everything. I wanted desperately to appreciate it all, but I didn't. I yearned to be back in New York, living in a dark, crummy apartment with George.

Posh though it was, I still had to carry my laundry to the basement. Al Capp, the *L'il Abner* cartoonist, lived one floor above us, and kept the same laundry schedule as I did. Most Tuesday and Thursday mornings when I entered the elevator, Mr. Capp was there to greet me and to offer to carry my basket. I recognized him from his photos and wished I'd been in a friendlier mood. But though his offer was genuine, and he was a large man, I felt if I piled my basket on top of his, it might cause his legs to give way. And my depression kept me from feeling sociable, so I always refused. But we did have a few conversations about New England weather.

Phillip and I visited Tracie at her foster home several times a week. After we found a larger apartment, we brought her home. As if she were handing me gold, Mrs. Merrick laid Tracie in my arms, then rushed back into the crib room and brought out a brown paper bag. "These are Tracie's things. She loves her little, yellow, rubber rabbit. I put a couple of diapers in, and a dress she looks so sweet in." She kissed Tracie's forehead and stroked her fingers.

"Well, I guess that's all." She walked out to her front porch and stood waving until we were out of sight. Mrs. Merrick had been Tracie's mother since birth. I knew from my daughter's happy disposition that she had been a loving one. At four months Tracie resembled me more than George. But I reminded myself that I was holding part of George. I did have that.

Phillip's family had to do some fast talking. The burden landed in his mother Portia's lap. It wasn't easy for this very socially prominent woman to make up bold-faced lies. A tiny, elegant blonde, she held her shoulders back and chin high, as she told her friends, "Karen can't have children, so when this lovely baby needed a home, they decided right away to give her one."

Phillip later told me his mother had to stand up against a lot of negative gossip about us. But she never once put me down, and she seemed genuinely fond of Tracie. After we returned from her beach club one day, she proudly reported, "Did you hear Evelyn? She said the baby looks like me!" Portia called Tracie, "Little Million Dollars." When she hugged her, which was often, she left the fragrance of her elegant perfume on my baby's clothes.

When Tracie was six months old, Portia helped me plan and carry out an extravagant christening party. The event was held at their three-story, twenty-room mansion, which stood at the top of a hill in a Boston suburb. The guest list was extensive, the day was sunny, and the food was perfect. Tracie was a hit with her happy smiles and infant jabber. We had chosen Woolie to be Tracie's godmother, and she held my baby proudly during the ritual.

A few weeks after the christening party, Phillip adopted Tracie. He was not a demonstrative man, but he always did what he thought was right. It was the legal procedure in those days to have an adopted child's original birth certificate sealed to the adoption papers. So the past was erased, and she now had a proper last name. Just not the one I'd hoped for. We settled into a hundred and fifty-year-old, saltbox cottage near Phillip's parents. A year later I gave birth to Tracie's brother.

For a while my life was busy mothering. In my effort to be a good wife to Phillip, I carefully avoided any New York theater news for three years. I did my best to forget George, but every time I looked at my daughter or heard a love song, I saw his face.

Then one afternoon I read an ad in the newspaper announcing that a new show, *Comes A Day*, was scheduled to come through Boston for tryouts on its way to New York. I saw George's name in the cast list. He'd made it. He would soon be on Broadway. His dreams had come true. A lot of emotions zapped through me. Neediness was one of them. The need to see him. I had to see him just one more time.

So, on an autumn Saturday I sat breathless in the audience of a Boston theater, watching George on stage. I had not lied to Phillip. He knew I was going to see the play. He was attending a football game. We planned to meet later at the cocktail lounge across the street from the theater.

Partially covering my face with my hand, I sat in the back row. Then I realized how foolish it was to hide. Silly lady, I thought. Sit up. Take your hand away from your face. Stop looking out of the corner of your eye. Nobody cares if you're here.

After the curtain call I realized I had no idea of what the play had been about. For me there had been no one else on stage but George. I sent a note backstage. "You were wonderful. Karen." He sent a note back. "Meet me at the corner bar across Boylston Street in half an hour."

My watch read three forty five. Phillip wasn't due to meet me for at least a half-hour, so I ran across the street to the bar and directly into the restroom. I combed and recombed my hair until it looked worse than it did when I arrived. When I emerged from the women's lounge, George was seated at the bar, looking wonderful in a black suit and white open collar shirt. I walked unsteadily toward him. He stood up, grinned, and opened his arms. I walked into them.

He did not hold me long. He guided me to a barstool.

"Can I buy you a drink?"

"Thank you. I'd like a glass of wine."

We sat and talked awkwardly about the play. I showed him a recent photo of our daughter. "She looks very sweet," he said.

"She is."

We sat for a moment in silence. Then he said, "I'm living with a wonderful woman and intend to marry her soon. Her name is Colleen Dewhurst. She's a marvelous actress, very skilled. I've learned a lot from her."

I could have handled it more easily if he had thrown a boulder at me. My insides turned to cold stone. But barely missing a beat, my actress side took over. With a steady voice, I said "I'm happy for you."

"Thank you. I gather your marriage is going well?"

"Oh, yes. Phillip is a good husband and good to Tracie."

"Well." The corners of his mouth went up but his eyes were cheerless. "That's good." He glanced again at the photo of Tracie, tapped it on the counter, looked again, and handed it back. He reached for a cocktail napkin and said, "I want to give you my agent's office telephone number in New York." He took out a pen, wrote a name and number on the napkin, and set it in front of me. "Her name is Jane Dacey. If you ever need anything, call her. She knows about you."

"Thank you."

I slipped the napkin into my handbag. I wasn't surprised his agent should know about me. George and I loved each other and always would.

I started to ask him about his life in New York, when Phillip walked in. How I resented him at that moment! He'd come to take me away. It was too soon. Just give me a few minutes longer, I thought. Please!

Phillip saw us, smiled, and walked to the bar. I introduced them. They shook hands, civil with no pleasantries.

After a few meaningless words were exchanged all around, George excused himself with a simple, "Goodbye."

"Good to see you," I said.

"Take care of yourself," he said politely. I felt dismissed.

"You, too," I replied.

I left with Phillip, feeling drained, and longing to touch my love again.

That night in the bathroom I removed the program and cocktail napkin from my handbag. I touched and kissed the photo of George's face in the program, which I tore into small pieces and placed in the pocket of my robe. I burned them in the fireplace the next morning. I kept the cocktail napkin in the back of my top dresser drawer next to the switchblade knife, that by then was rusted and wouldn't close, and the red belt Woolie gave me the day Tracie was born.

After seeing George, I had to escape from the constant pretense of loving Phillip. The day following my meeting with George was a Sunday, so I waited another painful twenty-four hours, not saying anything about my decision. I knew Phillip would do everything he could to stop me. In his comfortable life in a prominent family, he wasn't used to losing.

On Monday morning I called Tammy's sister, Nancy, who lived a few blocks away. I asked her if I could bring the children and stay in her basement bedroom until I could think things out. Nancy knew Phillip's family well, and though it put her in the middle of a bad situation, she opened her home to me. I didn't want the children to suffer, but I was certain that living in a loveless home would do them more harm than good in the long run.

I took the coward's way out and left Phillip a note.

> *Dear Phillip,*
>
> *I need to do some thinking about our marriage, and I can't do it living in the same house with you. The children and I will be at Nancy's for a few days.*
>
> *Please don't follow me.*
> *Karen*

I did not report anything to my family in Seattle. I didn't want to burden them with more disappointment, and I knew they'd pressure me to return to Phillip.

But pressure came from a different source. Phillip's mother and sister came to visit. We met in Nancy's kitchen over tea. His sister started gently.

"You may think you love George, but it's only that he's a glamorous actor. You'll get over it." Pat was a devout Catholic, the mother of three girls. She loved Phillip. To her, separation and divorce were only whispered words.

Portia spoke more directly and sternly.

"You know you belong with Phillip. And think what you are doing to those children."

They offered to obtain the services of a marriage counselor for me. After an hour and a half of listening to them telling me what I should do, I agreed to go. I had no choice in the matter. I had no money, no car, no way out.

Upon my arrival at the address of the "marriage counselor" in downtown Boston, I knew I'd been duped. The name on the door read "John P. Barnes, Attorney at Law." Why I didn't turn and run I have no idea, except that I'd promised to see him. A secretary ushered me into the inner sanctum and closed the heavy oak door behind her as she left. When I heard the door close, I had the same feeling of being trapped that I had had entering the Crittenden Home. Mr. Barnes was seated in his dark-paneled office behind a mahogany desk, busily writing.

"Sit down Karen," he said, without looking up. He might as well have said, "Sit down, while we prepare you for the execution."

I walked the mile across the room, sat down in the straight back chair across the desk from him, and waited. When he finally looked up and removed his reading glasses, he gave me a long, piercing look. When he spoke, he was brief.

"Karen, do you know how lucky you are to be married to Phillip?"

"Well, I ..."

He interrupted in a strong, firm voice, "Don't you think you should return home to him where you belong?" The prosecutor, judge, and jury had spoken.

"I guess." I nodded and stood. "Thank you." I left his office and returned with the children to Phillip that evening. He eventually forgave my "temporary lack of good judgment," and I resumed working at being the perfect wife.

I stayed with Phillip for the next twelve years. During that time George had leading roles in *The Hanging Tree; Anatomy of a Murder; The Hustler; The List Of Adrian Messenger; Dr Strangelove; The Yellow Rolls-Royce; Not with my Wife; You Don't, The Bible; The Flim Flam Man; Petula; The Savage Land* and *Patton*. Knowing it would be too painful to watch him on the screen, I didn't see any of them.

Sixteen

≈

Not long after I'd seen George that autumn, Phillip and I moved with the children to New Hampshire. He had purchased a year-round resort, where our lifestyle was busy and, to those looking in from the outside, glamorous. Most people figured I'd landed the best catch east of the Rockies. He was handsome, well bred, and an honest man. I really wanted to love him. I thought I might learn to love him by devoting myself to him and our family. To protect the family, I never told anyone about my connection to George.

A year after we moved to New Hampshire, our son Eric, was born. Living at the inn, with its tennis courts and swimming pool in the summer, and skiing and ice skating in the winter, made for an idyllic childhood for Tracie and her two brothers. I don't remember exactly when we told her she had been adopted, but she knew from a very young age. She had two adopted cousins in Seattle, so she knew it was not out of the ordinary.

When she was six, she made the happy discovery that one of her friends had also been adopted, and the two of them formed a close bond. Pam looked very much like her mother, and Pam's mom often remarked how much Tracie resembled me. It seemed to make the idea of adoption more comfortable for her, so I'd just nod and look pleased, though I was terrified to think someone might guess I really was her biological mother.

Our tow-headed, green-eyed little girl was popular, both with the inn staff and with our guests. One year she became the center of attention at the high school basketball games when the cheerleaders chose her to be their mascot. It was a happy and exciting time for her, both outside and inside our home. She had a close relationship with both of her brothers and Phillip.

Unfortunately, though, she suffered in school. When she reached the fourth grade she could barely read at all. Letters looked backwards to her "b's" and "d's" were reversed. When I tried to help her, it reminded me of the hours my mother had spent drilling me. My teachers told Mother, "She doesn't try." "She's lazy." "She won't pay attention." The other kids called me "stupid," and "the dummy." I developed a case of low self-esteem that I didn't overcome until I was well into adulthood. I hated the thought of my daughter going through the same torment I did, so we had her tested for learning disabilities. They found her to be a classic dyslexic and referred us to a teacher who specialized in the disorder.

Tracie's tutor and I were struck with *déjà vu* when we met, but neither of us could place when or where we had seen each other before. By our third meeting we knew. Howard had been the assistant set designer at the Toledo Zoo Theater the summer George and I had worked there. After we discovered the coincidence and spoke briefly about it, I avoided the subject, and he didn't ask questions. I didn't know how much he knew about George and me, but I was terrified of having the people in that small town discover the truth. I wasn't going to take any chances that he'd count up the years and figure out Tracie was George's daughter.

As part of my duties at the inn I formed a water ballet team for the children. Every Wednesday evening in the summer, crowds of our guests and townspeople gathered to watch the young swimmers. Our eleven-year-old diver, Gordy Clapp, was always a favorite with the audience. Gordy acted in the theater on our property when he was twelve. Forty years later he shared the stage with George when they each won Emmys, Gordon for *NYPD Blue* and George for *Twelve Angry Men*.

Even after eight years away from him, I still couldn't hear George's name without feeling a stab of pain. I stayed away from all of his movies and the articles written about him until one horrible day when I sat under the dryer at the beauty salon.

Flipping through the pages of a magazine, I came upon a full-page picture of George in his latest movie. I couldn't ignore it. I must have stared at that photo for three or four minutes, feeling jittery, weak and miserable.

Scanning the article, I came to a small subheading, "Where are they now?" As I read the words I realized the story was about me: the Stephens College theater student who had had George's baby. Where was she? My chest tightened. I felt my face flush. I looked around to see if anyone was watching me read the article. It was an overreaction, I knew, but in this small town of 5,000 everyone knew everyone's business, or tried to. They didn't know about my past or my connection with George. Only Phillip's family and mine had known that. Most important of all, Tracie did not know about her father. When the right time came, I'd tell her. But not now. She was only ten years old.

Forcing myself to sit quietly, I reasoned it out. No one knew of my connection with George and certainly not that I'd lived with him. That had been years ago and hundreds of miles away. No reason for concern. But as I read on, I began to panic. It reported accurately about George's father. About George's two years in the Marines. That he'd been a staff actor at Stephens College. His marriage to Carolyn and their daughter. "Scott lived in New York with a Stephens College student who was pregnant at the same time as his wife." The words on the page began to blur. That was a shock. I had not been aware that anyone knew we had even lived together, much less that I had been pregnant at the same time as Carolyn. "What happened to her? Where did she go? Scott refused to give any details. In fact, he slammed the door in this reporter's face."

A weakening dizziness swept over me. I wasn't sure I could make it to the door of the salon. Peering around, feeling like a criminal, I slipped the magazine into the bottom of my bag. Pushing the dryer back from my head, I removed the curlers.

The hairstylist rushed to my chair.

"But you're not half dry yet. Don't you want a comb out?"

"No thank you, Mia. I remembered I have an appointment."

I took a deep breath to control my shaking, stood up and walked to the front counter. I placed cash on the glass top, smiled at Mia and left the salon, walking slowly to my car. I opened the door, jumped into the seat, slammed the door, and locked it. My body shook violently. I was so lightheaded I thought I might faint. What should I do? It was only in one magazine. But that one magazine was sold everywhere. What if the story spread? I took deep breaths and hugged myself to control the shakes. My body finally calmed down, and I began to think logically. No one was going to put it all together. It would go away. But the only way I could be sure would be to buy all the magazines in town that carried the story.

There were two stores in the village that carried movie magazines. How silly and how guilty I must have looked, buying up their entire supply of the magazines, walking casually to my car then speeding off. If there had been any questions about my strange purchases that day, my friends never told me. And I'll never forget the relief I felt after the magazines had been reduced to ashes in our fireplace.

Phillip was a big hit with my parents. He had, after all, saved the family reputation from complete ruin and elevated me to a place of respect, and even envy. My parents came to New Hampshire every year for a visit, and Tracie captured their hearts. The subject of her biological father may not have been forgotten, but my mother and father never spoke of George again.

My father loved photography. He was especially fond of taking pictures of the New England autumn foliage, and he enjoyed bringing others along with him on his excursions. Tracie was ten years old when I decided to join him one day to try for a heart-to-heart talk with him. For years I had wanted to apologize to him for my hurtful actions. I wanted to look him in the eye, tell him I loved him, and ask for his forgiveness.

Before we left for the woods, stage fright set in. I must have walked back and forth in our driveway a dozen times, rehearsing what I'd say, until I heard my mother's voice.

"Karen, are you going to stand by the car all day talking to yourself? Daddy's ready."

She yelled back into the house. "Walter, get your camera and warm jacket. Karen's ready."

Daddy emerged from the house with three cameras on straps around his neck. He winked and smiled at me.

"I'm ready for our big day. There should be some fine color out there."

At least I knew he was in good humor for now. We drove the back roads, stopping every mile or so to take pictures.

"It surely beats the Pacific Northwest for its colorful autumns," my father observed. "Say, look, down there. The blue pond, white birch, and the orange and yellow leaves beyond. Now that's a shot! Let's stop here."

"This is a perfect place to have a picnic, Daddy. I'll bring the basket and the camp chairs." I watched as he hurried on ahead through the brush and over logs to get just the right angle for his pictures. My nerves set in again. Suppose he wouldn't listen to me or wouldn't accept my apology? What if I lost my courage? I followed him to the shore of the pond, set up the chairs, opened the basket, and pulled out two sodas.

"Well, well! How did you know I'd have a thirst after taking all those pictures?" He sat down, opened his soda, took a gulp and chuckled. "Yep. You even picked the kind I like." He looked fondly at me and again winked. "No help from your mother, I suppose. Too bad she isn't with us to enjoy this wonderful day."

Okay, he's obviously enjoying himself. It's now or never.

"Daddy, I ... There's something I want to talk to you about."

"And I'll bet I know what it is." He reached into his breast pocket, retrieved a cigar, and bit off the end. "You're wondering if Mother and I will be keeping the house or moving to one of those old folks' homes."

"No, Daddy. It's ..."

"Well, then, it's about one of the boys thinking he'd like to play football." He took out his lighter and lit the cigar. He took a deep pull on his cigar, chuckled, and shook his head. "I know. Mothers worry."

"No, Daddy. It's not about football." I took a deep breath before going on. "Daddy, I want to talk to you about me. I want to talk to you about what happened ten years ago. About me and George."

My father slammed the soda can down on his knee. It fell to

the ground, emptying the remaining dark fizz. He stood up and started to walk in the direction of the car.

"Daddy, please!" Without folding the chairs, I picked them up, along with the basket, and awkwardly hurried after him. By the time I caught up to him he was sitting in the front seat. I opened the trunk and threw in the chairs and basket, opened the front door, and sat beside him.

"Please, Daddy. Let me just say how sorry I ..."

"Start the car, Karen. We're going home." He turned his head toward the side window. I couldn't see his face, but his voice was hard and cold. "You were a wicked girl. You broke our hearts. We will never speak of this again."

"Please, Daddy. I want to say I'm sorry. Please forgive me. It was so long ago."

"Start the car."

I was devastated to see that he still harbored such anger. In his eyes I was no better than a slut. And to have a slut for a daughter was a degrading thing.

Tracie was eleven when my family invited her to Seattle for the summer. The night before she left I sat on the side of her bed. My only intention was to wish her a fun summer and to give her the usual motherly instructions about being a helpful houseguest. But looking at my daughter that evening, I saw George's face and knew it was time to tell her.

"Tracie, you know how much your dad and I love you?"

"Sure."

I had thought about telling her a hundred times. For both of us I had to follow through. Praying I was doing the right thing, I said, "Well, I have a special love for you."

"What do you mean?"

"I'm not your adopted mother. I'm your real mother." What a great relief I felt saying those words.

"I don't understand." She frowned and squinted her eyes exactly like her father. "You're both my adopted mom AND my real mom?"

"Yes. I gave birth to you."

She stared at me. "That's why I look like you. Everybody

always says I look just like you."

"Yes." I smiled.

"Is Dad my real father?"

"No, Dad adopted you."

"Who is my real father?"

"I'm not going to tell you that right now." *Dear God, am I saying the right thing?* "Someday I will, when I think you're ready."

"Why won't you tell me? Is he in jail or something?" She sat up.

"No, he's not in jail."

She studied the blanket before she asked in a little voice, "Does he hate me?"

"No, he doesn't hate you. He loves you."

Her eyes held mine. "Then, why won't you tell me?"

"It just isn't the time."

"Where does he live?"

This was worse than I had anticipated. "I'm not going to tell you until you're ready."

She sat very straight and jutted her chin out. "When do you think I'll be ready?"

"When you're old enough to understand."

"How old is that?" Her voice was rising.

"A few years from now." I tried to stay calm.

"If you tell me, I'll understand. Please!" she begged.

"I can't, honey." Now I was the one begging. "Isn't it enough for now that you know I'm your real mother?"

"I guess." She sat motionless for a short second. "Am I still going to Seattle tomorrow?"

"Of course. Everyone there is so happy you're coming. They all love you."

Another moment of silence. "And they all know you're my mother?"

"Yes."

"Do my cousins know?"

"I don't think so."

"I wish you were going too." Her eyes filled with tears.

"I'll miss you."

"I'll miss you, too." She reached for me, and we hugged for a long time.

While Tracie was in Seattle I asked myself a hundred times why I had told her. She had a right to know, but had I told her too soon? Or should I have told her years ago? Was I right not telling her who her father was? Was she too young to know any of it? I reproached myself for having shared my guilty secret with my little girl. I felt sure I'd made another huge mistake.

Three years later I received a call from my sister.

"Daddy is very ill. Come home now if you want to see him alive."

I took my youngest son, Eric, with me to Seattle for my last visit with my father. We had no heavy conversations, never referring to my past or to his failing health. When it was time for my brother-in-law to take us to the airport, my father sat down at the organ and played *Aloha* as we walked out the door. I had tried to apologize to him that day in the New Hampshire woods. But he could never bring himself to forgive me for the scandal I brought to his family.

Seventeen

≈

Tracie was totally confused. I was her mother, but who was her real father? Why hadn't I told her?

Then I caused her even more pain. I told her I was divorcing Phillip.

He was a nice man, but a controlling one, and had ignored my pleas for years to be a more attentive father and husband. When I asked Phillip for a divorce, he couldn't understand why. He hated to lose in anything and was outraged. He blamed everyone and everything, except the fact that we had never belonged together.

When I left, Tracie decided to stay with Phillip, and when she asked him for her biological father's name, he told her, even though Phillip and I had agreed I would be the one to tell her. I was angry, but the deed had been done.

She was thrilled, but not surprised. She had suspected it was someone famous because of my theater background and some celebrity photos I had left behind when I moved out.

Equipped with his name and the story of his mother's lost wedding ring, Tracie began her search. Beginning with Woolie, she made some phone calls, which led to other sources, and she was finally given a telephone number where she could reach him.

George had also moved on. After five marriages, twice to Colleen Dewhurst, he was married to actress Trish Van Devere and had five children. He would soon add a sixth to the pack.

Tracie called her father and introduced herself. George accepted her immediately, inviting her to join her half brothers and sisters in Mexico, where he was filming. It was a heady experience for a seventeen-year-old who had led a quiet life in a small village in New England. Years later George told me he knew Tracie would call one day. He'd been waiting for the call.

I didn't find out about their reunion for months, until Tracie wrote me a short letter. I was overjoyed for them both. I would have loved to see their first meeting. I visualized it often. How they must have searched each other's faces for a family resemblance. I wondered if he had asked, "How is your mother?" Then I'd scold myself for having had such a ridiculous thought. He didn't give a damn about me. But he loved our daughter! That was enough.

Over the next four years, when she wasn't at school, Tracie lived with George and Trish. During that time I married Dave, a charismatic helicopter pilot, ten years younger than I. Our marriage lasted only three years and probably shouldn't have happened at all. But I'm glad it did, because the reward I got was my son Davey. A few years later, my marriage to Dave came back to haunt me, when George became convinced I was enamored with younger men.

During my marriage to Dave, Tracie let me know in an angry letter that she wanted nothing to do with me. She disliked my new husband, and she resented me for having left Phillip. The hurt and anger I felt at losing her was tempered by the knowledge she had finally found the life she wanted with her father. I didn't try to reopen communication with her.

It was during this time that, with Phillip's blessing, George legally adopted Tracie. She kept Phillip's last name and added Scott, giving her the last name I'd wanted her to have for nineteen years.

He and Trish were good to her. They gave her everything she could want, including introductions to a host of celebrities and a college education. But as I discovered later, she craved her father's exclusive attention, and that led to problems with Trish and ultimately with George.

Dave loved the theater, as I did, and we went often. One evening, when I was eight months pregnant, we attended a production of the ACT theater in Seattle. One of the actors on stage looked familiar to me. When I checked the program, I recognized his name, as well as two others. One had been the director at the Toledo Zoo Theater and was now the director/producer of the ACT theater. The second was the director of the current production and had been at Stephens College when George and I were there. The third had been at the Toledo Zoo Theater that summer, playing Uncle Tom to George's Simon Legree.

After the show I went backstage and found the three of them. When I looked closely at them, I felt like Dorothy, in the *Wizard of Oz*, waking to see the tin man, lion and scarecrow. It was a delightful reunion until we came to a quiet, awkward moment when one said, "Well, George has certainly done well!" It struck me then that theater is like a small town with the usual gossip. They knew all about George and me and Tracie. And there I stood, eight months pregnant with Davey, reminding them of my shady past. We all looked at our watches, mumbled about how late it was getting, and Dave drove me home.

Eighteen

≈

By the late 1970's my two older sons had become disenchanted with their new stepfather and returned to live with Phillip. Shortly after they left, I received a surprise letter from Tracie. She asked if it was true Dave and I were divorcing. Overjoyed at seeing her handwriting, but wary about her reasons for sending it, I read the short note very carefully. Deciding she was sincerely reaching out, I had a letter ready for the return mail, assuring her it was true. Shortly after she received my letter, she called.

"Mother?"

"Tracie?"

"Yes."

Deep breath. "What a ... surprise. How are you?"

"I'm fine. How are you?

"Oh, just great. Fine." I picked up a pencil and began to doodle fast, a nervous habit that always helped me out of a tight spot.

"Is it really true Dave is out of your life?"

"Yes. It's true."

"I wanted to be sure, because I was thinking about visiting you."

This was all happening faster than I could take it in, but I wanted to give her a positive response. "I'd like that."

"Really?"

"Of course. And you could meet your little brother."

"Oh, yeah. The kid." She said, "kid" as if he were a bad smell. I let the comment pass. If I bristled, it might cause another rift between us. I felt sure when she got to know him, she'd love him.

"When will you be coming?"

There was a click on her end, and I heard George's voice. "Oh, you're on ... sorry."

Hearing his voice so unexpectedly after seventeen years sent tremors through my body. The receiver began to slip from my hand, but I held tight. I surely didn't want this man to think he still affected me in any way.

"Who was that?" I knew full well.

"Oh, just Daddy."

I sat on the floor, feeling weak and nauseous. For the rest of the conversation I spoke slowly – so she wouldn't hear my voice quiver – and methodically – so I'd make sense. We made plans for her visit and exchanged cordial goodbyes.

Then it hit me. In the last five minutes I'd spoken with my daughter, and I'd heard George's voice. I laughed out loud, wondering what he'd say if he knew his voice made me nauseous.

I sat on the floor, reviewing the call a dozen times. I tried to analyze why George had picked up the phone just at that time. Surely wealthy movie stars have more than one phone line. Did he know she was on? Did he know she was talking to me? And why would he care? He'd forgotten me long ago. Well, not forgotten me. Not when he lived with our daughter. But he clearly didn't feel any emotion for me. So I told myself to get over it, stop thinking about George, and make plans for my daughter's visit.

Three weeks after our conversation I met Tracie at the airport. We gave each other little waves of recognition, then a perfunctory hug, patting each other on the back. While we waited for her baggage, we feigned great interest in the other passengers and the luggage as it slid down the chute. When we reached the house in Tacoma, we busied ourselves with a tour of the rooms. We talked politely about her aunts, uncles and cousins.

I told her Davey would be home shortly, and she donned a polite smile. I was as nervous as hell. If they didn't like each other, and if I took my three-year-old son's side, I knew she'd leave again. I counted on Davey's charm and openness to save us all.

The door opened and Davey came bounding into the house, with his face wrapped in a huge smile. It only took minutes for Tracie to warm up. He was a funny little kid, and they were soon laughing together. Within days they had become pals.

The second week of her visit she asked about moving in with us for good. I was surprised. She was twenty-three at the time, and I figured she'd want her own life. But I was also very happy she wanted to be with us.

"We seem to be getting along well," I said. "Let's think about it."

In the evenings she told me about her life with George and Trish and about the mansion in Connecticut. She entertained me with stories of the exciting parties and backstage meetings with celebrities.

"I was in Daddy's kitchen pouring wine when I looked up and found Martin Sheen standing beside me."

She loved her perfect life. But if living on the East Coast was so exciting and glamorous, why did she want to stay with us in Tacoma? As she told her stories, I detected a continuing theme. She resented Trish for standing between her and her father. Did Trish make her so unhappy she'd leave her movie star father and move across the country to get away from her?

Whatever the reason, I was delighted she felt comfortable enough to raise the subject. One evening she said, "If you really want me to live with you, I could fly to Connecticut, get my things and drive back to Tacoma."

"I'd love it," I told her. My daughter was coming home.

One evening before she left, she told me George had told her about our life together before she was born. He quoted silly things I'd said and described my old fur coat. It amazed me he had remembered those details, and I had a hard time not showing my delight. Tracie and I had not yet discussed my own feelings for her father.

Tracie flew to Connecticut, calling me two days later to say George had given her a new car for the return trip. She'd drive across the country alone. The thought of her driving alone for four days worried me. I had just been reunited with my child. I didn't want to lose her to a road accident or a rapist. But though she was my child, she was a grown woman, and I had to treat her that way.

"Mom, I'll call you every night. You'll know where I am and

where I plan to be the next day. Please don't worry, or I'll begin to worry about you worrying about me."

"All right. Be careful. I love you." After so many years, it was wonderful to be free to say, "I love you" to my daughter.

Tracie's long drive was uneventful, and she arrived in Tacoma exhausted and proud of herself. The next days were filled with the realities of this special mother and daughter reunion. The territorial logistics worked smoothly. Davey and Tracie quickly bonded. But the leftover emotional scars did not go away. We sat together night after night, drinking too much and sniping at each other.

She often put me on trial, with her opening argument going something like this. "I don't understand why you don't feel any resentment toward my father."

"Because I was the one to leave him. And I loved him."

"If you loved him, why did you leave him?"

"I had to. I married Phillip."

"But I don't understand why you married Phillip." Her eyes would flash in anger.

I wanted to say, "Neither do I," But I'd always say, "Because I owed him so much. He was good to me."

"But you admit you didn't love him!" She'd stand then, spitting the words at me.

"That's right." I'd spit my words right back at her.

"You could have married my real father, and you married Phillip instead."

"Oh, God, Tracie, it wasn't that simple. I thought your father had turned his back on me."

"But you told me he came back, and the two of you went to the foster home to see me."

"Yes."

The redundant arguing would go on for hours, day after day, week after week, for months. We'd come to terms and be comrades for a while. Then her resentments would flare again, and we'd argue for days.

To add to the turmoil, every two or three months we'd receive a telephone call from George. He usually called when Tracie and I had come to an understanding. Sometimes I felt he knew we were in a peaceful spell and called to stir things up. At the beginning of the conversation, Tracie would be delighted to hear from him, often overwhelmed by his sweetness.

"Just calling to see how you are." "I've missed you." "Do you need anything?" Then the abusive language would begin. He blamed her for everything that ever went wrong in his life. We began to call these "dump calls," caused by his heavy drinking, Trish being out of town, and his having nothing better to do than to pour out his wrath on someone he loved.

After one of those phone calls Tracie told me he still seemed to harbor resentment about my having left him, although he carried a lot of guilt about those days himself.

A month after Tracie came back to live with us, I wrote George a brief letter.

> Dear George,
>
> Tracie and I are living happily together, and I want to thank you for sending her back to me.
>
> I was hoping after all these years you could forgive me for the decision I made to marry Phillip, but Tracie tells me you are still angry with me. Please let us both try to forgive, so we can get on with our lives, but more importantly, so our daughter can get on with hers.
> Karen

I had Tracie address the envelope and put her name in the space for the return address. I have no idea what happened to the letter. I asked him once if he remembered receiving it. He told me he hadn't. I wondered if he wouldn't admit receiving it, or if he just didn't remember.

In the spring of 1979 George called to invite Tracie to join him in Mississippi, where he would be directing a movie made for TV. She was ecstatic. We both were. It would be her first opportunity to be alone with her father for any length of time. We packed and repacked her luggage, wanting her to take just the right clothes, so she could feel relaxed and happy. When I left her at the Sea-Tac

Airport she looked beautiful in a new leather coat. She was giddy with excitement. I crossed my fingers that she and her dad would use the time to find and appreciate each other.

Not long after her arrival there, she called from Mississippi. "Everything is great, Mom. Daddy is on the set, and I'm home cooking dinner for him." Six hours later, George was fired off the set. He said he and the producer had had a heavy disagreement. But Tracie wondered if it had more to do with his heavy drinking.

Tracie and George packed up and flew to his home in Connecticut. Tracie told me later that Trish met them at the door, looked at her, and said, "What's she doing here?"

During the next two days I received some weepy phone calls from Tracie.

"I can't stay," she told me. "Trish is making it painfully obvious she doesn't want me here." She left Connecticut for Tacoma on the third day.

George called Tracie two or three times in the next few months. After she'd hung up from one of the calls, she tearfully reported he'd said, "I can't see you anymore because Trish doesn't like you."

When Tracie found her father, she also found the grandfather she'd always wanted. She visited him several times in Florida, and her Granddaddy Scott welcomed her as warmly as if he'd known her from infancy. She discovered during one of their long talks he had known about her since she was born. When Tracie told me that Granddaddy Scott knew about her, I was more than surprised to realize George hadn't kept her a secret.

He gave her several old and beloved photographs of her Grandmother Helena, pointing out Tracie's resemblance to the Scott family: flat ears, high forehead, and, of course, the Scott nose. She often proudly pointed to each feature.

As other people might doodle squares and circles, Tracie had always had a habit of doodling a profile of a face with a large nose. This began long before she found her father, and before her own face took on adult proportions. When I watched her draw, I wondered if she was drawing her face to be, or if she somehow remembered her father's face from his one visit shortly after she was born.

Of course, Granddaddy had been aware of me, and I had felt sure my name was held in pretty low regard. But Tracie assured me many times that he had no negative feelings toward me. In one of his letters when he asked her to say, "hello to your mother," I was surprised and touched. I wanted to respond, so she and I decided to send him a letter on tape. We spent long hours recording anecdotes of our life together and asked him to send one back. Several weeks later we received a tape from him, and I listened for the first time to George's father's charming, steady voice. And while I listened I realized, that he had forgiven me. Some members of my own family had never been able to do that.

Nineteen

≈

My daughter had a passion for shopping. Yard sales put her into a state of rapture. She could lose herself in malls for seven or eight hours with no trouble at all. I wasn't quite that passionate, but I enjoyed it, so shopping became our activity of choice. Our limited budget restricted us to second-hand and junk shops, but we loved it, since we both had a good eye for finding the under priced gem.

One Saturday into our fourth hour of junk searching, Tracie said, "You know, with all the time we spend shopping and buying junk, we should open our own shop." She held up a 1930s sieve and added it to our nearly full basket. "Look. A collectible."

"That would be fun," I said, "but we can't, for two reasons. One: I already have a Monday through Friday job with Head Start, and two: it would take a lot of money."

"Suppose we found the money, and I took care of the shop while you worked. That way I could be with Davey when he's not in school."

We pushed our baskets on to the book area where Davey sat on the floor looking through a comic. "Davey, how would you like us to have a shop full of junk and books?"

"Sorta okay ..."

"Well," I said, "we have two "sorta okays" and one vote to do it. Let's go home and talk about it."

Each day of the next week, the first thing in the morning, after I returned from work, after dinner, and late into the night, we discussed little else but having a shop. We became more excited by the hour. That was healthy for two reasons: it stopped us from arguing over why I left Phillip, and it kept our focus on the future. But we couldn't help returning to the depressing fact that we needed cash and a lot of it.

"Honey, it's a nice dream, but only a dream, and a dim, unrealistic one."

"Why?"

"I really don't think a bank would give a loan for starting an iffy business to a recently divorced, single mom, with a low-income Head Start job and no collateral."

"But, but, but ..."

"AND you're unemployed, and you have no credit history."

"BUT," she said, with her finger in the air imitating the wizard in *The Wizard of Oz*, "I do have a rich father."

"Oh, no. I won't ask George for money."

"You wouldn't be asking. I would."

"Tracie, we wouldn't be asking for a small loan. We'd need a LOT of money."

I poured us both a glass of wine, and we sat back down at the kitchen table where we had been for four hours.

"Come on, Mama, he's about our only hope. And we'd pay him back."

"It would take years to pay him back. We'd have to be very successful."

"Okay, so we'll work hard and be very successful. Why don't I call him?"

"I guess so. He seems to be our only answer. But it's too late to call him now."

"This is the time to call." She walked to the phone table. "He's always up late."

What in hell were we doing? Asking my old lover for money. I hate this, I thought. I really hate this. I opened my mouth to stop her from calling but she was already talking to him.

From Tracie's side, the conversation sounded loving. When she finally got around to telling him her reason for calling, he didn't hesitate to agree. He suggested we send him our written plans and needs.

Before she hung up, I heard her say, "She's fine. She's sitting right here, do you want to say hello?"

I panicked and left the room.

The next day we found a realtor and described our needs. She showed us several properties that were too big and too expensive. But she finally unlocked the door to the perfect place. The storefront faced the street and had three large rooms for merchandise. Our intended living quarters included two rooms in the back of the shop, a kitchen and two rooms on the floor below the shop. The lower floor opened onto a small yard. There was parking for two cars. The location was a bit out of the way, but it was on a busy street, so we were sure we could stop traffic with our signs and treasures sitting outside. The owners wanted a year's lease, but we were free to paint walls and floors as we wished. Best of all, the place was empty, and we could move right in.

We rushed home to work on a letter to George, which took us two nights to write. It still felt wrong to be asking George for money. He responded within the week by sending Tracie a check for $25,000. It was ten thousand more than we'd asked for. Two weeks later we signed a year's lease, paid the first and last month's rent and damage deposit, and moved into our new living quarters.

The few pieces of merchandise we had were pathetic. We knew it would take months of shopping to find the right stock locally, so, using the need for authentic antiques as an excuse, we flew to New England for a happy week of bargain hunting.

We drove from one old barn to the other, looking for those special antiques that could not be found in the Pacific Northwest. We knew the hidden places to go, and we'd planned our trip for the off-season, when it was a buyer's market.

We had two reunions. The first was with Phillip, who had sold his inn and was now in real estate. I hated the idea of returning to my old home, but Tracie wanted to see Phillip and her two older brothers. She'd stayed in touch, and there were no ill feelings between any of them. It was the opposite for me. Phillip and I had lots of ill feelings. I dreaded being in the same town with him, much less the same room. He still hated me for leaving him, and I'd heard through friends the unfair stories Phillip and his family had spread about me after I left.

Fortunately, the happy anticipation of spending time with my boys overshadowed any anxieties about seeing Phillip. We not only saw Phillip, we had dinner with him in the same house he and I had lived in. My sons set the table, placing their father at one end and me at the other. That hour was both horrible and sad. Eric, the younger of our two sons, stared at me with happy hope in his eyes. It wasn't hard to guess what he hoped for. Then someone suggested I sleep in Phillip's basement bedroom. That was enough for me. I found a motel for the night. After I returned to Seattle a week later, a friend wrote me that Phillip's new sweetheart had heard I was in town and feared I wanted back into his life. I could have saved the poor woman a lot of grief if she had just asked me.

The other reunion was the total opposite of my dinner with Phillip. We drove to Woolie and Luther's 200-year-old, white saltbox farmhouse, and were greeted warmly. We sat in the front room beside their huge, walk-in stone fireplace and sipped scotch. Luther took us to his greenhouse and proudly showed off his orchids. Woolie set out wooden bowls of vegetable stew and homemade bread on the trestle table.

They were interested in Tracie's life with George, and Woolie asked her to send her love to him. We didn't talk about the months before Tracie was born, but when I looked at Woolie across the table, she was looking at Tracie and me so tenderly I was certain we were sharing memories.

In 1989 Woolie called me. We'd kept up our correspondence, but we hadn't spoken by phone, so it came as a sudden surprise. We talked for a few minutes, bringing each other up to date on family. Then she said, "Goodbye, deah," and hung up. She died a few months later.

We finished our two-week shopping spree, packed up our New England treasures, and sent them to our new address in Tacoma. When we returned home, we were ready to receive them. The shop had freshly painted walls, clean carpets, and a beautiful blue and gold sign that read: "The Original Yankee. Antiques and Collectibles."

We unpacked our treasures and organized the rooms. One for

antiques, one for collectibles, and one for assorted junk. The day we hung the OPEN sign we stood proudly on the sidewalk, arms around each other, giggling like two little girls. We had done it! We'd worked together and pulled it off. We were proud of each other and of ourselves.

Five months later George called Tracie to invite her to dinner at a downtown hotel. He and Trish were in the area filming *The Changeling*. They wanted to drop by the shop the next morning between ten and eleven o'clock to check out their investment.

That morning I had no intention of going upstairs to see them. I knew George had not come to see me, and it wasn't my ambition to meet George's current wife. It was all arranged. I would stay below in the apartment, and Tracie would greet them and show them the shop.

Tracie went upstairs to the shop at nine-thirty. Needing something to keep myself occupied, I decided to clean the kitchen cupboards. I changed to my old paint-spattered jeans and a loose sweatshirt, and I began to scrub.

I heard voices upstairs at about fifteen minutes later. It didn't sound like George's voice was among them, so I assumed they were early customers. Tracie's attention would have to be focused on those people. I decided to go up and take the customers off her hands so she could be with her father. At least, that's what I told myself.

I walked up the stairs, opened the door to the shop, and there he was, standing not two feet from me. I panicked, very nearly slamming the door shut in his face. I couldn't breathe. My body froze. We stood looking at each other. I saw his grin and his eyes, and my voice shook when I said, "I don't know what to say to you."

"How about hello?"

"Hello," I said. He hadn't changed. I didn't see his gray hair. He looked the same to me.

He grinned again, stepped toward me, and held out his arms. I walked into them.

"Hello," he repeated. He held me a moment before adding, "My wife is in the other room with Tracie. I'd like you to meet her."

"Oh. Okay."

I carefully put one shaky foot in front of the other as he followed me into the secondhand room. And there she stood, like a beacon of beauty in the middle of tables of junk. If it had been a movie, a great light would have shown on her and a Tchaikovsky symphony would have swelled in the background. Her dark hair was pulled back in the most elegant way. Her slender body was covered head to ankle in mink, over a long-sleeved black wool dress that fit her like skin. There was a slight fragrance of exquisite perfume. I, on the other hand, looked and felt like a farmhand in ill-fitting jeans and shirt with my hair loose and scraggly.

About two gawky inches taller than Trish, I looked down as she offered her gloved hand. I couldn't blame her for keeping her gloves on. How could she be certain I wasn't carrying bugs? I was about to take her delicate hand in my large, rough, and red one, when I noticed her tiny feet, clad in fine leather boots, just inches away from my large, worn out sneakers. George mentioned both our names, and we both forced little smiles as we clasped hands. It felt like the longest handshake in history. Neither of us knew what to do next. Keep shaking? Come out fighting?

George interrupted the tension by asking politely, "Do you have any coffee in this house?"

I took a deep breath. "Yes. Come down to our apartment." I stepped to the front door, locked it, and turned the OPEN sign to CLOSED.

I'm not proud of what I did next. Tracie had told me Trish and their driver, Al, didn't get along well at all. And the social elite never invite the hired help into the house for social occasions. Cooks stay in their kitchens and drivers stay in their cars. So, I said, "Let's ask Al to join us. It's so cold out there."

George agreed it was a good idea. Trish didn't say a word. After giving me a side smile, Tracie went to the car for Al. Then we all traipsed down our dark, narrow back stairs to the apartment below, where George and Trish sat on our lumpy Salvation Army couch. Al stood, and Tracie sat on one of our two comfy secondhand chairs. There was another long silence while I made instant coffee.

As I poured coffee into our unmatched cups and mugs and

added sugar and milk from my grandmother's silver service, I said, "I'm sorry I don't have anything to serve with the coffee."

Trish and George spoke simultaneously.

"We're not hungry," he said.

"We had a big breakfast," she said.

I'll bet you did, I thought. Room service in a posh hotel. I sat down opposite Mr. and Mrs. Scott. I wanted to look at George again, but I didn't dare. I knew if I did, I wouldn't stop. So I looked out the window and said, "You know we don't usually have weather this cold."

"Oh, well, we're used to this," Trish said brightly. "When we left home it was much colder, with five inches of snow on the ground."

Home. Hers and George's home. *Thanks for reminding me, Trish.* A silence, until, God bless her, my cockapoo dog, Brandy, ran into the room to become the center of attention for five minutes. George was a dog lover and seemed delighted. Brandy, unfortunately, had a skin disease, which made her scratch and smell like dirty socks. She found comfort in rubbing against Trish's mink coat. Tracie and I caught each other's eyes as Brandy snuggled up to the mink, and I had to bite my lip very hard to keep from laughing. When my dog began to rub her privates against Trish's elegant leg, I gathered Brandy up and put her outdoors.

Polite silence followed. When I offered another cup of coffee, George and Trish looked at their watches and announced it was time to leave. We all traipsed back up the narrow dark stairs and through the shop again. The two of them hurried through the cold winter air to their car. As I watched Trish slide her delicate mink-wrapped body into the back seat, I felt a deeper jealousy than I had ever felt about anyone or anything in my life. She had George's love, she shared his life, she could touch him anytime she chose, feel his arms around her. I hated her. She had what should have belonged to me. His love, his home. He was MINE. No, I corrected myself. He didn't care about me. I concluded the only reason he'd come to the shop was to see his daughter and look at his investment. So be it. I worked hard the rest of that day, and the next, and the next. My only solace came from the snide remarks Tracie and I exchanged about George's wife.

Ten months later the shop went out of business. We blamed it on a lot of things: poor location, not enough advertising, each other. We finally faced the real reason. Neither of us had the slightest idea how to run a new business. We'd both worked hard, pouring as much money back into the shop as we could. But I had a day job, and Tracie needed money to live on, so we just slowly slid downhill.

We both dreaded having to tell George about the loss. But when Tracie called to tell him the awful news, he said, "I'm sorry to hear that, but don't worry, dear. I can take it off my taxes."

We were both relieved and grateful for his generosity. But I'd rather have had his love.

Twenty

≈

We split up the antiques. Davey and I moved into a five-room, Tudor cottage in north Tacoma. I continued to work at Head Start. Tracie found work in an eatery/bakery, renting an apartment nearby.

Life became peaceful and rewarding. Tracie and I developed a new relationship. We were becoming buddies. Good friends. We worked together on my house, painting and repairing. We dug a garden area for vegetables and flowers, each planting our favorite vegetable in our own section of the garden. We bought a rabbit for Davey and shared pride in his good grades at school. For the first time in years we were not living on the hope that George would call. We were content. It was a welcome feeling. We didn't expect or want anything to change.

In the spring of 1981 my mother died, and everything else changed as well. George began calling us again. And although Tracie and I had enjoyed the peace, George brought excitement to our lives, and we were drawn in again.

It was as if he'd turned on a telephone fountain. His calls became more and more frequent, were usually late at night, and he always sounded as if he'd had several drinks. The first time he asked to speak to me was a happy surprise, but I held down my excitement, assuming he wanted to talk about Tracie. We chatted for twenty minutes. His only mention of her was to ask me how she and I were getting along.

I was happy to report, "We've never been closer. Our lives are full, fun and busy."

"That's good, dear, I'm glad to hear that."

He asked me about my job with Head Start and how I liked working with children. That was followed by an awkward silence. Then we exchanged news of our dogs and the weather.

After that tentative conversation, we talked two or three times a week. At first we talked as old friends, about our youth, his career, my life, even the stock market. Soon he began to dump on me, several times reproaching me for having left him twenty-five years earlier. "Why did you leave me?" he asked. "You ruined my life." The next call would be filled with loving words and new promises of our being together. It was a very strange time. I didn't know what to think or how to feel. So I lived in the limbo of waiting.

In early December Tracie called in a very excited voice to announce, "Mom! Daddy just called. He's flying out here. He's on his way. He'll be at the airport in a few hours."

I took a deep breath. "That's great, honey, I'm very happy for you."

"Mom, I'm sure he'll want to see you, too."

My heart stopped at the thought. "I'm not counting on it. You just enjoy his company, and I'll call you in the morning."

"Well, okay."

"And drive carefully. It's foggy."

"I will. I love you, Mama."

"I love you, too."

I went upstairs and lay down, fully dressed, on top of my bed. I didn't sleep. I waited. How reminiscent of our early days in New York, when, exhausted, I'd force myself to stay awake, I waited for George to come home.

Around six a.m. I called Tracie. "Do you need any coffee or eggs?"

She knew it was a ploy. "Daddy is here, Mama. We've been talking all night. Why don't you come over?"

"Okay, I'll bring some food." When I hung up, I found my exhausted body shaking so hard I thought I might be sick. I sat on the side of the bed and hugged myself. After I finally calmed down, I panicked again. Removing my jeans and sweater, I began pulling clothes from my closet. Not too dressy and not too casual. I changed several times before I decided I looked appropriate in jeans and a sweater. I woke Davey and told him I'd be at his sister's for an hour. Then I brushed my hair a dozen times, sprayed myself with cologne, picked up the food, and drove to Tracie's apartment.

Sitting in the car for a few moments, trying to calm my nerves, I repeated a mantra. Taking several deep breaths, I counted backwards. Nothing helped. I was too excited, and I didn't want to waste any more time when I could be with George. I also didn't want to lose my courage, so I jumped out of the car and ran up the steps.

I tapped meekly on her door in case she wanted to grab the food and shoo me away. She opened the door. "Hi, Mama! Come on in."

My heart pounded. I walked slowly down the short hall toward her living room. Suppose he didn't want to see me? I knew he'd make it evident, and I'd make my visit brief. Suppose he was indifferent to me? Maybe I should just go home and try to forget the whole thing. But if I left, he'd think I didn't want to see him, and maybe he did want to see me. Or suppose ... This was far worse than stage fright. I leaned against the wall, took three deep breaths, and quickly turned the corner into her living room.

George stood in front of the sofa. We stared at each other. He was wearing jeans and a heavy weave white cotton shirt with the cuffs rolled up. My heart stood still.

"Hello," I said.

"Hello," he replied in his sexy, raspy voice. There were dark circles around his eyes from lack of sleep, but his mouth wore that beautiful sideways grin that had always taken my breath way.

After another long moment of staring at each other, he said, "Aren't you going to sit down?"

"Yes." I took the chair across from him.

He sat, patting the sofa pillow next to him. "I mean, here, by me."

I sat beside him.

Tracie came out of the kitchen and sat on his other side. There we were, after twenty-five years, together again. We started grinning at each other and laughing.

"It's good to see you," I said.

He studied me. "You'll never know how wonderful it is to see you." He spoke slowly and emphasized every word.

I contemplated him and saw the same face I'd loved my whole life. With a beard! I'd never seen him in a beard. "You haven't changed," I said, "You look the same." It was embarrassing how loud my heart thumped.

He laughed. "Look again. I'm an old man." He squinted at me. "But you, you're still as beautiful as you were twenty years ago."

"George, YOU look again."

"I am," he answered quietly. Then I saw sadness in his eyes.

Tracie cleared her throat. "AH, um. Hello? I'm still here, sitting on the couch. Hello?"

We turned our attention to our daughter. She was staring at us as if she'd never seen us before. "You're beautiful, too," I said.

"Anybody hungry?" Tracie asked.

"Not me."

He looked back at me. "Not yet. I'm still looking at your mother." He put his arm around my shoulders and looked at his daughter. "You were our love baby, you know."

"I see that now," she said.

"So, Mr. Scott," I said, "How long are you staying?"

"As long as you'll have me," he sighed contentedly.

It was nearing time to get eight-year-old Davey off to school so we all left Tracie's apartment and drove the half-mile to my house. When we opened the front door Davey was in his pajamas, eating a bowl of cereal.

"Davey, this is my dad," Tracie said.

"Hi."

George shook his hand. "I'm glad to meet you, Davey."

"You want some cereal?" Davey asked him.

"No thanks."

Davey finished his breakfast, dressed, and as I walked him to his bus stop, he said, "Is he really Tracie's dad?"

"Yes."

"Oh. Is he staying with us?"

"For a day or so."

"Okay."

When I returned, George was lying on the sofa, about to take a nap.

"While you rest, Tracie and I can do some grocery shopping for dinner."

He reached into his pocket and withdrew a hundred-dollar bill. "Will this be enough for food for dinner?" he asked.

At that time in my life a hundred dollars bought groceries for two weeks. But at that moment I didn't want him to know how poor I was. So when he handed me the money, I accepted it with cool nonchalance. "Yes, thank you." I said.

We returned from the supermarket loaded with food, drink, and a new chess set for Davey. We knew George was a chess fan, and we hoped if he played a game with Davey they'd get to know each other a bit. George was curled up on the couch napping, his face relaxed. He looked much as he had twenty-five years earlier.

Tracie and I had been up for nearly two days, but a nap was the last thing on our agenda. We were both so chipper and slaphappy that it was hard to stay quiet and allow George to sleep. We hummed, giggled and hugged while we prepared *hors d'oeuvres*, drinks and dinner. I changed clothes, brushed my hair several times, and sat watching George, wishing he'd wake up. It was weird and wonderful, seeing him there in my home with our grown up daughter in the next room.

He woke suddenly, sat up and looked around, saw me and grinned. "Tell me this isn't a dream."

"It's not."

"Well, who's got a drink?"

"I do, Daddy." Tracie handed him vodka on the rocks. He lit up a Lucky Strike, and said, "May I look around your house?"

"Of course," I said. I poured myself a glass of wine and watched him inspect my collection of framed photos and prints of nineteenth century ladies and children. He seemed taken with the famous print of Pinkie, touching the glass as he outlined her feet.

"Look at those dainty feet in those sweet ballet shoes. That's lovely, just lovely." He turned and smiled sweetly at me. "Why don't you and I take a walk in your backyard?" He reached for my hand.

It was a chilly, drizzly day, and I wrapped myself in my warmest coat. We were walking through my vegetable garden when he stopped suddenly. "Baby, why do you wear that ratty old coat? It reminds me of your Stephens College coat, and it looks like shit."

I was amazed that he'd remembered my old coat but offended at the criticism. I shoved my hands deep into my pockets and gave him a feisty glare. "Well, sir, I can't afford anything else. I purchase my wardrobe at second hand stores. Besides, I like this coat."

"Jesus, that's got to stop. You're too beautiful to be wearing rags."

That comment melted me, but I still felt hurt. "Thank you, George. I had no idea I looked so trashy."

"Not to me, you don't. And don't ever put you and the word 'trashy' in the same sentence again." He reached out, gathered me in his arms, and kissed me.

Our first kiss in twenty-two years! If he hadn't continued to hold me for the next three minutes, I would have collapsed on the ground.

We continued our walk through the garden. "What vegetables do you grow?"

Overwhelmed by his kiss, my foggy mind couldn't remember, "Oh, you know, just plain vegetables. And flowers, lots of flowers." I couldn't remember the flowers, either, so I changed the subject. "Would you like to see our rabbit?"

"Yes, my darling, I'd very much like to see your rabbit."

He followed me to the laundry area, where we kept the hutch. A huge grin covered his face, and he chuckled as he reached in and stroked the fur on Davey's twenty pound all white bunny. "Well, well, well."

"You still have a love for animals, don't you?"

"Yes, dear, I do. I trust animals." He stroked the fur tenderly. "They're honest. They won't betray you."

We walked back out to the muddy garden.

"You work hard out here, don't you?" he asked.

"Yes, and I love it. It relaxes me."

"We'll have a garden when we're together."

Had he just said those words? When we're together! I looked at him. For a moment there was no gray in his hair, his skin was firm, and his body was slender. I saw the young man I'd fallen in love with twenty-five years earlier. He'd never really left me. Then we kissed again, a long and tender embrace. We held each other for a long time, not noticing that the drizzle had turned to heavy rain. We were getting soaked. We walked into the house holding hands. Tracie looked at our clasped hands and smiled.

We settled down to drinking and nibbling, never getting around to actually eating a meal. When I asked George if he was hungry, he said, "I'll never be hungry again if I can be with you." I was sure I'd heard that comment in a movie once. "Besides," he gave his stomach a spank and laughed, "with this gut I have enough fat to live on for a long, long time." I hadn't even noticed he'd gained a few pounds.

We were happy together. Giggly together. Tracie and I took photos of each other with George until the film ran out.

Davey was excited about his new chess set, and George seemed delighted to play a game with him. So for the next hour, while Tracie and I popped corn and prepared dinner, they got to know each other over the chessboard. It was a warm family scene and made me realize what George and I had missed all those years.

Tracie and George talked about Granddaddy Scott's health, and then Tracie asked. "Where do you want to be buried, Daddy?"

George put his arm around my shoulders. "Right next to your mother, if she'll have me."

I was surprised and deeply touched. "And we can be together forever."

"I'm going to be buried at Arlington," he said. "So we'll have to be married for you to join me."

"Oh. Well."

He grinned and interrupted me. "Will you marry me?"

My heart rate increased. "You're already married," I said. "As soon as you're free, I will. But as of this moment, I commit myself to you."

He took my hand, kissed it, and didn't let go for several minutes.

I was absolutely sure he meant the words. He'd said them in front of our daughter. I was positive we'd eventually be married. Positive, thrilled, overjoyed, and out of this world happy. And calm. I felt no surprise, almost as though I'd known this would be.

We told Tracie about our life in New York before she was born. George entertained us with funny movie star stories and struck his famous Barrymore profile pose for a photo.

"Is there anyone in films and theater you don't know?" I asked.

"Many," he answered. "But I've got a story about someone you know." He pulled me down on to his lap. "I walked into my dressing room one night after a show and saw Jake Dengel staring at our daughter."

"Jakey? Our Jake Dengel?" For a moment I thought he was making the story up.

"Our Jakey." George looked at Tracie and winked.

"What was he doing in your dressing room, and why was he staring at our daughter?"

George finished his drink and poured another from the bottle in front of him. "He had seen the show that night and came back stage. He walked in, and there she was. If you think you're surprised, imagine how he felt. At first glance, he thought he might be seeing a ghost. 'Is this who I think it is?' he said. Then I introduced them, and his color returned."

"Since neither one of you had ever mentioned him before, it was a weird feeling for me to have this stranger staring at me like that," Tracie said.

"So, Tracie, you've finally met our friend Jake. Did your father tell you he lived with us in New York?"

"Oh, sure. It was just weird, meeting him right then."

"I can imagine. It's weird for me to hear about it."

I turned to George. "Do you still see him?"

"Once in a while."

"How is he?"

"He's fine. Just fine."

"Does he work? In the theater I mean?"

George nodded and smiled. "Jake does just fine."

I stood up and walked the room, seeing Jake in my mind. My dear Jakey. "I can't believe it. Our Jakey! We should call him!"

"I don't have a number," George said. "Maybe some other time."

"When you see him, please give him my love."

"I will, dear."

We refreshed our drinks and finger-nibbled the food while we conjured up silly dreams of the future. "Let's build a house," George suggested.

"Where?" I loved his wonderful mood. He was getting playful.

He raised his arms as though he were cheering. "On a ranch. Away from everybody," Then he rested his hand on the back of Tracie's chair, slapped the table with the other and gave a delighted laugh.

"And we'll only tell family where we are," I said.

"Well, maybe not all of them," George grinned.

"A great big house, so I can have my own suite," Tracie chimed in.

"You can have whatever you want, dear." He looked at her with a sweet fatherly smile and stroked her hair.

Taking in my tiny wreck of a kitchen, I added, "And we'll have a kitchen bigger than this house, filled with food from our own garden. And we'll have chickens. I love chickens."

"And don't forget the kennels and runs for the dogs," George added. He looked at Tracie. "We'll give you your own pool and a movie theater."

"How will we keep the world out?" I asked. I was definitely getting giddy.

"At the beginning of our driveway we'll have a giant billboard that sits on the ground and looks like the continuation of the road. When people try to drive to the house, they'll drive through the billboard and right over a cliff on the other side." George looked at us proudly, raised his eyebrows and waited for a response.

"They'll never find us!" Tracie giggled.

"The world will leave us alone!" George reached for my hand and pulled me down on his lap again. "We'll live in peace forever." He laced his fingers in mine and kissed my hand.

"It will be awful for you to leave your estate in Connecticut," I said. "I know how much you love it."

He smoothed my hair back. "Not as much as I love you."

For a moment we were quiet. Our silly dream seemed to have satisfied some need we all had.

Finally, about two a.m., George said, "I'm taking your mother upstairs now."

Tracie looked at us as if we were two teenagers about to do

something she didn't approve of. She said, "Oh ... well I'll see you in a few hours then."

"I didn't bring a thing but me." George guided me toward the back hall. "Do you have an extra toothbrush in the house?"

"I'm so glad you brought you." I said, "And yes, I have a spare toothbrush. Do you still brush the hell out of your tongue?"

"You remember that?" He chucked.

"How could I forget? I'd lie in bed and watch you at the sink, scrubbing your tongue for all you were worth."

He chuckled. "It couldn't have been a pretty sight."

"I loved watching everything you did."

"You were a sweet girl. Yes, I still brush my tongue."

I had been proud of my cottage, working on it for long hours, painting and repairing. Now, as we climbed the narrow, creaky, wooden stairs to my cold bedroom, I remembered Tracie telling me of the grandeur of George's mansion, and I was ashamed. "It's cold and not very spacious," I opened the door on the bedroom I'd worked so hard on. "It's surely not what you're used to." I walked to my bedside table and turned on the lamp. There it was, a room not much bigger than a large closet with a cold, bare floor.

He followed me in. "I think it's charming."

The chilly air did not allow for coyness. We removed our clothes and jumped under the covers.

"It's so cold. I'm sorry."

"I didn't jump in bed because it's cold," he said, wrapping his arms around me. "I'm twenty-five years older than the last time you saw me."

"If you are, I am, too. But I am sorry I don't have heat up here."

He drew me into his arms. "We'll just have to keep each other warm."

"I'm happy you're here," I said.

"And I'm just so happy to see you." He rested his head on one hand and leaned his head so close our noses nearly touched.

"What made you decide to fly out here?"

"I've been thinking about it since I saw you in the antique shop. I've thought about you every minute. God! It's driven me crazy!" I was glad I'd left the light on so I could see his wonderful face when he said, "This time I'll never leave you. Get over here and keep me warm."

"I am."

He pulled me closer, rested my head on his shoulder, tilted my chin up and kissed my forehead. "You'll never be close enough." He laid his head back. "How's Tracie been?"

"She'd fine. She has a job, as you know."

"I wish she'd find herself a life," he said gruffly. "She's always there, in the middle of things."

"She missed having a childhood with you."

"I'm aware of that. God! How I'm aware of that. But I've tried to make it up to her. I'm still trying to make it up to her." He combed his fingers through his hair. "She's a good kid, But Christ, she can't seem to stick to anything. I wouldn't care if she chose to be a meat cutter, as long as she stuck to it."

"She's been through a lot," I said. "She needs time to find herself."

"Well, maybe she will find herself if I cut off the five grand I send her every year. I don't think I'm doing her any favors."

"That will be hard on her." I didn't say more. It would be a sad shock for Tracie, but he was the father, and it was his gift. I think if I had been able to convince her to find a life apart from her father, it might have saved their relationship. But she was twenty-five years old, and I was only the mother. I felt like I had failed her again.

"But I owe you, Baby. While you were living like this, I went through twenty-five million bucks. God knows I owe you." He stared at the ceiling.

"I've missed you so much," I said. "After I heard your voice that first phone call, I had a hard time standing up."

"I knew Tracie was calling you. I told her it was time. I picked it up so I could hear you. I'd been waiting to hear your voice for years."

"You could never know how much I wanted to hear yours," I admitted.

"I've wanted to be with you since we came to the shop, but I couldn't until your mother died." Still holding me, he covered his face with his free arm. "Jesus, how I hated her."

"She felt the same way about you. Your name was not

mentioned in her house for twenty-five years."

"When Tracie told me her grandmother was dead and you were divorced, I began to close in."

"I'm so glad you did. I wish it hadn't taken so long." I wrapped my arm around his chest. "You'll never know how I longed for you."

He told me again how guilty he felt for spending so many millions of dollars and not a cent on me after I'd supported him in New York.

"I'm taking Trish on an around-the-world cruise for her fortieth birthday. When I get back, our marriage will be over. I'd end it now, but I promised, and I owe her. She's stayed married to me for ten years, and put up with a lot. She's a good woman. She's the only wife I never cheated on."

This was confusing. I thought his coming to us meant he'd left her. Or was I about to break up another of his marriages? I pushed the horrible thought from my mind.

He stroked my hand that lay on his chest. "I've always known where you were. Every week of every year."

"How?"

"I've got my ways, Baby."

It sounded to me a little like a line from a movie.

"Colleen was jealous of you."

Oh, sure, I thought. Colleen Dewhurst, jealous of me. That I didn't believe. But his mood was mellow and he seemed open to my asking some questions. "Why did you turn down the Academy Award?"

"They're a sham. I'm no better than a hundred other actors are. "But," he kissed me lightly, "if I ever do go to the Awards, it will be with you." He pulled my hair back, and put his mouth close to mine. "Oh, my baby, I owe you so much."

Beneath the warm covers in the icy cold room, we made love. But this time it wasn't a couple of kids making fast love in the heat of passion. It was two adults aware that after twenty-five years we'd been given the gift of each other again.

Tracie and I drove George to the airport the next morning for his return trip on his personal jet. The three of us stood outside the car for final goodbyes. He kissed and hugged Tracie. I walked a few yards with him toward the hangars.

He stopped and circled me with his arms. "Here we are, saying good-bye again,"

"And I'm wearing an old fur coat and weeping."

I asked him how long it would be before we could be together. "Ninety days after the cruise, Baby. I promise." He swept my hair back and kissed me

"Will you stay in touch?"

"I'll write you from every port in the world. I'll write so many post cards you'll get sick of reading them." He walked to the private plane terminal without looking back.

Tracie and I stopped at the market on the way home. We bought wine and cigarettes to chase away our fears. The fear he would change his mind about the future, and the fear he wouldn't call again. But he did call that evening. "Just to hear your voice and tell you I love you."

A few days later he called to say he'd spoken to Trish, and she "wanted to make amends." Two days later he called to say he was going through with the cruise he'd promised Trish for her birthday. "I owe her that much. After the trip, that will be it." There was one more phone call after that, "just to hear your voice. I'll be back soon. Then it'll be quits with Trish, and we'll be together."

Twenty One

≈

G eorge didn't write post cards from every port in the world. He didn't write at all. We didn't hear from him for nearly six months. I did a lot of heavy sighing. One week I'd eat nothing but chocolate. The next week I'd eat nothing. Luckily, neither my hair nor teeth fell out. Every time the phone rang I picked it up on the second ring. When the mail arrived, I ran for it. High hopes followed by deep disappointment became part of my life.

We posted a map of the world in our kitchen, trying to guess where he was and trying not to imagine the two of them happily together. We were living in limbo and began searching for clues about what would happen in the months ahead. We read our daily horoscope, had our palms read, and bought the horoscope magazine every month, searching for a happy prediction.

In January we told my married sisters and their families George had been with us in December. They greeted the news with mixed reactions. Some of them were supportive. "We want only your happiness. Just be careful," they told us.

The others were sure we were making a big mistake by letting George back into our lives and told us so. "Karen, it's just another one of George's deals."

"Tracie, what are you doing? Hanging around for the bucks?"

We were determined not to listen to their negative remarks, and we decided not to tell anyone else about our relationship with George. We were trying hard to hang on to our dreams, and we didn't need anyone undermining them. What a joke, I thought at the time. For years I'd kept my connection with George a secret for the sake of family. Now, again, because of family, I had to go back into hiding. And most ironic of all, George had become so famous that if I were to tell anyone outside the family, no one would believe me.

Tracie joined me every evening after work, and we took solace in each other. We had to believe George meant his promises. If we doubted him it would mean we'd have to go back to the way it was before his visit. And that seemed impossible. So we believed. We held the faith. When doubts pushed in, I pushed them out. I convinced myself we'd be together again.

We became devotees of the TV show, *Entertainment Tonight*, hoping for a glimpse of George's face. We worked out some of our frustrations by dancing nightly with Davey to the tunes on the *Muppet Show*. We laughed at the antics of *Our Gang*, and I began to watch George's old movies.

After listening to our "poor us" woes one evening, Davey gave a heavy sigh, clasped his hands behind his head, stretched out on the couch, and mused, "Life is life, and food is food." I posted his words beside the map of the world, and the words of my eight-year-old son became our family motto.

And there were many ugly nights. Tracie would keep me up well after midnight, demanding more information about my relationship with George. She claimed she had a "birthright" to know all about it. Before his Christmas visit, she had been sure George and I had had a one-night stand. It took weeks and a pile of promises to convince her otherwise. It was degrading to have her look at me as if I was a prostitute. It reminded me of the way my father had looked at me when he demanded I marry Phillip.

She blamed me for her illegitimacy, telling me, "You couldn't possibly know how it feels to be illegitimate. I've had to go through life this way. You got away with everything, and I had to take the brunt of it."

I hadn't, of course, gotten away with anything, which I tried to explain to her. And when she asked me over and over if I'd ever thought of aborting her, I answered, "No." But I couldn't tell her about George's reaction to my pregnancy.

One evening in late May, George's agent called me. "Karen, you don't know me, my name is Jane Dacey."

I tried to cover the shock and thrill I felt, and I hoped I wasn't talking too loud, a habit I had if I got overly excited. "Yes, I know who you are. George told me about you. In fact, I've had your telephone number written on a cocktail napkin for years."

"He wanted me to call and tell you he's in the hospital. He had eye surgery for a torn retina."

Weakness set in, and I knelt by the phone table. "How is he?"

"He's all right. He just wanted you to know."

"How do I get in touch with him?"

She gave me her address at her New York office. "I'll forward your letters to him. It's been good to talk to you, Karen. I've known about you for years. I'm glad you're back in his life."

What a relief! The waiting was over, and he loved me. He was okay, and he loved me. That evening Tracie and I celebrated with champagne and hugs, certain our lives were about to begin again.

For the next few weeks we flooded Jane's office with get well cards and letters for George. He called once to tell us he was going into rehearsals for *Present Laughter*. He'd be both directing and taking the leading role.

Tracie remembered from her time living with him that you didn't bother George when he was in rehearsals. So we stopped the letters and cards, with one exception. Tracie sent him a card for Father's Day, together with a coffee cup with a drawing of a chicken on it. It was a reminder of the chicken ranch the three of us had conjured up that Christmas. Tracie asked him later if he'd received the card and mug. He didn't remember the card, had lost the mug, and the chicken didn't connect at all. Poor Tracie. She had tried so hard, and he had stepped on her pride without giving it a thought.

Present Laughter opened to great reviews. I sent George a note of congratulations. He responded with a phone call, telling me Trish had left to work in Massachusetts. "I'm feeling very good, dear. The show is more successful than I had anticipated."

"How's your health?"

"Better than ever. I'm playing a lot of golf, and I've lost some weight."

"And your eye?"

"Fine, dear, just fine." He sounded irritated. "Don't ask me any more about my health." He hung up.

He called the next evening after the show. He was loving, kind and chatty. I had the feeling he didn't remember the previous call.

The calls became frequent. Some loving. Others dumping on me. I never knew what to expect. "I miss you more than I can say. We'll be together soon." "Why the fuck did you ever leave me?" "You ruined my life." "If we'd been married I know it would have worked out. I would have stayed with you. We'd have made a go of it." "Jesus, we lost so many years. How could you do that to us?" He asked me several times, "How many other men have there been?" Once he said, "Why do you want to take on a one-eyed, overweight has-been?"

"Because I love him," I answered.

During one call he said, "Do you three want to come to New York for the Christmas holidays?"

I didn't even consider giving him a controlled, casual reply. "YES!"

"That's good. I'll have Jane make the arrangements. I love you, Baby."

Christmas in New York with George! The thought brought back so many memories and a physical reaction that I surely had not expected. I felt nauseous, just like when I was pregnant.

Tracie and I talked of little else but Christmas in New York, and it became a reality when he sent us a check "to buy some pretty clothes." In another letter Jane sent us our airline tickets.

Wanting to give George a special gift for Christmas, I decided to knit him a sweater. I asked Jane to try to get his measurements. She called me two or three days later. "Karen, it wasn't easy," she laughed. "I'm sure his tailor thinks I'm the one knitting the sweater. But here they are. Good luck."

The anticipation of that trip made the days achingly long. But shopping for new clothes helped to make them tolerable. My greatest find was a black cocktail dress with a lace insert under a V-neck, and a waistline that made mine look tiny. I fell madly in love with that dress and hoped I'd have it for years.

We didn't tell the family about our trip until Thanksgiving. They were curious about the movie star side of him, asking Tracie questions about the years she had lived with him. But they were not convinced he was sincere about wanting me in his life. They didn't believe this trip would bring anything but heartbreak. They also knew that if they started making nasty cracks again we'd walk out the door. He was, after all, Tracie's father and the man I'd always loved.

Twenty Two

≈

We left Tacoma dreaming of chestnuts roasting on an open fire, hot chocolate, and chilly walks in Central Park. Bundled up in our new heavy sweaters, winter coats, hats and gloves, we arrived in New York City, where the temperature was an unseasonable 70 degrees.

Jane met us with a limo. It was strange to finally meet the woman whose telephone number I'd had on a napkin in the back of my drawer for twenty-five years. Small, dark and sixtyish, wearing a brown suit and brown comfortable shoes, she didn't look at all like the jaded theater agent I'd expected. I liked her immediately. She may have had a tough core, but she was welcoming and kind to us.

She laughed and told us, "George told me to order the longest limousine I could find in New York City. Well, this is it."

I had only been to New York once since I lived there with George. And now, sitting next to our daughter, I was returning to be with him again. The memories returned so vividly I might have been watching a movie. We drove to the Plaza Hotel, where George had booked a suite. In those early days I would never have had the courage to walk through the front door of The Plaza.

There had apparently been some confusion about our reservation. Tracie and Davey's rooms were down the hall from the suite. The desk clerk apologized and said, "You're first on the list when a suite with two bedrooms opens up." That was fine with us, but Jane seemed worried. "I hope this doesn't upset George," she said.

Phillip had been in the hotel business, and I had stayed at some pretty wonderful places, but knowing that George had reserved this magnificent room for us made it especially thrilling. When I entered the room and saw the antique French furniture and the view of Central Park from the huge window, I was tempted to stand in the center of the room and shout, "I love this. It's gorgeous!" But to Jane it was just another hotel room and another day in her life as George's agent. I took a quick look and said in a moderately enthusiastic voice, "This is beautiful," while I followed the bellman carrying my luggage into one of the bedrooms.

Jane led Tracie and Davey to their room, and I closed my door. Then I ogled. I gazed at the tapestry window dressings framing another huge view window, the mahogany side tables, dressers and writing desk. I looked at the double bed and wondered if I'd be sharing it with George.

Jane tapped on my door, urging me to hurry so we could get to the theater in time for the opening curtain. This would be the night for my new black dress. I wanted him to see me looking wonderful. Half an hour later, when I opened my door and saw the admiring look on Jane's face and heard her words, "Oh, my, what a change. You look beautiful," I was sure George would be pleased.

We arrived at the theater just in time for the first act of *Present Laughter*. George was recreating the part of Gary Essendine, whom he'd played in Toledo summer stock twenty-six years earlier. I had played opposite him in the part of Joanna Lyppiatt, and it was like watching ghosts. He had fine-tuned his comic delivery, and his timing was perfect. The audience loved him, and I wanted to stand up and shout, "This man loves me! Isn't he wonderful? And he loves ME."

Since Tracie had been backstage many times after the show, she proudly led us through cold gray corridors to George's dressing room. The room was surprisingly small and crowded for that of a superstar. It contained a cot, a small table stacked high with trinkets, fan mail, and manuscripts and barely had space for a makeup table. I saw George's chessboard, a closet and a bathroom.

When I walked in, George stood at his closet, half dressed and sweating heavily. As I crossed to him with the intention of giving him a hug, he backed away. Feeling embarrassed and clumsy, I retreated to the hallway. He and Tracie were chattering away when he noticed me standing in the doorway. "You're welcome to come in and sit down," he said as though speaking to a fan.

He sat at his dressing table cluttered with photos of his children, the cast of *Present Laughter*, and Trish. Next to the photo of Trish sat a pile of our letters and cards. He had two drinks of vodka while he dressed and continued talking with Tracie. With the exception of one or two quick looks my way, George totally ignored me. I became more confused by the second. What should I say to him, "How are you?" "How was your cruise around the world?" This was the man who had called me night after night, proclaiming his love. A year ago he'd asked me to marry him. Had I dreamed it all?

After he finished dressing, we followed him back down the hall and up to the lobby, where a man and a woman waited to congratulate him. On the upper lobby another group was waiting for his autograph. Tracie kept walking to the car. "Never stand waiting for him, "she said. "He doesn't like that."

We waited in the car. When George finally joined us, Al, his driver, drove us to Gallagher's. As we entered the restaurant, George introduced us to the headwaiter, "This is Tracie, my daughter, her mother, and her son, David."

My gosh! I thought, he not only knows I'm here, but he introduced me. That's a beginning.

At our table George's chair was a foot or so away from mine. During the first twenty minutes, while the conversation revolved around the history of Gallagher's and the photos of the celebrities that covered the walls, I noticed him inching his chair closer to mine. He finally pulled his chair to touch mine, and we began to sneak peeks at each other out of the corner of our eyes. The second half-hour, we sat with silly grins, gazing at each other.

Davey ordered a hamburger. The waiter asked him if it would be all right to serve it on toast. "Sure," Davey said. After the waiter left us, Davey giggled and said, "I guess New York doesn't know any better." When it was time for dessert, Davey ordered a bowl of chocolate ice cream. The waiter brought him a giant banana split, and I gathered by Davey's smile, that he'd changed his mind about New York.

"David, do you still like chess?" George asked.

"Yeah. A lot."

"I have an extra electronic set, and I'm going to give it to you."

"Wow!" Davey's eyes lit up. He was thrilled, more than George could know. But Davey was still shy with George and not expansive in his thank you.

The waiters didn't hover, but they catered to our every whim. When I rose to find my way to the ladies room, two waiters tried to escort me. I was feeling woozy from three quick glasses of wine. George referred later to my condition as a case of the vapors. The last thing I wanted was everyone's full attention as I wove my way to the restroom. The return trip was worse. The waiters had been waiting for me. They followed me back to the table as I concentrated on looking sober and walking a straight path.

We stayed late. In fact, we were the last to leave the restaurant, except for three older ladies seated at the bar. I think they had been waiting for George to finish his meal, because as we rose to leave they bounded across the room toward him. They were silly, tipsy, and giggled like teenagers as they asked for his autograph. He seemed to enjoy the scene and took his time asking them their first names.

While we waited for George, the manager asked me if we'd like a tour of the restaurant. He led us to the back area and pointed out tables that were always reserved for special celebrities. I made a reverent stop at Henry Fonda's table, touched the seat, and took my time gazing at the handsome photo of him that hung on the wall behind the table.

On the drive back to the hotel, we asked George when we'd see him again. "Probably on the weekend," he said. "Maybe you'd all like to come to my house in Connecticut next Monday and Tuesday."

Tracie spoke up, expressing my thoughts. "That's two days away. Won't we see you until then?"

"Well, if you really want to."

Was he pretending shyness or testing our sincerity? Did he want to be begged?

"Of course we want to. Please be with us when you can," I said.

"Done! I'll be there!" He spoke in his Gary Essendine character. I gathered it was easier for him to hide behind the character than show his vulnerability. It didn't matter. We'd see him the next evening.

They moved all of us to a larger suite the next morning. Settling in and strolling along the streets of New York took most of the day. The temperature was still in the high 60's. Chestnuts roasting on an open fire no longer seemed so appealing. When George knocked on our door late that evening, we were ready with his vodka and a room service snack. For an hour he was warm and funny, telling stories about the show. Then abruptly he got up to leave.

As I walked to the elevator with him he said, "I hate it when you flirt with other men."

I wasn't sure I'd heard him right.

"What? When did I flirt with another man?"

"At Gallagher's. With the waiter."

"George, please, I'd never do that. Please don't think ..."

"You like younger men, don't you?"

"No, I ..." It had been so tentative between us up until then, I couldn't just blurt out, "I love you and only you." So I just stood there as he gave me a sterile kiss on the cheek and stepped into the elevator. When I finally thought of something to say, the elevator door had closed.

I thought back to the restaurant and remembered he'd been watching me closely. I thought it was admiration, but he'd evidently been watching to see if I smiled at the waiter. Of course, I'd smiled at the waiter. He'd gone out of his way to please Davey.

Sunday evening George's son drove the three of us to Connecticut. Alex was amiable, and we chatted easily. He had attended a school not far from Tacoma, so we had something in common. Watching this sensitive young man, I thought, I'm his sister's mother, back in his father's life. It can't be easy for him. But then, he was probably used to his father's unpredictable lifestyle.

Greenwich, Connecticut, features one huge mansion after another. Just driving down the road is a real estate delight. But when we drove up George's driveway to his stately, colonial brick manor, it was an unexpected thrill. I hadn't thought about his wealth until then. We walked up the front steps and entered the immense hallway. My first impression was of elegant comfort. Trish and George obviously had very good taste. The wide hardwood floors were covered with imported Asian carpets. Authentic antiques were everywhere. We followed George to the kitchen, where a circular stairway led up to the second floor. I concluded the house was so vast they needed short cuts.

We'd been in the kitchen briefly when Ellie Mae, George's housekeeper, walked in. A senior citizen with happy brown eyes, she'd known Tracie from the years she'd lived with George and Trish. She hugged her as if she were her own daughter. She welcomed me as a long lost friend. "I'm so glad you've come. I think he needs you," she whispered. Tracie had told me Ellie Mae and Trish didn't get along, so I felt I had an ally.

I hadn't asked George about his marital arrangement with Trish. I assumed they were divorcing and that he was living there alone. But after I'd been there for five minutes, I reversed my thinking. Reminders of Trish were everywhere. Tracie pointed out her favorite Neil Diamond tapes that were stacked in the kitchen. Photos of her were on the tables: Trish and George, Trish and her horse, Trish and the dogs. Her paints and easel occupied a third floor room. Her jacket wrapped the back of a kitchen chair, as though she'd just stepped out for a minute.

Surrounded by Trish's presence, I felt unwelcome and misplaced. What was I doing here? Was he trying to make me uncomfortable? My discomfort didn't seem to bother George. Was he waiting to see if I'd fit into his lifestyle? And if I did, would he leave Trish? If not, would he ask her to come home? Or, was she really just visiting the coast, and he'd timed it so we'd be gone when she returned? I had so many unanswered questions.

When Tracie asked about Trish, he answered, "She's on the coast for awhile." When Tracie asked when she'd return, he changed the subject.

He carried my bags to a guestroom, and I was reminded again that everything belonged to Trish, when he said, "I wouldn't feel right sleeping in the bed Trish and I share. We'll sleep in one of the other bedrooms." Not anxious for Davey to see us disappear into a bedroom together I was relieved when he led me to a room located in another part of the house away from the kids.

As we all started back downstairs, I began to have very uncomfortable feelings. I couldn't believe he felt right having us in the house. I began to think Trish knew we were there and was waiting for George to tell her which one of us he wanted. I felt like someone had covered my eyes with a blindfold and spun me around and around until I was too dizzy to think.

We had settled down in the kitchen/great room area when the phone rang. Alex picked up the receiver. "Hi, Trishy!" He may have said more, but I was too stunned to hear it. George took the phone and spoke cordially, with her for some time, making no attempt at privacy.

I left the room for the bar and poured myself a glass of excellent French wine. After two sips it hit me. I was drinking Trish's excellent French wine. Alex had followed me into the bar and patted my shoulder. Here stood Colleen Dewhurst's son, comforting me while my lover, his father, talked to Trish, his stepmother, as I drank her wine.

After George finished his conversation with Trish, he went on with the evening as if there had been no interruption. I didn't ask about it, and he didn't offer. Nothing about the situation surprised me anymore. I wasn't sure if I had stepped into a dream or a nightmare. Or maybe fallen down the rabbit hole with Alice in Wonderland.

Davey discovered George's chess set in his study and asked if he could play it. George told him to go ahead and again promised, "I've got an extra set I'll give you." And again Davey's eyes lit up.

After an hour of drinking more of Trish's French wine and snacking on cheese and fruit, we all climbed the stairs to our rooms. When George showed us the other guest rooms, he pointed out another electronic chess set in a box, saying to Davey, "That's the one I'm going to send to you in Tacoma." Davey's eyes were so big I thought they'd burst.

When George and I finally closed the door behind us in the guestroom, he grabbed me in a harsh embrace and said, "I hate that you were married to a younger man. And I hate it when you flirt with waiters! You're mine. You've always been mine." The next kiss was so hard it felt like he was branding me.

"George, how could you think I'd flirt with a waiter when you were sitting next to me? Besides, I don't flirt with waiters." He got into bed and turned away. I guessed that was my cue to be quiet and go to sleep. When I put my hand under the pillow I felt something cold and heavy. I pulled my hand out fast, jumped out of bed, and took two giant leaps to the wall. "George, is that a gun under the pillow?"

"It's a gun, Baby. And what's your hand doing under my pillow?"

"That's beside the point. A gun! Why?"

"I always sleep with a gun under my pillow."

"Why?"

"I've had threats." He said the words offhandedly as if they were unimportant. Then changed his mood. "Not everybody loves me like you do. Now come back to bed and let me take care of you."

That was fine with me. I climbed back into bed, and we held each other until we fell asleep.

During the night I awoke to see George holding his gun, staring out the window at the grounds below. My first inclination was to cower under the sheet, but if my love was in trouble, I should help, so I jumped out of bed and ran to him. "What's the matter?"

"I thought I heard someone out there."

"Do you see anyone?"

"No. There's no one."

"Do you really think it's necessary to keep a gun?"

"Baby, I've found people in the house."

"Stealing?"

"Not necessarily. Some people just want to see me. Just be here."

"That's pretty creepy."

"Come on, let's go back to bed."

I went back to bed but not to sleep. The gun under the pillow and the suspicion somebody was outside made for jittery nerves.

George rested the next day while Davey, Tracie and I walked his property and relaxed. After living there for four years, my daughter knew her way around. We followed her back to the stables and down the long drive to the stone bridge built over the driveway for the horses. She was proud of being his daughter and knowing her way around. She'd found what she'd always wanted, and I was very happy for her.

George invited his friends Rose and Tony to spend the evening with us. A small pretty woman, Rose brought her own utensils. We watched her as she made her own pasta and created a wonderful Italian meal. We spent three hours in the kitchen helping her and taking silly photos of each other. When the meal was ready, we savored every delicious bite.

George seemed very proud of Rose and kept asking, "Isn't it the best Italian meal you've ever had?" Tony, who reminded me of Columbo, seemed to be always smiling. He beamed when George gave Rose compliments. We were a happy group.

As if on cue, as soon as the kitchen was cleaned up George set up the card table. Tony opened a drawer and brought out two decks of cards. Rose asked me if I liked to play bridge. I was about to give her an honest answer, but George interrupted and said, "Of course she does. She played backstage at Stephens. She was a very good player." He looked at me. "And don't worry, dear. I'll be your partner and help you. Not that you're going to need any help."

"And," said Tony, "we just play for fun."

I felt desperate. "George, Stephens was a long time ago. I haven't played since then. And I really don't –" But the table was up, the chairs were being placed around it, and there seemed no way out. We took our seats. As soon as I had cards in my hand, my mind went blank from terror. I couldn't remember how to bid. I couldn't keep track of the tricks. The longer we played, the more muddled my mind got, and they didn't hide their own expertise at the game. To add to my feelings of being an outsider, their bits of conversation showed a genuine fondness for Trish.

"Have you been playing bridge with George for a long time?" I asked.

"Oh, yes,' Rose said cheerily, "George, Trish, Tony and I have been playing together for years."

"She called yesterday," George said offhandedly.

"Oh? How is she?" Rose asked eagerly.

They were talking about Trish as if I weren't in the room.

About halfway through the game we heard a strange sound at the front door. George and Tony jumped up. Tony bounded for the door. George caught up to him, pushed him out of the way, and opened the door. George stood in the doorway, looking out into the night. Tony yanked him out of the way and slammed the door. "George, you were a perfect target. That was a stupid thing to do."

There hadn't been anyone there. But the scare was real, and after the recent shooting of John Lennon, George's carelessness had been especially foolish. We refreshed our drinks and returned to the table. Before continuing the game, we talked about the incident. "I'm well aware of the crazies out there," George said. "I've found them in my house, and I've received plenty of weird mail. But," he looked at Tony, "if they're after me, I'll be the one who gets it, not my friends."

We continued the bridge game, and even though they all assured me I played very well, I knew there were many times they wanted to tip the table onto my lap. When I finally made it through to the end of the game, grateful relief swept over me. I wanted to jump up and shout, "Never again!"

But as they were leaving, plans were made for the next game. "The more you play, the better you'll be," Tony said to me. I was sure he was trying to make me feel better, but my heart sank. After they left, George did not lock the door for the night. He didn't lock the door but kept a gun under his pillow. I didn't even try to figure that one out.

My heart sank again the next day, when I removed our clothes from Trish's basement dryer. In an early morning fog I had gathered our things in a hurry, and without taking time to sort, had stuffed them into the washer. An hour later I pulled them out of the washer, plopped them into the dryer and set the timer for fifty minutes.

When I removed them, I saw to my horror that my gorgeous new black dress had been reduced to a doll's size. No amount of pulling would stretch the fabric. Tracie walked down the basement stairs and found me holding the shrunken dress to my breast as I moaned. If she saw the humor, she didn't laugh. She came to me and gave me a very sweet hug.

In mid afternoon, a friend of Alex's drove us into New York. We made plans to see George after the show the next evening. We dropped him off at the theater and returned to our room at the

Plaza.

Jane had found a nanny to watch Davey for the two weeks so he was happily busy with magic shows and sightseeing. This gave Tracie and me the freedom to do some heavy Christmas shopping and see a Broadway show. That evening we saw *Woman of the Year*, with Raquel Welch. Jane had urged us to see another new show, *Cats*. But ignorant me said, "Who wants to see a show about a bunch of cats?"

When we told George the show we'd seen, he said, "Ah, Rocky. She's a good person and a good actress," and added, "by comparison to Julie Christie. I could never figure out where SHE was coming from."

When George arrived at the suite after the show that evening, he was charming and funny, except for one moment when he became very serious. "I lost a word tonight. I've never done that before." When we began to commiserate, he shut us off by saying he didn't want to talk about it.

Drinking heavily that night, George had run out of liquor by two a.m. He called the bar to have more delivered. When they refused him, he became belligerent, shouting into the phone and cursing them. But they held to their policy. He finally smashed the receiver down. "Daddy, you're tired anyway. We don't need another drink," Tracie said, trying to calm him.

"How the fuckin' hell do you know if I need another drink or not?" he growled at her. "Mind your own business. I don't need you telling me what to do."

Her face dropped. I wanted to go to her, but he turned and started for the bedroom door. I thought if I didn't go with him he'd take it out on Tracie.

The next evening when George came to the suite after the show, we ordered dinner from room service. He was drinking that evening, but not as heavily. He seemed at ease and looking forward to the show's closing. Davey had gone to bed early and George and Tracie were getting along well. They began to discuss the future. It started as a fun father-daughter talk about the ranch we'd all live on. I went to use the bathroom, and when I returned he was standing over her, yelling at her and calling her names. She was sitting on the couch, crying. The tirade continued for five or ten minutes until I was able to talk George into coming to bed. Tracie was left there alone, sitting in the corner of the couch, looking frightened and dejected.

In the bedroom George kept muttering to himself until he fell asleep. "What in hell does she want from me? She's always there, always in the middle of things, why doesn't she give me a break?"

"She loves you."

The next evening he said to me, "I want you to come to Connecticut next Monday, alone. We need time to get to know each other again, and we can't do it with the kids around." He suggested I hire a car and spend Monday and Tuesday with him. Tracie did not greet the news happily, but she knew her father had spoken.

Sunday evening the temperature finally dropped, a light snow had fallen, and by Monday morning the grounds around George's home had been dusted with a fluffy coat of white. The house appeared to rise above the cloud I was floating on.

The cab driver was in the middle of telling me about all the movie and stage stars he'd seen, when I told him to turn into George's driveway. "Hey, look! I think I see George C. Scott standing on that front porch."

"That's right," I said. I paid him, opened the door, and stepped out. His mouth opened, but he didn't speak. He just stared at the famous person standing at the open front door in his robe and bare feet, arms wide in welcoming.

George hugged me and said, "Hello."

I looked up at him. "Hello." I felt my heart leap when I looked into his gentle, merry eyes. My sweet George had returned.

He escorted me, as he had when Tracie and Davey were there, to the guest room on the third floor, reminding me he didn't think it right for us to sleep in Trish's bed. I agreed with him. The bed was a heavy wood antique piece, high off the floor and very comfortable. I did not ask if he and Trish had ever slept in it together.

After I unpacked, he said, "How about you making some of those perfect square sandwiches?"

"You remember that?"

"I remember everything about us." He pulled my hair back and leaned his face close to mine. "You're mine. You always were and always will be."

While we sat in his kitchen eating our sandwiches he told me that the old apartment hotel was still there. "I've driven by it many times," he said. "We ought to take Tracie by so she can see where she was conceived."

In the afternoon, we walked down the backside of his vast property. "I'm going to Monterey, California for the Crosby Pro/Am Golf Tournament at the end of January," he announced. "I'd like you to come with me."

He wants ME to go with him! I very nearly slipped on the snowy slope. He took my hand to steady me, and as I recovered my balance, I thought of my responsibilities at home. "I'd love to come. You must know I'd love to come. But I have a job ... and Davey. How long would we be there?"

"If you have to ask that, forget it."

"I want to go. Can you give me a few days after we get back home to see if I can make arrangements?"

He pulled me close to him. "My darling, I'll wait forever." I loved hearing him say that, but I was fairly certain I'd heard the line in a movie.

On the walk back to the house he talked more about the Pro/Am and asked me if I played golf. "No. Do I need to?"

He stopped walking and wrapped his arms around me. "No, my darling, you don't need to. It might be more fun for you if you knew something about the game though."

Later he changed to his jeans and sweater and asked if I'd like to ride with him to the liquor store. "I'd love to," I replied.

"I love you," he said.

As he opened the door of his car for me, he spotted some discarded beer cans under the front seat. Pretending great embarrassment, he hurried to get them to the garbage can. He started the car, acting the role of the befuddled limo driver and sneaking quick peeks at me. He seemed more relaxed and happy than I'd seen him since we arrived in New York.

As we drove to the village shopping center I realized this was the first really normal thing we'd done together in nearly thirty years. Just two middle age folks doing their shopping. What might have been, I thought.

We stopped at the liquor store and then the food market. We walked back to the car and he helped me inside. Then as he walked around the front of the car he looked through the front window and gave me one of his big sideways grins. So reminiscent of our early days when he sat in the car waiting for me.

That evening we drove to Tony and Rose's home for dinner. George was silly and respectful, rushing to my door to help me out, bowing deeply as he offered his arm, and kissing me softly. For a while the young George had returned and was courting me.

Our host and hostess opened their front door before we rang. When we stepped into their spacious, colorful front room we were greeted with the aroma of herbs and garlic cooking in the kitchen.

George's mood was comic and expansive. He raved about the meal as though he'd fallen in love with the pasta. I was feeling a twinge of jealousy, so I tried to top his compliments with huge tributes of my own. We were getting sillier and sillier as we ate and drank. But I honestly had to admit to myself that her cooking was chef grade.

We lingered over the meal for two and a half hours. During that time George invited them to join us in Pebble Beach. They excitedly accepted, noting all the evenings we'd be able to play bridge, and all the days to play golf. Pebble Beach was beginning to feel like a threat.

When we finally rose from the table and helped clean up, I hoped it might be too late for bridge. I inquired if we shouldn't skip the game for one night.

"Of course not!" George shouted with a happy smile. "There's always time for bridge!"

Rose seemed to be warmer to me that evening. I thought perhaps I could win her for a friend. I knew George would be happy if the four of us were fond of each other. But it was an odd thing. She was small, about Trish's height. I could see the two of them, arm in arm, doing the shops together. I was at least three inches taller than either of them, and I couldn't see Rose and me walking arm and arm. I knew it wouldn't work. She may have been shorter, but I felt she looked down on me.

Before we left there were hugs and kisses all around. Tony told me he felt I was the woman for George. He said, "I've never seen him happier or more relaxed."

George had a lot to drink that evening, and remembering the young George, I feared he'd insist on driving. But as we walked to his car, he handed me the keys. I felt both relieved and privileged to be trusted with his beloved Mercedes.

I put my driving glasses on, and as I carefully studied the road, I felt him carefully studying me. "You are very sexy with glasses on," he said. "You should wear them all the time."

By the time we got home George's demon was returning. After several more drinks he began to rant about my leaving him years before. "You turned your back on me. I loved you more than life, and you turned your back on me! You ruined my life! No excuse for it!"

I wanted to say, "You've never given a thought to what I went through all those years. I don't think becoming an internationally famous and fabulously wealthy movie star is such a bad life." But in his condition I didn't dare fight back. He finally went to bed and immediately passed out.

Early in the morning we went down to the kitchen together. George was cheerful and attentive. Not wanting to spoil a minute of our precious time together I didn't mention his ugly mood of the night before. For a while we watched George's favorite cartoons on television. Then we sat at the table talking about the miracle of our finding each other again. We didn't kiss. We held our hands toward each other and lightly touched fingertips across the table. It was the closest moment we'd had in many years.

Later that morning he took me to the second floor and I sat beside him while he played quiet music for me on his electric organ. As he played *The Second Time Around*, he said, "For the past year I've played this music and thought about you."

That moment was perfect. Everything was so perfect that I suddenly had a terrible panic I'd lose it all. I put my arms around him and said, "I'm so afraid something will tear us apart."

He stopped playing and held me tightly for several minutes

"No, babe, never. We'll never be parted again."

He napped most of that day, eating a small meal about four in the afternoon. Then George's driver Al drove us into the city. George and I made plans to meet after his show on Wednesday, and Al delivered him to the theater. Then he let me off at The Plaza. I thought to myself, "What an awful life. Always waiting for your boss. I'd hate to be a driver." Al was a fine, loyal man, and I was sorry to learn later that he and George had split company. I guess I liked him partly because Trish didn't like him, and the feeling was mutual.

Jane Dacey called several times during those ten days, asking if she could do anything to make our stay in New York more fun or comfortable and reminding us of our Christmas Eve dinner date with her. She was a caring person. But at the same time she was another teammate. A few weeks later I discovered she was caring because he'd ordered her to be. She and Trish didn't get along at all.

On Christmas Eve Jane hired a limo to drive us to her country club, about an hour upstate. Again, the driver had to wait for three hours while we were enjoying ourselves. When I saw that his tip amounted to about a hundred dollars, I stopped feeling sorry for drivers.

The stone exterior of the stately brick clubhouse was covered in ivy and trimmed tastefully with blue lights. As the front door was opened, we walked onto a thick red carpet that led us past a twenty-foot Christmas tree decorated with hundreds of tiny red lights, antique toys, and bows.

At one end of the mahogany paneled dining hall, a small platform held a string quartet, softly playing Christmas melodies. I was thankful we'd taken special care to look our best for the occasion. I think even Davey was glad I had forced him into a dress jacket.

As Jane introduced us to her friends, I had the impression our personal history had preceded us. "Oh yes, Jane has told us about you." Whatever they'd been told, we were treated like royalty, and it made for a lovely evening.

The oysters, champagne, fish, duck, delicate pastries, sorbet and dessert wine were served on fine china and set on Irish linen. The company and charming music set me at ease, and I ate more than I had all week.

On the way back to the Plaza we parked and waited for George in the alley behind the theater. As he emerged from the stage door, a large group of fans met him with pens and papers. He looked very tired but smiled and gave each one his autograph.

When we returned to the hotel, George ordered a light supper with champagne and several bottles of vodka. We listened to the noisy celebration in the streets, had kisses all around, and went to bed.

George and I lay in bed holding each other close. He raised himself on one elbow, and said, "You're mine. You'll always be mine." He said the words harshly and as if he were trying to convince me. He lay down, and we held each other again. I didn't put my hand under the pillow, afraid of what I might find.

Tracie and I tried to make Christmas morning traditional. We'd placed our gifts under a giant poinsettia plant. Of course, the famous light beige, cable knit, cardigan golf sweater was there to surprise George. He was surprised when he opened the package. I hadn't had time to finish the project, so inside the box he found one and a half sleeves, half a back, and the two front sides.

"I'm going to finish it soon," I said. "But I wanted to show it to you now and see if it's going to fit."

"Well, well, thank you, dear." His pleasant smile belied the fact that he wasn't thrilled.

He wasn't interested in the gift ritual and didn't reciprocate. He told us he didn't give gifts at gift giving time. That was reminiscent of that first Christmas in our New York dingy apartment, so many years before. But he was giving us ten days in a suite at the Plaza. That was gift enough.

Tracie gave him a plaid cap in return for one he'd put on her head when he'd been with us in Tacoma. He delighted in exchanging hats, and performed the ritual often with those persons close to him. He seemed touched by her gift, putting it on and not removing it. It was the only gift he took with him from the celebration.

While he watched us unwrapping our presents, he rubbed our feet. He was a great masseur of feet. "A foot! I need a foot!" I loved sitting on the sofa next to him with my feet on his knee while he gently rubbed away. If he felt at ease when he entered a room, he'd rub the shoulders of the nearest available person. His touch was endearing.

We ordered a huge Christmas breakfast with champagne, and we watched Davey play funny war games with the new robots we'd bought for him. George was relaxed and funny. He gave everyone a hug before he left late that afternoon and crept out on tiptoe like Bugs Bunny.

Tracie and I went once again to *Present Laughter*. The experience was different from the night we'd arrived. I had been too nervous to enjoy the other actors or George's directing skills. This time as I sat in the audience I picked up on the nuances and truly appreciated his performance. As I watched George on stage, it was impossible to separate the man I loved from the actor. I remembered during one of George's dump calls he had suggested I loved the celebrity and not the man. At the time I had not argued the point, but I knew now there was no separating them. It was a compliment, not an insult, to the man.

After the show, George escorted us again to Gallagher's. Alex joined us for a short time, telling us about his wedding plans. George said he was delighted with the girl who would soon be his daughter-in-law. Alex was as charming and sensitive as he had been in Connecticut, kissing us both before he left. "I'm sure I'll be seeing you again," he said.

The day Tracie, Davey and I were scheduled to leave, we had breakfast with George. During that final hour over our third Bloody Mary, George asked me to go with him to Hong Kong in late February. "I'll be filming a television movie. It might be fun for you, and I want you to be with me."

Again I was filled with happiness, until I looked at Tracie's sad face.

She was a strong lady and wasn't going to be left out. "I'd like to go. I'm not just chopped liver you know."

He hesitated, but only for a second, and then shrugged, "Sure.

Why don't you all come?" He'd said it, and the kids had heard it. Our daughter beamed, and I hoped he wouldn't go back on his promise.

That day Tracie planned to fly to Florida to see her ailing Granddaddy Scott. Tracie asked George what she should tell her grandfather about the past two weeks.

"Tell him everything," he replied.

She seemed surprised "Are you sure you mean everything?"

He nodded. "Everything," he said in a quiet, firm voice.

Then Tracie urged him to call his father since he hadn't spoken to him in months. "Absolutely not!" he bellowed and refused to discuss it further. When George made up his mind, it was final.

We stood at the door before he left the hotel room, and he took his hat off and placed it on my head. One of the hats he gave us had belonged to James Cagney and was his pride and joy. I don't remember which one it was. At the time I didn't care. I wasn't in love with James Cagney.

George and I walked to the door together, and I watched as he walked down the hall and stepped into the elevator. I closed the door and sat on the floor against the wall, hugging his hat and sobbing. Being separated from him tortured me, especially now after we'd renewed our love.

The next morning, packed and ready to leave, I opened my wallet for bills to tip the housekeeping staff. Except for enough to pay a cab in Tacoma I had only a few coins. The tip would average out to ten cents a day for those lovely hard working ladies. I felt like a thief as I skulked out of the suite, hoping not to see any of the housekeeping staff.

We stood by the front desk as Jane paid the hotel bill. It totaled $17,000, and the maids received $1.40! I was too embarrassed to ask Jane to include a tip for them, but I'm sure she did. She took care of every detail. For months, whenever I thought of those poor maids who probably thought I'd stiffed them on purpose, I was embarrassed all over again.

Jane had booked a limo for Davey and me. She paid for it and tipped the driver. Davey loved riding in the limo and spent his time opening and shutting the many windows. The driver had the radio on. The song that was playing was the theme to *Chariots of Fire*. I saw a man, dressed in white pants and shirt, running along the side of the road. I thought, "What a coincidence. He's running while that music is playing."

Limos and *Chariots of Fire* would forever remind me of our two weeks in New York with George.

Twenty Three

≈

George's show closed the Sunday after we left. He called on Monday to say he would be going to Los Angeles on business. "Don't worry, Baby. I'm not going near Trish. I'll check into a hotel. I love you."

I read in *The Inquirer* a week later that Trish had "fled from him" and wouldn't let him in their Los Angeles house. So who was telling the real story? I didn't want to know.

George called twice during the next week, once during a heavy snowstorm in Connecticut. "It's very pretty to look at. I wish you were here." He had nothing to do but read scripts and talk on the phone. So we did, twice that day, for two and a half hours each time. He urged me to make up my mind about going to Hong Kong, and he said he was proud of Tracie for the way she handled things in Florida when his father was so sick. He intended to take her shopping in Hong Kong and buy her something nice.

He asked me if I'd tried acting again. I told him about a few jobs I'd had in Tacoma and my one big brush with fame. "Otto Preminger came to Boston looking at actors for small parts for his next movie. I drove down from New Hampshire and auditioned."

"I'll bet you got the part on the first reading," George said proudly.

"No. But I got a call back and drove all the way back to Boston the next day."

"That's my girl!"

"They sent me in to talk with Mr. Preminger. I was so scared I couldn't talk."

"He can be a scary man."

"He was sitting in the center of a darkened room on a raised platform and told me to stand in the one spotlight," I explained. "I did, and he asked, "Vot have you done?" I answered, "Nothing," but I felt like saying, "I just wet my pants."

George laughed for minutes and finally said, "I gather you didn't get the part."

"You gather right, my love."

"Oh, my darling, I'd forgotten what fun we used to have together. I'm just so grateful we found each other again, my baby. You've no idea how I've missed you."

We hung on the phone, neither one wanting to say goodbye. "We'll never say goodbye again," he said. "We'll say 'so long,' but never goodbye." I was absolutely sure I'd heard THAT line in a movie. But it was a nice line, and he sounded so sincere and sweet I didn't want to tease him.

He called every evening the next three weeks. These calls were loving and chatty.

No more berating me for having left him. Even if he'd obviously had a lot to drink, he stayed gentle and loving. He sent me money for more clothes and "some decent luggage." Several times he asked me if I'd made up my mind about the Hong Kong trip. I told him I needed a little more time.

Besides working at my Head Start job and preparing for the Monterey trip, I was cramming. I checked out "How to Play Golf" books from the library and asked everyone I knew about the game. I wouldn't become a golfer in three easy lessons sitting in a chair, but at least I could learn the language and scoring. When I wasn't studying golf I sat at the folding table with four bridge hands spread in front of me. I didn't tell George about my cramming. If I played bridge better in Monterey, I might tell him then.

In mid-January George's sister, Helen, called looking for Tracie. When she discovered she was talking to Tracie's mother, she became chatty. "Tracie is a lovely girl. You did a wonderful job raising her."

"Thank you."

"Maybe some time you and I can meet."

"I'd like that very much."

She made no reference to my relationship with her brother, but her warm voice made me feel like family.

Tracie called several times from Florida while she was caring for her grandfather. During one of the calls she gave the receiver to him, and I said, "Hello, Mr. Scott."

"Call me Granddaddy," he said. "And why aren't you here with your daughter?"

"If I were," I answered, "I'd like to give you a hug."

"And I'd give you one back," he said in a warm, happy voice.

After I hung up, I suddenly ached to hear my own father saying loving words to me. But he was long dead and had gone to his grave ashamed of me.

The more George urged me to make up my mind about the trip, the more muddled I became about my future. As much as I wanted to go to Hong Kong, it was not an easy decision. I couldn't leave my job for a short absence without a good reason, and I didn't think my boss would consider taking a trip with a married alcoholic to be an acceptable reason. I had no vacation time coming until summer. I would have to quit my job with little notice. That would be equal to burning my bridges. I was close to being vested. If I quit my job, I'd lose my retirement fund. Was George sincere in his promises? Did he plan to finally divorce Trish? Where did I stand? What was I doing?

Sleep became impossible one night, so the practical side of me took over, and I sat up and made pro and con lists. The con list far outnumbered the pro list, so I threw it away. I needed to confide in someone.

My supervisor at work was a levelheaded woman who had always been fair. I knew I could trust Eleanor. One rainy lunch hour as we sat in my car, I gathered up my courage and told her about my past and present with George. Up to then I had not shared my story with anyone in Tacoma except family. I told her about the decisions I had to make and asked her advice.

"You can't go on keeping one foot in one life and the one foot in the other," she said. "It will wear on you, and you'll trip and fall."

The next day I met with our county director, Stanton Rogers. I told him I was quitting my job. "Have you found other work?" he asked.

"No. I'm not going to another job."

"Is there anything we can do or say to change your mind? "

"There isn't. I've loved working for Head Start."

"You know you only have three months to go until you are vested. You'll lose all that."

"I know."

"Please reconsider."

"Thank you, but I'm quitting for personal reasons."

There I was again. Turning down a sure thing for an iffy future with George. Once again this lovesick, pitiful person was throwing security away to run off with a married man. The same alcoholic actor. I wrote my official letter of resignation, collected my final paycheck, shook my boss's hand, hugged Eleanor, and set myself adrift.

When George called me that evening he asked me again, this time he was gruff and impatient. "Are you or aren't you going to Hong Kong? Make up your mind now or forget it."

"Yes."

"That's my baby."

Hong Kong would soon be a wonderful reality but now it was time for the reality of Pebble Beach. Jane sent my plane ticket, I bought some sporty clothes, and I began to pack for my departure in three days. George had said he'd call with final arrangements, but I hadn't heard from him in six days. Not even a dump call, which wasn't like him at all.

When I phoned Jane, she reported he was in LA but didn't have a number, which sounded odd to me. Jane always knew how to find George. I had decided to telephone George's friend Tony, when Tony called me. "Have you heard from George?" he asked. "We haven't heard a word in three weeks. We're all packed and ready to go, but now we're not quite sure what we should do. Are you sure Pebble Beach is still on?"

Not knowing anything more than he did, I assured him everything was set and that I intended to go ahead with my plans. I'd let him know when I heard from George. But I wasn't at all sure of anything. He was in LA. Maybe he was on a week long drunk. Maybe with Trish. Divorce? Reconciliation? Or maybe he was in trouble somewhere. Well, I couldn't exactly send out an all points bulletin for George C. Scott. Who would believe me? They'd just think this poor, single, lonely mother in Tacoma was stalking a movie star.

That evening I received a collect call from George. I was relieved but surprised, since he always insisted on paying for everything. "I'm sorry I had to call you collect, babe, but I had no other way of getting you."

"Don't worry about that. Just tell me where you are."

"I drove up the coast from LA. It's raining like shit. Some of the roads are washed out. I'm in a motel."

"Where?"

"I don't know where the Christ it is!"

"Are we still meeting in Pebble Beach?"

"Of course, dear. Don't worry. Just call Tony and Rose and tell them everything is fine and I'll meet their plane when they get in."

I hung up, called Tony and Rose, and gave them the news. "We'll see you soon. We'll bring the cards."

I could have done without the card comment, but I looked forward to seeing them.

Two days later, wearing my new navy blue pantsuit, and my hair freshly streaked, I flew to San Francisco, and then took a small commuter flight to Monterey. The evening city lights glittered as we flew in low over the field and small terminal. Those wonderful butterflies filled my stomach when I saw George standing on the back deck watching my plane set down.

I climbed the stairs to the deck, and we walked toward each other as if we were in a slow motion film. It reminded me of the days when I would meet him in his car in Missouri. The anticipation of holding him was so great it hurt. But about two feet away from me, he stopped. He did not hold his arms out in greeting, nor did he kiss me. "Hello, dear," he said. "I'm so glad to see you." The cool greeting confused me.

I soon discovered why he'd been reluctant to show his affection in public. Autograph seekers stopped him constantly. Fans continually interrupted our meals and walks to speak to him wherever he went. If I'd thought he'd be mine alone those two weeks, I was mistaken.

He took my carry on bag and led me to the inside baggage area. As he gathered my bags, he said, "Nice luggage."

"Thank you. You paid for it," I smiled up at him.

He chuckled. "Well, I've got good taste."

We drove to his rented house, a gorgeous, low spreading home a block or two away from the golf course. He showed me around, ending our tour in the master bedroom. I was about to bring my bags into the room when he stopped me. "We're not sleeping in here, dear."

"Why?" Again, no master suite for Karen.

"I want Rose and Tony to have the best room."

"Oh, of course. I agree."

"I'm glad you do. They're my best friends."

I wondered what number I was on his list of important people. So ... where are we sleeping?"

"We'll be staying in the guest house. Do you mind?"

"Of course, I don't mind." I'd have been happy in a small tent in the back yard if I were with him.

We picked up my luggage and walked to the far corner of the back yard. The guesthouse was dark inside. The exterior looked more like a large storage shed. George went to the front door and tried to open it. He tried all seven keys on the ring he'd taken from the hook in the house. He tried jiggling the handle, then pushing with his shoulder. It wouldn't budge, no matter how many times he pushed or how many foul words he used. Finally he said, "I wonder if the window is open."

The window opened easily to about two feet. "Okay, Baby, you climb in there and go around and open the door."

"ME?"

"Well, I wouldn't fit. Here, I'll give you a hand up."

"George, I've never been athletic, and anything could be in there. Don't you care if I fall over something?"

"Be brave, Baby. Here, put your foot on my hand."

There was no way out. I knew he'd go on insisting. "Okay. But I really hate this." I put my foot in his hand, and he immediately pushed up. I wasn't ready, and nearly sailed off his hand. "Hold still, George."

"I'm trying. You're heavier than you used to be."

"I am not! Besides, how can you remember how heavy I was twenty-five years ago?"

"You were light as a kitten the night I boosted you over the Stephen's college fence."

"I haven't gained an ounce since then."

"Just get inside the window."

"Okay. Now let me get a hold on the window sill." I grabbed the sill and pulled half my body inside the window. "I need another push. I'm halfway in. I haven't got any leverage and don't see anything to grab on to. In fact, I don't see anything. It's dark in here. I don't want to go any further."

"You can't stop now. Here, I'll give you another shove."

"OH, NO, Please NO!"

He shoved. I glided right in and landed on something soft. My eyes adjusted, and I found the something soft was a mattress. I had slid into the bedroom. "Okay. I'm in." I turned on the bedside lamp and walked cautiously to the front door. "I'm at the front door," I yelled.

"Well, open it," he bellowed.

"What'll you give me?"

"I'll go back to the house."

"NO. I'm opening the door."

The guesthouse interior was a cozy, wood-paneled, carpeted room with a double bed, a dresser, closet, two side tables, and a bathroom. A telephone sat on one side table. I picked up the phone and listened for a dial tone. "I promised Tracie I'd call when I arrived. I'd better do that."

"She can wait until we've got some food and drink in this place."

In the main house we found a stocked refrigerator and bar. We filled a tray with crackers, cheese, vegetable dip, cookies, candy, bottles of wine, liquor and beer, and returned to the cottage. "Now I really have to call Tracie."

"Go ahead, my love. But that better be the last call home. This trip was for us, remember?" He filled both our glasses while I dialed.

"Hello, Tracie?"

"Hello, Mom. How's everything?"

"Everything is wonderful. I'm sitting here beside your father, and were having our cocktail hour."

"It's eleven o'clock, kinda late for a cocktail hour isn't it?'

"I just got in about an hour ago. How's Davey?"

"Fine. How's Daddy?"

"He's fine."

"Can I speak to him?"

I looked at George and pointed to the phone. He walked to the other side of the room shaking his head.

"Daddy's in the bathroom. I'll get him."

George grabbed the phone. "Hi, dear. How's everything? Good. And it's good to talk to you, too. I have to go now. You, too." He hung up, gritted his teeth, and glared at me. "Don't ever do that again!"

"I'm sorry, she just wanted to talk to you."

We talked all night. He wanted to know more about my life "between" and asked again if I was over Dave. Was I sure I wanted an old man in my life? Why had I left him?

I was getting irritated at being blamed for our breakup so many years before and reminded him I had gone through years of pain.

"It's hard to believe you'd marry a man you didn't love," he said. "You have such great capacity for love."

We decided to stop blaming each other for the past and only think about our future. "We love we!" he said. "We love we."

While I cleaned up the cottage bathroom the next morning, I saw a bottle of George's prescription pills. Since we were together now, I thought I should know about his health, so I asked him about them at breakfast.

"None of your business. And stay out of my personal things."

"I was just ..."

"Leave my things alone!"

After breakfast George showed me a huge box that had been waiting for him at the house when he arrived the day before. "Go ahead and open it if you want to, Baby. It's just a box of advertisements they give to everybody who plays in the Pro/Am.

I opened the box and took inventory. I found a pair of golf shoes, a pullover red cashmere sweater, a lightweight golf jacket, several bottles of liquor, drinking glasses, two golf shirts, ash trays, cartons of cigarettes and boxes of candy. The saying "He who has, gets" was true.

That day George golfed, and I drove his cart. At first I was nervous about driving it. After all, it was the Monterey Golf Course, he was George C. Scott, and people would be watching. But as always, George's confidence in me chased the fears away, and I found it easy and fun. I resolved to pay no attention to bystanders, though I couldn't help noticing people watch us when he'd step back into the cart and kiss me.

"Does that bother you, that people are watching us?" I asked.

"No, my darling. I'm making a statement." He held my face in his hands. "After all these years, you're still my girl ... still my girl." And he kissed me again. "Would my lady care to join me for an evening out?" He was his old charming self.

"I'd be more than honored, sir."

I wished for the hundredth time I had been more careful with my laundry in Greenwich. This evening called for that wonderful little black dress. The one my teddy bear was now wearing, as he sat on my bed in Tacoma. Lucky teddy bear.

George and I had a quiet dinner that evening at a Mexican restaurant, where George could hide from the crowds in the back corner. Even so, a few of his fans found him. He was relaxed and jovial, actually eating his food. He proudly introduced me to everyone who came to the table, making me feel like his superstar.

I told him more about my life in the past few years. He was grateful to Phillip for raising Tracie, but on the subject of my second marriage he again expressed his resentment. He knew that Dave was ten years younger than I. "You like 'em young, don't you, Baby?" Denying would do no good. I changed the subject.

The next day we drove to the airport and picked up Rose and Tony. They were pleased when we showed them the huge master bedroom with French doors opening out on to their own private brick patio. I didn't blame them.

"Why didn't you two take this room?" Rose asked.

"We're very happy in the guest cottage." I used my most cheerful voice to convince both her *and* me.

They changed to casual clothes, and we headed for the golf course. As they played, I proudly drove George's cart and took photos of them. But golf was another activity I didn't share with them. I began to wonder if I'd ever fit into his lifestyle.

For the next three days it rained heavily, so we stayed indoors at the bridge table. In the evenings we cooked dinner together, following Rose's instructions. George cooked some meals himself. One evening he and Tony cooked a pork roast. They trusted me to cut tomatoes for the salad, eventually earning a promotion to preparing the entire salad.

Then it was back to the bridge table. For hours. They were gentle and encouraging, but I wasn't any better than I'd been in Connecticut. If anything, I'd gotten worse under my self-imposed pressure.

George seemed to feel it was his duty to keep us all amused and happy. He slept little at night and rose tired in the morning. But when I asked him how he felt, he answered with a smile. "I've never felt better in my life." A phrase he always used that meant he was totally exhausted.

His days were almost business as usual. Scripts arrived every day, and decisions had to be made. He gave me the script for the sequel to *Patton* to read, and I found someone had already made notes on it. I asked him about it.

"Oh, yes, that was Trish's copy," he replied casually.

I was tempted to make notes on top of hers, but I restrained myself. If I planned to be a helpmate to George, I had to get used to things like that.

The story was sweet and sensitive, showing the inner man, with flashbacks of the general's early life and his relationship with his wife. It ended with the general's death.

George had great respect and reverence for General Patton. He wanted the film to be perfect. "I won't cut corners. But Christ, I don't know how I'm going to find the money."

He asked for my judgment of the script. "It's lovely," I told him. "But beyond that I can't give an opinion. I'm not in the film business and don't know enough about it. I just want to be your wife, take care of you and not interfere with your career."

He attempted a slight smile at my words, but suddenly he turned angry and roared, "Don't you know I want you to give an opinion? Just you. No one else. Just you!"

After the rains stopped we spent the next two days on the golf course. George was preparing for the tournament and took practice very seriously. But each time he slid back into the cart beside me, he'd say lovingly, "I've missed you. Where have you been?"

Before we went to our cottage for the evening, George and I often took a moonlight walk. We'd kiss and laugh and dance on the grass, feeling young again. One evening he stopped in the middle of our silliness and, in a very serious, intense voice, said, "You're still my girl. After all these years, still my girl. This time I'll never let you go."

"Are you sure?"

He held my hair back from my forehead. "I've made up my mind. I won't change it." When he kissed me it was hard, as though to seal his promise. I began to feel our future together was no longer just a dream.

At the end of the first week we gave a dinner party. We all helped Chef Rose. George's task was to trim the ends off the asparagus. He sat on a high stool, seeming to concentrate. He knew he had a captive audience and made each piece a comic set.

I was elevated to removing centers from mushrooms and spooning in one of Rose's special fillings. I got to make the salad and the garlic bread all by myself.

The guests were invited for six-thirty. At six-twenty five George announced, "I told everyone to wear jeans. I forgot to tell you, I'm sorry, dear."

I looked down at my best black skirt and white silk blouse, trimmed in lace. I had been so sure my outfit would be perfect for the evening, and now I hated the way I looked. I didn't play golf. I was hopeless at bridge. Now I was overdressed at my own party. I wanted to choke George, but there wasn't time. People were arriving.

The first to arrive were George's good friends and publicists, Jim and Pat Mahoney. I always trusted men who had white beards, and Jim had one. Pat, short, cute and genuine, came into the kitchen as George and I were making drinks. George put his arm around me. "Pat, this is the woman I have always loved."

She hugged me. "Our dear Karen, welcome." I had a friend! I stayed close to her for the rest of the evening.

We settled down to drinks and *hors d'oeuvres*. About an hour into the party Jack and Felicia Lemmon arrived. It was then I committed my second *faux pas*. Trying to be chatty with Felicia, the best I could think to say was, "Do you have any children?" She smiled a gracious smile, but obviously thought me a jerk and mumbled something about, "The bathroom," and got up and left. Then I stood up too quickly and backed into one of the tables, nearly knocking the tray of *hors d'oeuvres* to the floor.

Jack Lemmon was much smaller than I thought he'd be. In fact, he looked shriveled. He sat on the floor in front of Felicia and talked across the room to George. Jack had already had his share to drink before they arrived and was in a soulful, almost weepy, mood, pointing several times to George and referring to him as, "the king."

George returned the compliment. Pointing to Jack, he'd insist, "Oh, no. There sits the king!" Which prompted a response in kind from Jack. And so it went with the two superstars. Jack finally admitted to being worried that he might not work in films again. George assured him he would. But Jack worked on gathering more sympathy until the subject changed to golf.

I knew that Phillip had been one of Jack's friends when they were in school in New York. So I sat down beside him and asked if he remembered the family. "Do you remember putting their piano on the back of an open truck and playing and singing while you were driven up Broadway?" He looked at me with a blank stare and turned away. Apparently, he was either embarrassed by the memory, too drunk to comprehend it, or just being rude. Felicia struck me as a sweet person, though she was so quiet that evening I wondered if she ever said anything. I excused myself and headed for the kitchen to see if any more mushrooms needed stuffing.

One activity this group of celebrities loved was having their pictures taken. You'd think movie stars would get enough of that, but so long as there was film in the camera they'd pose. Everyone brightened up at the prospect of having their pictures taken. Jack and Felicia took a wooden fork decoration from the wall to do an impression of a Grant Wood masterpiece. Then everybody took pictures of everyone else.

Dinnertime was fun and noisy. Rose got a load of compliments on her cooking. I was envious as hell, knowing full well I wasn't half as talented as Rose in the kitchen.

My chair was halfway down the table from George. A few minutes after we had begun to eat he asked me to bring my chair and sit close to him. "I don't want you that far away. I need you here beside me."

During dessert Jack and I argued about the minimum wage. As a Head Start employee I felt I had the experience to present a case for higher wages, so I made a few rude comments about "the wealthy not knowing or caring." We argued until George told me to back off. We sat at the table for a few more drinks until conversation waned and the guests decided it was time for them to leave.

I had learned from Tracie there is one drink you NEVER give George after he's had a few. But this time, after he was well on his way to drunkenness, he poured himself a glass of Remy Martin. When Rose and Tony saw George bring out the bottle, they didn't stay to watch. They'd seen George waste himself many times and had not been entertained. They went to bed.

"You'll stay with me, won't you, Baby?"

He looked lonely, and I thought he needed me. "For a little while. But I'm tired. It's been a long day."

He stayed at the table, drinking and mumbling about the evening and how he liked Jack. Then, after another drink or two, he began mumbling obscenities at me. I got up to leave, but he grabbed my wrist and pulled me back down. "Shit down, mother-fucker. Aren't you gonna stay and keep me company?"

His fierce gaze bore into me. He was beginning to frighten me. "I'm tired. I really want to go to bed."

I watched as his face became transformed into the same ugly

mask I'd seen twenty-five years earlier when he'd tried to kill us. His eyes bulged, his skin went taut, and he erupted in rage. He appeared and sounded as if he were out of his mind. But at the same time he looked lost and sad like a beaten animal. He spouted a stream of the foulest language I'd ever heard.

Terrified, I told him again I was going to bed. He tried to grab me, but his movements were sluggish and slow. I ran out of the room. But I knew if I were alone in the guesthouse I'd be vulnerable, so I crept into one of the bedrooms in the main house.

He continued to sit at the table for about five or ten minutes. Then I heard his footsteps, as he went through the house, turning off lights, talking to himself, mumbling, raging, shouting, "Mother fucking bitch. Where are you?"

I had never been so frightened. I felt like I'd been transported into the Jack Nicholson movie *The Shining.* I kept reminding myself this was not George, but his demon. I had nothing to protect myself with, and if the demon found me, he'd probably try to kill me. He was completely drunk and crazy. I wasn't fully sober myself, but my mind was sharper and I could move more quickly.

"Shlut!"

I gathered he was addressing me. I crawled into the closet, closed the door, and sat in the corner, hugging my legs and trying to make myself as small as possible. He wandered from room to room, roaring obscenities. But he obviously was aware enough not to go near Rose and Tony's bedroom at the end of the hall. They knew better than to come out, and I was too frightened to care if they heard him.

I heard the door to the bedroom flung open. "Pissh on you, shlut. Shlut who likes young men. Where the fucking shit are you? I'll fineja."

He left the room. I heard him walking from room to room, banging into walls, slamming doors, and bellowing. Then suddenly the house was quiet. I surmised he'd passed out on one of the beds. But I didn't trust he wouldn't find me if I left my hiding place. I fell asleep curled up in the closet.

The next morning I ran to the guesthouse and crept in, hoping George wasn't there. He was, but he had passed out and seemed to be sleeping quietly. I knew the demon had gone, and I was safe again. I showered and tried to make my face up so I didn't look quite so tired. I walked to the house and found Rose and Tony in the kitchen.

"Good morning, gang." I tried to sound rested and cheerful. "How did everyone sleep?"

Rose stood at the juice squeezer. "Very well, thanks."

"How about you Tony?"

"I had a good sleep." Tony put his paper down. "You?"

"No. George got terribly drunk and chased me all over the house. It was awful."

"That's why we went to bed when we did. We knew what was coming," Rose said.

She handed me a glass of juice and I sat down at the table with Tony. "He really scared me."

Tony chuckled. "He's a great guy and my best friend. But I sure wouldn't want to be a woman in love with him."

Moments later George walked into the kitchen. He was in a lighthearted mood, doing a little dance, and singing, "Love's so lovely, the second time around."

I countered with, "Love's so shitty with both feet on the ground."

He just grinned at me and took the orange juice Rose offered him. I knew he'd either forgotten about his drunken tirade, or wanted to forget it by pretending it never happened. Either way, I knew Mr. Hyde had left, and there was nothing more to fear from Dr. Jekyll this morning. He sat down, and we all enjoyed a big breakfast.

Rose and Tony decided they'd, "take a ride for the day." George went into the living room to take a nap. When I followed him a half-hour later I found him curled up, with no cover, shivering like a small child. I asked him to come to the cottage to nap with me. I missed him and wanted to be near him.

"No," he said. "You're mad at me. You really don't want to be near me."

I stroked his forehead and kissed his cheek. "Of course I do. Please come." I offered my hand, and he finally took it.

After a long nap in the cottage, we both felt better and hungry again. We heated canned soup in the kitchen, bringing back happy memories of our starving days in New York, and we laughed at how long ago that was. "We may have been starving, but we were together," he said.

When we'd finished our soup, I asked him if he was aware of how he'd behaved the night before.

"What do you mean, *behaved*?"

"It happens when you've had a lot to drink. You become another person, a very scary one. You did the same thing when we lived together in New York."

He reached across the table for my hand. "Don't you know I'd never hurt you? You of all people? I love you. I promise you, Baby. I promise you."

I don't believe George had any idea of the extent of his madness when his demons emerged. I don't think he'd have been able to live with himself if he'd known.

Tracie called every evening to ask how things were going and to find out when I'd be home. George spoke to her only once, briefly, said a sweet fatherly goodbye, then slammed the phone down. "Why can't that grown up woman leave us alone?" I felt torn and guilty. I wanted to be with George, but she loved him, too. I loved her, and she was at home caring for her brother, which I should have been doing. I didn't argue the point. I was afraid of setting him off again.

The first morning of the tournament George had an early tee time, so we didn't stay up as late as usual the night before. He still had a fitful sleep and awoke irritable and tired. Tony, Rose and I drove with him to the clubhouse and waited while he checked in. For a movie buff like me, standing close to all those famous people was heaven. I had lots of film in my camera and in my pockets, so I happily clicked away, taking pictures of Clint Eastwood, Ephraim Zimbalist, Jr., Charlie Pride, Johnny Mathis and Pat Boone.

As George played, I followed on the upper trail. He'd look up, grin and give me thumbs up. Watching him do anything always thrilled me, and I took it for granted he did it well.

Twice that day I was asked if I was Mrs. Scott. Once I almost lied, and the second time I mumbled, "No, I'm his significant other." Then I realized I was calling myself his mistress. I decided next time to merely say, "No."

The day was hot, and George began to sit on his portable chair every chance he got. Rose, Tony and I were able to buy cold drinks set up along the way, but there was no water or food for the players. So by the time he reached the eighteenth hole he was dragging.

As the players emerged from the gate, their fans swarmed around them. When George came out the large crowd overwhelmed him. I couldn't find him. Finally, I saw him hold out his hand to me as he yelled, "Get me out of here, fast."

I had to pull with my full strength to get him out of the crush of fans. People were giving me harsh looks as if I had no right to interrupt their opportunity to be near a star. We were close to escaping when the media caught up to him and asked for an interview. The five or ten minutes it took seemed to be the last straw for George. When they finally let him go, he was ashen and shaking. "Just get me to the fucking car," he said. They loaded us onto a bus and headed for the parking lot. When the bus stopped and we got off, we discovered we were at the wrong parking lot. While we waited for his entourage to get the car, we sat George on his portable seat. He was dehydrated, and he told me he thought he might pass out.

When we got back to the house he drank several beers and took a nap. We were talking about calling a doctor when George marched into the kitchen and announced, "I've never felt better in my life. Now, how about a game of bridge?"

The cards were dealt, and we played for two hours, George using up his energies trying to be the great host. But when we finally crawled into bed, he admitted he was exhausted and afraid he'd oversleep and be late for his tee time the next morning. So I stayed awake and watched over him. He had a habit of leaving the radio on all night to listen to soft music. That night the station played 50s music. When I heard *Stranger In Paradise*, I began to cry. He turned in his sleep and held me, murmuring, "Baby, Baby, I love you, forever and beyond."

The morning I left, George opened his luggage and handed me several real estate books advertising premier properties for sale in Connecticut, Delaware, New Jersey and upstate New York. "Choose the one you want, Baby. Just not too far from New York," he said.

This came as an exciting shock. He hadn't mentioned anything about buying a house for us. He'd gone from calling me a slut one night to talk of buying a house for us two days later. The man was full of surprises.

I dreaded leaving. I decided to wait until George left for the tournament and busied myself with logistics, making sure his caddy knew George needed cigarettes and plenty of liquids. Before he left, he reached to hug me, and I pushed him away.

There was a flash of anger and surprise in his eyes. "Why?"

"I'll cry if you hug me. I don't want to cry now. I want to send you off to your tournament relaxed and happy."

He understood. "Oh, my poor Baby." He got into his car and drove away.

Tony and Rose drove me to San Francisco, bought me lunch, and left me at the airport. I had grown fond of them, and it was hard to say goodbye. But I was sure we'd meet again soon and see each other often.

Twenty Four

≈

The first two weeks of February, the phone calls were daily, long, and loving. Each time he'd say, "Darling I can't wait to see you. We'll never be parted again." During one call I asked him if he'd sent the chess set he'd promised Davey. "Oh, I'll look into that," he said.

Jane called several times to firm up plans for the Hong Kong trip. George and Tracie would fly over together with some of the crew in mid-February. Davey and I would follow a week later. A week after we arrived, Tracie and Davey would fly back, and I'd stay on for another week with George.

Tracie's dreams were coming true, a week alone with her father, watching him film. I was excited for her. She and I had formed a warm relationship that I felt sure would last.

Davey's teacher gave him only one assignment: to keep a daily journal of his trip. Two weeks in Hong Kong with a famous movie star, and no homework but writing in a diary. It was heaven for a nine-year-old kid. Everything was perfect. The future looked wonderful in every way.

Two nights before we left, Tracie called with the name of George's doctor and the prescription number for his blood pressure pills. He needed a renewal. Would I have it filled? It was a sudden and huge request, since his doctor was in New York and I had no proof of anything. Luckily, I had a friend whose husband was a physician, and though it wasn't exactly ethical, if not actually illegal, he wrote out a new prescription, and I had it filled. After all, it was for George C. Scott.

Before our plane took off, Davey and I sat at Sea-Tac Airport with my best friends and cousins, Dick and Jackie. They had driven up to see me off, and, as always, to offer their loving support. We discussed Hong Kong and the logistics of the trip. They asked me if George still drank as much.

I had to be honest. "Yes."

"Which is a lot," Jackie said.

"Yes."

"Do you really know what you're doing, getting mixed up with an alcoholic?" Dick asked.

"Yes," I said in a firm voice. "This time I do. I love him, and I trust him."

My flight number was called, and they walked us to the gate. Jackie kissed me. "Take care of yourself."

"I really hope you know what you're doing," Dick said.

"I do." I headed to my gate.

The fifteen-hour flight had one stop in Japan before Hong Kong. Flying in first class was so luxurious I could have stayed on the plane another fifteen hours if I hadn't been on my way to see my love. Davey slept and played with his electronic games. I read and thought about our future as a family. George seemed fond of Davey. He surely had been good to him, including him in our trips and celebrations. George and Tracie had formed a new bond. Tracie and I were close and loving. George and I loved each other. At long last we were a family.

The Hong Kong airport was steamy, hot, and jammed with people. After customs, we saw Tracie and George waving to us. My heart stopped. It always did when he grinned at me. This time he was not reluctant to hug me in public. A big, warm, bear hug. I would have flown another hundred hours for a hug like that from the man I loved.

We filled the cab with luggage, and Davey climbed in to sit between George and me. George picked him up, sat him on his other side, put his arm around me, and pulled me to him. Certain that he was being romantic, I snuggled close, until I heard him whisper hoarsely, "What in hell have you done with your hair?"

At first I thought he meant it looked messy, so I began to

search for my comb. But he made himself clear when he added, "I hate the color."

"Oh. I didn't want the roots to show while I was here, so I thought I'd go brown instead of blond."

"Well, change it back!"

"Yes. Okay."

George had booked four rooms at the Peninsula Hotel. He had a suite where we ate our meals and gathered in the evenings. Tracie's, Davey's, and my rooms were halfway down the hall from his. Davey loved having a room of his own, and I was next door, close enough to keep my eyes and ears on him.

As we entered the lobby, I heard two or three people greet George with, "Hi, General!" It was the first time I thought about his being famous outside of the United States.

After unpacking, Davey and I met Tracie and George in the living room of his elegant suite. The front wall, almost entirely windows, had a view of the thousands of lights of Hong Kong and the bay beyond. The room was equipped with several silk-upholstered chairs and two sofas, a teak dining table, desk, and a bar filled with smoked salmon, pates of all kinds, cakes and candies, and a bar, loaded with assorted wines and liquors. Behind the bar a five-foot, gold-framed mirror hung on the wall. I stood in the middle of the grandeur, looking at George, Tracie, and Davey, and thought, this is the most glorious moment of my life. Tracie's excitement spilled into chatter about her new friends on the movie crew, and George seemed happy for her. He also seemed pleased that the movie was going well.

As we sat on the sofa they told me about the Big Surprise. The next morning, as George's treat, we were scheduled to board a three-masted schooner, the *Osprey*, and sail for two days around Hong Kong Bay. As we stood together at the bar refreshing our drinks, Tracie whispered, "Daddy has been so excited for your arrival. He scheduled the trip for tomorrow, so you could come."

George and I sat together. As he rubbed my feet, we all chattered for an hour about the exciting day ahead. I could see George getting sleepy, and I was exhausted as well. We left him and went to our rooms. The phone rang as soon as I entered my room.

"Are you alone?" George asked.

"Yes."

"Then get yourself back up here as soon as you can." He hung up.

I grabbed the key to the room, my cosmetic case, and opened my door. I was about to step into the hall when I saw three men in hotel uniforms, standing with their backs against the wall across from George's room. Thinking it would look improper for me to be seen returning to George's suite, I waited five minutes and peeked out again. They were still there. Lined up, as if guarding his room.

I finally decided they intended to stay, so I put my shoulders back and walked casually up the hall, nodding to each one as I passed, and knocked on George's door. He opened it, pulled me in, and grabbed me in a hug. "What kept you?"

"There are three men in the hall across from your room. I didn't want them to see me coming back."

He laughed, took my hand, and led me into his bedroom. "You'll have to get used to them. They're always there in case someone rings in the middle of the night." He sat down on the bed and pulled me down beside him. "But it's just us now, and I can't tell you how happy I am to see you."

"I've missed you somethin' just awful, my lord," I said.

"And I you, my lady. We must not let it happen again."

"But wait, my lord. I've a gift for you from the United States." I opened my cosmetic case and pulled out his blood pressure pills. He looked at the bottle for a moment. "Thank you, dear. I'll take one tomorrow." He enclosed me in his arms. "Tonight is for us."

In the morning, while room service set up breakfast and we waited for Tracie and Davey to join us, I stood with my coffee and watched the sampans and junks in the bay and the thousands of people and cars in the streets. I was anxious to get down there, to join them and investigate the city. But then I felt George's arms around my waist and his kiss on the back of my neck, and I didn't want the moment to end.

There was a knock at the door, and Tracie, Davey and room service all arrived at once. The cart was loaded with so much food

I didn't know how the man maneuvered it. George was always generous when he ordered. The food was enough to feed a dozen people. Most of it went back to the kitchen.

After our hearty breakfast together, George left for the set. The rest of us would board the ship, sail around Hong Kong Harbor, and pick up George and Dell, George's makeup man, when they finished their day of filming to continue our cruise.

When Tracie, Davey and I boarded, we were met by Robert Halmi, the producer of *China Rose*, the film George was doing. On board as well were Halmi's wife, Esther, and Jane Dacey.

I had become quite fond of Jane. George had warned me with kind of an "or else" statement that none of his wives got along with her, and I'd better like her. I told him he could stop worrying, that I found her easy to like, and I thought she genuinely liked me.

The 175-foot boat was a glorious sight, with her tall masts and shiny wooden decks. Boarding offered us an exciting moment. As the crew brought our luggage on, we followed them down to the cabins. George and I were to sleep in the large cabin at one end of the ship, and the others would take the smaller sleeping quarters. The spacious cabin, with its teakwood bunks and thick carpet, looked like something out of a twenties movie. Romantic and gorgeous, the room made me feel like an exotic movie queen one minute and a bubbly sixteen-year-old the next.

I found Tracie, Davey, and the rest of the gang, including Jane and Lee, her assistant, on the deck where Robert Halmi, who had been in Hong Kong several times, pointed out the sights. He referred to it as Never, Never Land. He directed our attention to the sampans and junks and told us about the boat people of Aberdeen, who live their entire lives on their boats.

The weather was chilly with spitting rain, but we stayed on deck the entire afternoon, until we circled back to pick up George and Dell to anchor for the night. When George came aboard he grabbed me and held me as though we hadn't seen each other for weeks. He opened his jacket and said, "Come here next to me. Let me zip you in and keep you here forever. I don't want you more than an inch away from me."

As soon as they were on board, the liquor flowed, *hors d'oeuvres* were spread, and the crew of eight waited on us and prepared our dinner. They let Davey hang around with them during the day and have dinner with them that night in the crew's galley. They made him feel important and kept him busy so he didn't have to sit in the corner and watch the adults drink. Grateful that they were so sensitive to Davey, I spoke to one young crewmen, thanking him. That was a gesture I'd pay for later.

George insisted I sit with our chairs touching. He watched my every move. By dinnertime he was weaving when he walked and slurring his words. He ate little. Shortly after dinner he asked for cognac. The crew, eager to please and unaware of the consequences, brought him a glass. George pointed to spot in front of him on the table. "Just put the bottle here."

Unfortunately, they obeyed.

The conversation turned to Esther Halmi's hardships growing up in Hungary, and how her family had suffered. A lovely woman, she seemed self-conscious about her lack of fluency in English. So we all made an effort to help her feel more comfortable.

Except George. He suddenly turned to her and shouted, "You bitch. I don't give a fuck where the hell you came from, and I don't give a shit about your family."

There was a moment of shocked silence. She stared at him in disbelief. It was apparent she had understood every word. She sat frozen, either too stunned to respond, or aware no one talked back to the king, no matter how loutish and disgusting he acted. Her husband needed George to finish the film. It wouldn't do to have the producer's wife tangle with the star, so she said nothing. Someone changed the subject to the plans for the next day. George calmed down, too drunk to realize how brutal his outburst had been.

Soon after his explosion, the group began to leave the table for their cabins, most of us aware that if George had no drinking companion he would eventually find his way to bed, too. Robert and George stayed at the table discussing George's plans for *Patton II*. George did most of the talking, declaring over and over again he'd spare nothing for the film. Robert left for bed, and I was about to suggest to George that we go to our cabin or he would be sitting alone, when Davey came out.

He'd been awakened by the loud voices. Now George had

someone new to attack. "You spoiled little fucker. You have no manners. Little mommy's boy. Little cock sucking mamma's boy." Davey, his eyes huge with surprise and fear, sat pushing his back up against his chair as though he might find an escape hatch. Sleepy and confused, he had walked right into a screaming maniac!

At that moment I hated George. I was ashamed of myself for putting my son in this terrible situation and not being able to stop it. I stood up, gave George a stern look and announced, "I'm taking my son to his cabin."

George opened his mouth to say something but closed it and glared at me.

My heart broke for Davey. There was no way to erase or explain what had just happened. I didn't understand it myself. In that brief moment I hated George. No matter what he'd said or done in the past twenty-five years, I had never felt that hatred.

When I returned from settling Davey, George let me have it. "You dirty, fucking, bitch. You can't stop flirting can you? Did you stop and say hello to the redhead? Can't stay away from the young men." He continued his usual tirade, including Davey's father several times.

"George, you can sit alone and scream all night. I don't care. But I'm not going to listen to any more of your crap. I'm going to bed." I headed toward the galley door when Tracie stepped in. "Take care of your dear father," I said. "Just be careful. He's in a pissy mood and very drunk."

Within a few minutes Tracie delivered him to our cabin and left. He lay down on the floor next to our bunk and continued mumbling about the young redheaded crewmen. "You just can't stay away from young men." As he stared at me I saw Mr. Hyde emerging, with his bulging eyes. He got up and started toward me but fell into another bunk and passed out.

I stayed in the cabin, watching him for the few hours remaining of the night. I'd been through this often enough to know the man who woke up would be my George again, and not Mr. Hyde.

When he awoke early the next morning, I told him his other self had been there. He seemed surprised. "Oh, Baby, you know I'd never hurt you. You, of all people. I'm so sorry. You've no idea how sorry I am. Here, let me hold you." We slept for an hour or so, holding each other. When we woke up again he was gentle and contrite.

When we went up for breakfast our friends were seated at the table. Everyone seemed happy and chatty. If George's tirade the evening before had not been forgotten, at least no one mentioned it. It had been a long night, and my empty stomach was growling. We sat down, and unfortunately the young redheaded man appeared again as our server. The platters of scrambled eggs, sausage, muffins and fruit looked wonderful, and tasted better than any breakfast I could remember. So when our waiter poured my second cup of coffee I was rather expansive with my thank you. George pulled away, and in his loudest stage voice, said, "You just can't stop can you? You have to flirt with every young man you see." There was another uncomfortable short silence, followed by everyone chattering at once. I might have been embarrassed except I was used to his behavior.

After breakfast the crew set sail. Some of them climbed so high in the rigging we had to lie on our backs to watch them. As soon as the sails were up, the wind began to blow, and the boat began to rock. We clung to each other and the railings for support, yelled above the wind to be heard, and laughed at everything. We took pictures of each other, the crew and each other again. I felt free and full of energy and silly thoughts.

The roll of the boat became more severe, and we soon retreated to the lower deck for warmth and safety. Big mistake. Stomachs began to churn, and we had to take turns using the head. It became a game to see how fast we could run and how many times in a half-hour we had to throw up. We told unfunny vomit jokes. We tried sitting quietly. We tried standing on deck. We all wished we had not eaten breakfast. Through it all, George kept right on drinking. Davey, on the other hand, as he reminded us many times in the next few days, didn't even feel nauseous.

At thirty-eight knots the captain decided to lower the sails, but by then, we were so sick it didn't matter. For the remainder of the trip we tended to our poor stomachs and to packing our bags. In the late afternoon we anchored, and the crew motored us to shore. I was relieved to see the redhead was not on our boat.

George slid in the waiting car beside me "Babe," he said, "if you'll just stay with me, I'll be all right. I could even stop drinking." I wasn't sure if he was kidding or admitting to a drinking problem and would actually try to stop.

Then he looked at me with his most charming sideways grin and said, "Do you want to mmmmaaaaay...me?"

I told him he sounded like the Fonz on *Happy Days*, trying to say, "I love you."

Hong Kong 1983 - George
(left) and George and Karen
(below left) on a boat. Karen,
George and Davey
sightseeing (below right).

Karen and George
playing coy with
each other.

Twenty Five

≈

Davey and I spent the next two days sightseeing while Tracie kept busy with her new movie-crew friends. After George finished filming for the day, we met in the popular Peninsula lobby cocktail lounge, crowded with business people and celebrities sitting at small round tables placed close together. I made an effort not to star gaze. When Tracie jabbed my ribs and nodded her head toward the next table I noticed George Hamilton sitting about three feet away. I stared at his white teeth as he smiled at his friends. His deeply tanned face framed his twinkling eyes, and he laughed a lot. Lucky for me, my George was talking to some men at another table, or he would surely have seen me watching George Hamilton, and there'd have been hell to pay.

During those cocktail hours I had the feeling a lot of big deals were being made. Men in dark suits carrying briefcases filled the place, and a man at one of the tables waved to George. He rose, went to their table, sat down, spoke to the men for a few minutes, shook hands, and returned to our table. I guessed that he had been invited because he was a famous star and they wanted to have his attention for a few minutes. Or maybe they were talking about investing in *Patton II*. I hoped for the latter, George wanted to do the movie so badly.

Our rooms had not been changed, so I continued to commute between my room and George's suite under the close watch of the hall security. If they were giggling about the Scott mistress, they kept straight faces as I passed them. In the morning another group would be at their station to see me return to my room. The stoic look on their faces reminded me of the Buckingham Palace guards.

The first three nights after the schooner trip, George and I talked our way through most of the night. He confessed that his friends, the Mahoneys, whom I'd met at the party in Pebble Beach, had loaned him the money for that first, spur of the moment, December trip to Tacoma. We reminisced and dreamed about our future. But then I asked him about the men in the Peninsula cocktail lounge. He was suddenly angry. "That's none of your business."

George looked terribly tired each morning, dragging himself out of bed. The fourth day, before he left, I followed him to the door. "I can see you're exhausted. Why don't we skip this evening together and you get some sleep?"

"My darling, I've never felt better in my life." He kissed me and left.

Tension was growing between Tracie and me, between Tracie and George, and between George and me. I thought the reason was fatigue. I didn't know Tracie wanted to stay in Hong Kong longer, and that her father had promised she could travel with him and work on *Patton II*. And she didn't know he had promised me that he and I would travel together and stop in Hawaii for R and R on the way home.

George's mood swings became troubling and confusing. Unsure what would upset him, I felt ill at ease most of the time, afraid that whatever I said would send him into a tirade.

Tracie urged me to find a tutor for Davey so he could stay longer, which meant she wouldn't have to return to Tacoma with him. At the same time, Jane advised me to send the kids home and stay with George. I became more confused by the hour. I realized I wouldn't be able to please everyone.

The fourth day George asked Davey and me to spend some time on the set watching him film. He sent his driver, Chung, in a tan Rolls Royce that had been reserved for George and his family. The day was humid, misty and gray, and the ancient, foreboding-looking, welfare hospital that was our destination only added to the bleakness. Chung pointed out the window and smiled. "See there, your husband is waiting for you." The word husband came as a surprise, but I didn't correct him. When I looked up and saw

George leaning out one of the windows of the hospital, grinning at me, with his arms outstretched, I felt the same butterflies I'd felt for twenty-five years.

We had arrived at lunch break. Jane and an assistant were setting up tuna sandwiches and hot soup. George greeted me with a hug, then settled down to his lunch and the newspaper crossword puzzle. Davey and I sat across the room on huge, ornately carved antique wooden chairs. The hot soup was welcome in that cold, dank place. The crew wandered in and out for their lunch, talking in hushed tones, respectful of George's rest hour.

That day I had a brief handshake and hello with Ali McGraw, George's co-star. She sat on the step of her trailer relaxing and studying her script. She gave Tracie and me a warm greeting. Knowing George was Tracie's father, Ali surmised he was also Davey's. "Are you having fun in Hong Kong with your dad?" she asked.

Davey didn't try to explain. "Yeah, it's great."

Ali had a child close in age to Davey, so we spoke briefly of sharing a tutor. When we left her, we were sure we'd see each other again.

After lunch Davey and I sat with Jane and watched them film and re-film the same scene what seemed a dozen times or more. I began to realize George earned his money.

The next afternoon George invited us again to the set to watch the filming, this time at the base of a cemetery hill. Because of the lack of cemetery space, Hong Kong has had to bury its dead in layers for generations. Coffins piled one on another with earth between became high hills. Tracie and I decided to climb one of the hills and look at the photographs of the deceased. It took about an hour to reach the top. Once we did, I knew it had been a mistake to drink an extra cup of coffee before we started our hike. It would take too long to get to the base of the hill, there were no bathrooms in sight and no spaces between the graves and I surely didn't want to go on a grave. Finally we reached the top of the hill. So here stood "Mrs. George C. Scott," at the top of a cemetery in Hong Kong, lifting her skirt to pee. Tracie stood several feet away, doubled in laughter, trying to pretend she didn't know me. I didn't blame her. I didn't want to know me at that moment either. That was one of the closest moments she and I had had in weeks.

Saturday we met George and some of the crew for lunch in a posh restaurant, thickly decorated with exotic potted plants. Jane arrived shortly after I did and sat beside me. We both admired the plants and began to discuss our mutual love of gardening and cooking. We had a warm, friendly girl talk, and by the time George arrived we were deep into planning how we'd help each other with our future gardens and exchange recipes.

As George and I were leaving, he leaned over to me. "I'm very pleased to see you and Jane are getting along. It means a lot to me."

"I like her a lot," I said truthfully. "I don't think we'll have any trouble with a friendship."

"I hope not. She and my other wives never got along."

He'd mentioned this so often I wanted to put his mind at rest. "I promise you Jane and I will be fine."

"You'd better," he said.

Almost as if to prove something to George, Jane invited Davey and me for a boat ride the next day to see Aberdeen up close. It was a remarkable tour to see all those people who never left their sampans, bartering for food and wares from the delivery junks. They were not happy to see us watching them, so we didn't stay long. But during the two or three hours we had together, Jane and I talked more about the future.

Sunday the cast and crew rested from filming. I ordered breakfast, and George ate very little. He said nothing to me, and then sat at his chess set. I left for my room to change and found a message from Jane saying she wanted to talk. She came right up and offered to take Tracie and Davey to the circus for the day. "You and George need time alone."

I went back to the suite and asked George if he wanted me to go or stay.

"I do not care!" he growled and turned back to his chess.

Again I returned to my room. By now I was giving the guards friendly little waves as I passed. I called Jane to tell her I had decided to go with her and the kids to the circus.

"I think you should stay," she said. "He needs someone with him, to be near him."

Back down the hall I went. I told George I was staying and would be in my room if he needed anything.

"Just stop changing your mind!" he growled at me.

An hour later I went to his room to collect his laundry, as I had done all week. He came into the bedroom as I knelt by his closet. "What's going on here?" he roared.

George loomed above me. Leaning forward, he looked huge. I felt like a small child who had just been caught stealing something from her daddy. I looked up at him and spoke in a small apologetic voice. "I'm sorting your laundry."

"I don't need you to sort my laundry. I am capable of doing that myself."

He'd been pleased when I took care of him in New York and Monterey. His new attitude shocked and hurt me. "But I always do it when we're together."

"I do not need you to sort my laundry or anything else!" he shouted.

I began to put the clothes back where I'd found them.

"Leave them alone!" He stood watching me until I left the bedroom.

Without a nod to the guards I hurried down the hall to my room, where I stayed, trying to figure out how everything had gone so wrong. Finally, by five in the afternoon I had worked up enough courage to return to the suite. He was watching tennis on television. I sat on the floor in front of him.

Tracie and Davey arrived soon after, and we ordered dinner. They'd had a great time and were full of talk. George wasn't interested in anything they said. While we waited for dinner, the mood of the room varied from playful to hostile. Davey sat on a footstool in front of George, and they preformed the ritual of exchanging eyeglasses as they had done many times in New York.

Then George began to curse Davey. Quietly at first. It almost sounded like silly teasing. He smiled and said quietly, "You dammed little spoiled brat." Davey smiled. But George continued with, "You little mama's boy, pretending you're sick so mommy'll pay attention to you. You miserable little cocksucker." He picked up the paper and began to read.

That was enough! I was furious and about to tell George so, but I stopped myself. Something in Davey's eyes that told me this was a showdown, and his deal. If I stood up for him, it would hurt his pride. Silence filled the room. I was reminded of the showdown at the OK Corral. Davey slowly backed the stool away from George and turned it around until his back was to him. George put his paper aside and watched Davey as he lay back on the stool, looked upside down at George, and said in a quiet but firm voice, "I don't care, George, I really was sick." He got up, walked to me and sat down. He'd finally spoken back to the king! Something I hadn't been able to do. I wanted to cheer, but I knew what wrath that would have brought.

The evening went downhill from there. George seemed to think he had to take sides between Tracie and me. No matter what we said to each other he'd growl at one of us. "Leave your mother alone," or "Give the kid a break."

When I walked Davey to his room, I told him how sorry I was for the way George treated him. I asked him how he felt about George. "It's okay, mom," he said. "It's all over. He's okay, I guess. But he sure can be mean sometimes."

Tracie had left for the night when I returned to the suite. As I walked in George said, "Christ, why can't that woman find a life of her own?" It depressed me that they hadn't found the warm relationship I knew they both wanted. I knew Tracie loved her father and still yearned for attention and understanding. If only he could give her that, she'd feel secure and could step out to find her own life. And she needed to love him with a lighter touch. But I also knew neither one of them understood this. The tug-of-war would probably continue.

That night I asked George if he wanted me to stay with him. "Do as you please. But sleep in the other bed." He rolled to the wall and didn't say another word.

I lay on the other bed but didn't sleep, in case he needed me. He had a fitful sleep, mumbling and turning. In the middle of the night he went to the other room. When I peeked out, he was playing chess on his electronic set. He did not return to bed.

The next morning I ordered breakfast as usual. The kids

arrived. George came into the living room, but he did not go near the service table. He walked to his desk, picked up his script, looked at us and said quietly, "I'd appreciate it if you all left by the end of the week." He gave us a cold, stage smile and added, "Too much turmoil. Jane will make reservations. I'd rather not see you in this room again." He gathered his things and left.

That was it. We were being expelled. If he had suddenly hit me in the chest with a golf club it couldn't have hurt more. But with his mood swings it didn't really come as a surprise. Both Tracie and I were stunned. "I can't believe he's doing this," I said.

"I think Daddy is so overtired he doesn't know what he's saying," Tracie said. "He'll change his mind. He'll rest up, rethink, and everything will go back to the way it was."

"I think he meant it," I said.

Tracie left for the set to be with her friends on the crew. Davey and I went to my room to watch television and wonder what to do next. An hour or so later Jane called. I gathered she'd received her instructions. In her most cheerful voice, she spoke of making reservations for our trip home as though it were going to be just another leg on this fun adventure. "In the meantime, if there is anything you'd like to do or see during the next four days, I'll be happy to arrange it."

Twenty Six

≈

I saw George three times the remainder of that week. Once after he'd made his pronouncement, during an evening filming, and just outside our rooms. The crew and paraphernalia were strewn throughout the hallway in front of the elevator. When I walked by, it was obvious everyone had heard the news. They either looked quickly away, or straight through me. No one spoke to me. Just a day before when I'd been the chosen one, everyone was friendly and helpful. Now I was a disease.

As I waited for the elevator, I kept my head down, trying to pretend I wasn't there. I stood in the midst of this nightmarish scene when George came around the corner wearing pajamas for the night scene. He stopped, obviously surprised to see me and not at all pleased. There was a flicker of a second while he decided what to do. All eyes were now on the drama, and he played to his audience. He walked directly to me and smiled. "How's the sightseeing going?"

"Fine, thank you," I replied without a smile. He's wearing pajamas, I thought. He looks awful in pajamas.

Thank goodness the elevator door opened at that moment and ended my suffering.

Jane kept her promise and kept us busy with tickets to the aquarium and the museum. One day Chung drove us to the top of a mountain to visit an ancient fortune-teller. He looked about a hundred and fifty years old and had the aura of a great sage as he sat in a high, carved wooden chair. Through a translator he told me, "The man you are with now will not be your future." Then he revealed to me the year I would die. The trip did not cheer me up.

As I unlocked the door to my room that afternoon, Ali McGraw was coming down the hall. Certain that she'd want to avoid any contact with me, I hurried to open the door to save us both the embarrassment. But when she saw me, she called my name and walked directly to me. She took my hand and said, "I think you're a fine woman. I know it's difficult to travel with a well-known person under these circumstances, and being a movie star is hell. It does awful things to you." Then she gave me a warm hug, and we said a fond goodbye. What a fine, classy woman you are, I thought. I wish more celebrities were like you.

One evening as I was leaving Davey's room, I saw George for the second time. My son had had a long day, was very tired, and it had taken him some time get to sleep. After I closed his door, I discovered I'd left both our room keys in his room. I didn't want to wake him again, so I started up the hall looking for one of those nice guards to help me.

George came out of his suite at just the wrong moment. He saw me and quickly averted his eyes as if he'd seen something disgusting. There was no place for me to run, and he was moving closer. I had a feeling if he got near enough he'd step on me. And not by accident. I rang the bell for hall service. In the quiet it sounded like a fire alarm. He walked past without looking at me. "Good evening," He said in a harsh, cold voice and continued down the hall.

I wanted either to put my foot out and trip him or scream, "WHY ARE YOU BEING SO MEAN?" But I didn't have the courage. Finally, one of the hall guards appeared and unlocked my door. I lay down on the bed for a few minutes and turned on the television, trying not to think or feel. But it was impossible. Several times I was ready to search George out and beat him up. But as much as he needed it, you just didn't do that to the king. He was an expensive object. Besides, he had too many people protecting him. Instead I ordered wine and paced my room.

I began to think, if I begged him to let me stay ... I laughed out loud at that one. Once the king has made up his mind, he does not change it. Which meant, of course, he had never made up his mind to marry me. There were moments I was afraid I'd kill myself. I'd jump from the hotel window or slash my wrists. But the thought of Davey brought me back. Little did Davey know how he saved my life that night. Crying or gnashing my teeth didn't help. It was over. Cursing didn't help. Hitting my head against the wall didn't help.

It was over.

Nothing spelled the finality of it all more clearly than Jane Dacey coming to my room the next morning. "How are you doing?" she asked gently.

"Fine," I answered.

She held out a check for five thousand dollars, written to me. "George wanted me to give you this."

Surprised and angry, I wanted to yell, "Oh, it's pay-off time!" and rip it up and stuff it in her mouth. But she was only the messenger, and I wasn't that crazy. If I were to go back home, I needed some money.

Then I took what I gathered to be my last opportunity to ask about the chess set. She said, "I'll look into that and let you know. I know it's there, but it may need repair."

She told me she'd made reservations for that Friday and asked if I'd like a day trip to China on Thursday. I accepted. What else was there to do? Sit around and feel sorry for myself? Pick yourself up, Karen. Go look at China.

Davey and I walked down the dock on Thursday to the hovercraft that would carry us to Macau. I saw a large crowd of people standing just inside, pointing and shouting in my direction. I turned to look behind me, but no one was there. As I boarded the boat the crowd surrounded me, holding out napkins, bits of paper, hats and pens. I must have looked how I felt: confused. A young man tugged at my arm. "We heard an American movie star was going to be on this boat. Is it you?" He shoved his pencil and paper in my hand and said, "Please sign here, thank you."

Well, I thought, why not? If they want a movie star, they've got one. At that time my name was Karen Eastman, and that's what I signed. Thirty times. Poor people, I'm sure they wondered who the hell Karen Eastman was. I wish I'd signed Marilyn Monroe. Then they could tell all their friends she wasn't really dead.

The tour was cold, muddy, and I'm sure would have been

interesting, if I'd cared. I paid little attention to the sights and watched Davey enjoying himself. He deserved a happy day.

One incident did catch my attention. As we were crossing the border into China, the bus stopped and several armed, uniformed men boarded. They shouted, waved their guns at us, and poked their bayonets under the seats. Davey, who had been pretty lively up to then, raised his legs off the floor and sat rigidly still, looking straight ahead. He had had lots of experience with one scary man in the past two weeks, I guessed he knew how to handle a few more. The tour guide said, "Please stay in your seats. These men are searching for contraband. They will not harm you." They did the same drill before we left China.

That night in my room I felt more desperate than I had the night before. We were leaving the next morning. We were really leaving. After all these years, he'd finally turned his back on me. And I knew in my heart it was for good. Again, I paced my room most of the night, wanting to kill myself and afraid I'd do it. About five a.m. I called Tracie.

She came to my room and sat with me for an hour. Loving and frustrated, she couldn't find the words to comfort me. She still couldn't believe what George was doing to me. I didn't know that she still thought it was only me he was pushing from his life, and that he'd keep his promise for her to work on his next film.

She left at seven, going to her room to dress and pack. We planned to meet later in the day to prepare for our 8 p.m. flight. I went to Davey's room to pack his things and order breakfast. During the day Davey and I shopped for last minute gifts and took more photos of the city. We returned at three for a room service snack. At about four-thirty Tracie called to say, "I'm with daddy. We're having a farewell drink. Do you want to join us?"

What was this? I thought. Does he really want to see me? Or humiliate me again? Either way, I wanted to see and talk to him one more time. I dressed and combed my hair the way he liked it. I looked at my bags ready for the trip, and I thought, "Maybe I'll be back to unpack you. Maybe it isn't the end after all." I walked up the hall filled with a mixture of the dread of goodbye and a spark of hope for a new beginning.

I tapped on his door. "It's open. Come on in," Tracie yelled.

George sat at his desk reading a letter. "It's from Trish," he said. "She had an accident horseback riding. She badly scratched her face. I'm terribly worried about her."

He's hiding behind Trish again, I thought. Or, maybe it's just a prop, an empty sheet of paper. "Oh, that's too bad," I said.

I stood on one side his desk, feeling totally awkward, while he stayed seated. The hapless prisoner standing in front of the judge, he did not ask me to sit down. "So," he said as he smiled his cold stage smile, "Jane has arranged everything for your trip?"

"Yes, she's taken good care of us." This was more like an interview than a final goodbye to my lover.

"Well, that's fine. If you need anything you can always call Jane." He was talking to me in the same tone of voice he used when he ordered fresh towels. "I'll be in Hungary working on *Patton II* after July."

"I'll be in my room," Tracie said and left.

I called Davey's room and asked him to come up to the suite and say goodbye. There were three or four awkward moments, while I stood in front of George's desk and he sat, head down, reading his script. Finally Davey knocked at the door. He walked to George, gave him a hug and said, "Thank you for everything."

"You're welcome." George looked up briefly and gave him a weak stage smile.

"Mom, I'll be in my room with Tracie," Davey said.

George and I were alone again. "Thank you for everything," I began. "It was generous ..."

He interrupted with, "This is not goodbye."

That was my opportunity to say, "Oh yes it is, you S.O.B.!" But I just stood there with that teeny tiny bit of hope in my heart. He rose slowly from his chair and walked to me. We hugged, and I tried to kiss him. But he turned his head.

"I love you. You're quite a guy."

"I love you. You are a magnificent woman."

I walked to the door. He stood in the center of the floor. "Safe journey," he said as though he were reading his shopping list.

"Safe journey to you." I went out, quietly closing the door behind me.

Twenty Seven

≈

The trip home was long and bleak. Though Tracie and I didn't say the words, at that time, we each harbored resentment of the other for causing the "turmoil." In Tacoma, we shared a cab. There was little conversation. Tracie went to her apartment. Davey and I went to our house. Tracie and I didn't communicate for a week. Davey worked on making up his schoolwork. I worked on trying to pull myself together.

Apparently during those last few days before we left Hong Kong, George had been stirring up some turmoil of his own. A member of his entourage had contacted *The Inquirer* to report that he and Ali McGraw had fallen in love. *The Inquirer* had recently published an article about George and Trish breaking up, so they were happy to photograph the lovebirds sitting together in the Peninsula lounge. A "good friend of the couple" carefully quoted it all.

     The story appeared a few days later, in time for me to see it at the checkout stand on my first trip to the grocery store in Tacoma. At first it was a jolt. Then I realized it had to be a plant. Even George couldn't have had an affair that quickly after I left his bed. And I couldn't believe it of Ali McGraw.

     Tracie came for dinner one evening in high spirits. She announced her plans to sell all her stuff and be ready when her father called about working on *Patton II*. Sure his anger was only with me, not with her, she believed she'd be hearing from him any day.

     She didn't get her call, but I received one.

"Karen, this is Tony ..."

"Tony. What a surprise. How are you?"

"I'm okay. I'm in Hong Kong. It seems after you left, George went on a two day drunk and held up shooting. He locked himself in his room and caused all kinds of headaches. They called me to come out here and help get him on his feet."

"I don't know what to say, Tony. He told us to leave."

"Yeah, I know. Listen, Karen, get rid of the girl, and we'll all be back playing bridge in a week."

"I can't do that. She's my daughter."

"If you don't get rid of her, you'll never see him again."

"I'm sorry. I just can't do that."

"It's your life."

About three weeks after the article exposing the Scott/ McGraw love affair, and two weeks after Tony called, I received a call from an *Inquirer* reporter. He had been contacted by a source who told him what really happened in Hong Kong, who we were and where he could find us. The reporter's name was David, and he asked if he might fly up from Florida in the next couple of days to talk to us. "We'll pay you, and the interview won't take more than an hour or two."

"I'll talk to my daughter and let you know," I said. "The more I thought about it, the better it sounded. I could actually get paid for venting my anger.

But Tracie was wary. She still waited for her father's call about *Patton II* and didn't want to ruin her chances by saying something negative about him. She finally agreed if we taped the interview and went in disguise. The disguise seemed kind of much, but why not?

When the reporter called back, we agreed to be interviewed the following day. We'd meet him at a picnic table at in a nearby park. He would recognize us by our tan raincoats. Getting into the clandestine mood, it's a wonder I didn't say, "Carrying black attaché cases."

The afternoon was warm and sunny, but we still thought it best to wear our tan raincoats, slouch hats, and large, dark glasses. Tracie carried the tape recorder. We had heard it's best to record everything said, so we can prove our innocence later. We'd seen enough spy movies to know about this sort of thing. David, the professional journalist and gentleman, did not laugh out loud when he met us. We shook hands, sat down, and turned on our tape recorders.

Tracie refused to say anything negative about her father for fear it would ruin her chances with him. I didn't want to be the baddy, or maybe in my heart I also hoped for another chance. So all David got were two hours of a boring, sugary version of our lives with George.

Q: "Tracie, tell me about his temper."

A: "He's really not so bad."

Q: "Karen, is it true you and his first wife were pregnant at the same time?"

A: "Ah, yes, I think so."

Q: "Tracie, why did you leave Hong Kong so suddenly?"

A: "It was time to come home."

Q: "Karen, how do you feel about him now?"

A: "We'll always be friends."

Poor rag mag journalist. He'd come all the way from Florida for a big nasty story and had to return with nothing. When the interview was over and David had gone his way, we pulled our hats down over our faces and slunk back to the car feeling like mysterious celebrities and secretly hoping others would think so, too.

Tracie was afraid if her father saw the article he would be angry, so she called and told him about it. After she'd given him the details, she put me on the phone, and he said, "I'll kill the article. You don't need that shit."

Oh my, the power of G.C. Scott!

The last week in March, 1983, Davey and I lined our chairs up in front of the TV to watch the academy awards. Tracie watched from her apartment. I remembered George's words, "If I attend, it'll be with you, Baby." So I was positive he wouldn't be in the audience. We were relaxed, enjoying the show and our popcorn, when the cameras suddenly focused on George and Trish, sitting together in the audience. It was lucky Davey held the bowl of popcorn, because an abrupt tremor passed through my body. I don't know why I was surprised. I should have expected it. But I was still vulnerable, and it hurt worse than if he'd walked into the room and stabbed me.

Ten minutes later they showed the happy twosome again. I think the director wanted the audience to get the message that the man who had refused the award in 1970 was back in the fold. Or maybe George asked to be shown twice on camera to send another message – that he and Trish were back together.

If other people didn't get the message, I did.

Neither Tracie nor I heard from George again. After a few months, our anger at each other dissipated, and we were again close. Both needing a fresh beginning, we moved north to a small town near the Canadian border, where we tried to put the past behind us and get on with our lives. Eventually, Tracie moved to Hawaii, I remarried, and it seemed George had settled back down to wedded bliss with Trish.

On that September day in 1999, when I received the call from Tracie telling me George had died, it had been nearly sixteen years since we had seen or heard from him. As I walked the beach that day, I realized my grieving was for someone who for me had died a long time ago. I grieved for the young man in Missouri with dreams of working on Broadway. The silly young man who danced down the street singing "Yellow Brick Road." The funny young man who stood by the subway grinning, with his arms outstretched to me. The young father who held his baby daughter so tenderly when we were sitting on the couch at the foster home. And had I made a different decision back then, all of our lives might have been different.

I said goodbye to George that day in my own way on the beach. And when I did, I felt as if I'd finally shed that old Stephens College fur coat. I felt light and free. I drove home and found my husband mowing the front lawn. He smiled and waved at me. I smiled and waved back. It was a simple, loving greeting. I walked into the house and knew I was finally home where I belonged.

———

About the Author ...

Karen Riehl's 30-year career in community and professional theater includes acting opposite George C. Scott, and directing Emmy award-winner Gordon Clapp in water shows. Her many acting awards include Indiana's AACT Theater/Fest '93 Best Supporting Performer.

An accomplished playwright, her children's play, *Alice in Cyberland* (Meriwether) was published in 2000 after winning her a national award in the Southwest Festival of New Plays. The Brown Bag Players of Mission Viejo, CA produced her parodies of *The Princess and the Pea* and *The Golden Goose. Getting Out of Salem* is Karen's newest play.

Love and Madness is Karen's second book. Her novel, *Saturday Night Dance Club* (SANDS Publishing), was published in 2001. Karen has completed her third book and is currently working on her fourth.

Karen lives in southern California with her editor-husband Richard and their tortoise Seabiscuit.